Jackie Cochran

Florida A&M University, Tallahassee
Florida Atlantic University, Boca Raton
Florida Gulf Coast University, Ft. Myers
Florida International University, Miami
Florida State University, Tallahassee
University of Central Florida, Orlando
University of Florida, Gainesville
University of North Florida, Jacksonville
University of South Florida, Tampa
University of West Florida, Pensacola

UNIVERSITY PRESS OF FLORIDA

Gainesville · Tallahassee · Tampa · Boca Raton · Pensacola · Orlando · Miami · Jacksonville · Ft. Myers

DORIS L. RICH

Jackie Cochran

Pilot in the Fastest Lane

Printed in the United States of America on acid-free paper

12 11 10 09 08 07 6 5 4 3 2 1

Library of Congress Cataloging-in-Publication Data
Rich, Doris L.
Jackie Cochran: pilot in the fastest lane / Doris L. Rich.
p. cm.
Includes bibliographical references and index.
ISBN–13: 978-0-8130-3043-2 (alk. paper)
1. Cochran, Jacqueline. 2. Air pilots—United States—Biography. 3. Women air pilot—United States—Biography.
I. Title.
TL540.C63R53 2007
629.13092—dc22
[B] 2006023029

The University Press of Florida is the scholarly publishing agency for the State University System of Florida, comprising Florida A&M University, Florida Atlantic University, Florida Gulf Coast University, Florida International University, Florida State University, University of Central Florida, University of Florida, University of North Florida, University of South Florida, and University of West Florida.

University Press of Florida
15 Northwest 15th Street
Gainesville, FL 32611-2079
http://www.upf.com

Contents

Foreword

> Why do I want to fly? Because half-way between the earth and sky, one seems to be closer to God. There is a peace of mind and heart, a satisfaction which walls can not give. When I see an airplane flying I just ache all over to be up there. It isn't for a fad, or a thrill, or pride. Women are seeking freedom. Freedom in the skies! They are soaring above temperamental tendencies of their sex which have kept them earth-bound. Flying is a symbol of freedom from limitation.

No, the above is not a quote from Jacqueline Cochran but rather from an article in the June 1930 issue of *Pictorial Review* by a pilot and author named Margery Brown. But the final sentence—"Flying is a symbol of freedom from limitation"—could well sum up much of Jacqueline Cochran's motivation to become a pilot in 1932 and to devote her life to aviation until her death in 1980.

Limitation was probably not a word Cochran added to her ever increasing vocabulary. She recognized no limits. She taught herself to read. She learned to fly to promote her growing cosmetics business. She always went for the records set by men, knowing that records set by women would probably soon be bested by men. Through her husband's wealth and her own friendships with politicians and military brass, she created opportunities for herself to obtain positions of authority and to fly high-performance aircraft—something other pilots could not attain.

Doris Rich, who has previously authored excellent biographies of Amelia Earhart and Bessie Coleman, has produced a book that answers many of the questions lingering about this fascinating figure in aviation history. This work belies some myths that have swirled around Cochran (her family background, for one) and substantiates others (the doll won, lost, and regained). It is well rounded in the way it treats the various aspects of Cochran's very interesting life: impoverished young child, young woman establishing her own business, fledgling pilot, wife of one of the most powerful men in the United States, leader of the WASPs, one of the most respected pilots in the world. At the time of her death in 1980, Cochran held more speed, altitude, and distance records than any other pilot, male or female, in aviation history.

Doris Rich has done the best job of anyone who has attempted a biography of this complicated and complex individual. She and her late husband, Stanley, conducted years of exhaustive research and interviews. For the first time, members of Cochran's family agreed to talk with an author. No important source was overlooked. When Rich needs to use technical terms regarding aircraft, she describes them well for the general reader.

Much about Cochran is contradictory. Though she herself achieved so much, she hated the women's movement and did not believe that women should go into combat or become astronauts. As she grew more and more famous, she almost always took the time to fix her makeup and hair before getting out of her aircraft, knowing that photographers would most likely be waiting. A contemporary of hers once told me that Cochran's tough side disappeared whenever she was with her beloved husband, Floyd Odlum. Certainly Odlum's money and Cochran's fame gave her access to aircraft other women of her time did not have, but she still had to make the record flights herself.

Cochran's close friend Amelia Earhart is, of course, the first name mentioned when the subject of women pilots arises. Earhart's disappearance in 1937 remains a mystery and no doubt adds much to her fame. Cochran died quietly in California in 1980, and her funeral was attended by few. But as readers of this book will see, it is Cochran whose name should be on people's lips when a discussion of women pilots is taking place. Cochran deserves this book.

Claudia M. Oakes
Chief Operating Officer
Cradle of Aviation Museum
Garden City, New York
August 2006

Acknowledgments

Much of the material in this book came from the papers of Jacqueline Cochran at the Dwight D. Eisenhower Library in Abilene, Kansas. Other libraries and archives providing information include the Library of Congress; Texas Woman's University; the Lyndon Baines Johnson Library; the U.S. Air Force Academy, Archives Branch at Maxwell AFB; the Oral History Collection, Columbia University; the International Women's Air and Space Museum; Coachella Valley Historical Society; the Alabama and Georgia State Departments of Archives; the Florida State Archives; and the National Air and Space Museum in Washington, D.C. Staff members at all of these institutions assisted me with their guidance. Especially helpful were those at the National Air and Space Museum, including Dorothy Cochrane, Tom Crouch, Kate Igoe, Kristine Kaske, and Melissa Keiser.

For information on Jackie Cochran's early years, I am indebted to Billie P. Ayers, to members of the Waters family—Quinten, Jack, Alice Jean, and Dr. Kathleen Sander, all of whom I interviewed—and to Ann Lewis for her extensive research.

I am grateful for interviews with Wil Hanson, Claudia Oakes, Judith Odlum, Beverly Hanson Sfingi, Virginia Waring, Dr. John E. Wickman, and Ann Wood-Kelly. Others who granted me interviews were Margaret Kerr Boylan, Jan Conner, Connie Cowan, Iris C. Critchell, Dr. Deborah G. Douglas, Mary Feik, Robert J. Gilliland, Kristen Norstad Jaffe, Bill and Violet Kersteiner, Laurel Ladevich, Barbara E. London, Isabell Norstad, Jean Howard Phelan, Mrs. Joseph C. Shaw, Arnold Steele, Nancy Livingston Stratford, Jane Straughan, Colonel Jack Tetrick, and Dr. Earl A. Thompson.

Thanks also to the following people who provided me with information through correspondence and telephone conversations: Richard Sanders Allen, Harold Cousins, Jane L. Cunningham, Dik Daso, Beth Dees, Donald C. Ferguson, Dr. Murray Green, Mona Kendrick, Dora Dougherty McKeown, Roger G. Miller, Jasper L. Moore, Patricia Newcomer, Mike Ravnitsky, Durane

Reed, David Schwartz, Henry D. Steele, Jane Straughan, Bobbi Trout, Eleanor Wagner, and Vernon M. Welsh.

For editorial assistance, I thank my daughter, Chris Rich, and my friend Nancy Orban. For his unfailing guidance and encouragement, I thank my agent, Felix C. Lowe. Finally, for sharing the four years of research and thousands of miles on the road in search of the "real" Jackie, I am indebted to my husband of almost sixty years, the late Stanley Rich, journalist and retired foreign service officer.

Jackie Cochran

One

Sawdust Road

The child stood in the open door of the kitchen at the rear of the company dining hall, her bare feet planted firmly on the rough wooden floor. She was small for a four-year-old, but sturdy. Her dress, made from flour sacking, revealed bare arms and legs tanned by the Florida sun. Her skin was flawless, almost luminous, and large brown eyes dominated the lovely little face.

"Bessie," she announced in a voice ringing with the nasal twang and drawl of the Florida panhandle, "wants biscuits. Biscuits with gravy!" She paused, as if considering her own request, then added, "Please?"

Little Bessie's mother, Mollie Pittman, sighed. Chief cook at the lumber camp, Mollie stood before the huge old wood-burning stove, her twelve-year-old assistant, Virginia Jernigan, nearby. "She's always hungry, Ginny," Mollie growled. "That child has a stomach with no bottom." Nodding at Bessie, she said, "Come on then," and handed Virginia a tin plate with three biscuits from the warming shelf. "Help her, Ginny."

Virginia took the plate and placed it on one of the long trestle tables, waiting for Bessie to climb up and kneel on the bench, her chin barely clearing the table. After Virginia dredged a biscuit in a bowl of gravy, Bessie took a few bites, then handed it back to the older girl. "More gravy, Ginny. More gravy," repeating the request until she had finished all three biscuits. Wiping her mouth with the back of a now-greasy hand, she clambered down from the bench and shouted her thanks as she bolted out the door into the bright tropical sunshine.

Mollie looked at Virginia and smiled. "Bessie sure as all get-out knows what she wants, and most often as not she gets it."[1]

On a May day in 1910, a census taker arrived in the township of Pine Barren, Florida. Bulldozed into the rolling hills of Florida's panhandle, Pine Barren was a bedroom community for employees of the Southern States Lumber Company in nearby Muscogee. From the moment that the stranger with the clipboard under his arm stopped at the Pittmans' unpainted pineboard house, one of many lining the sandy, unpaved path, little Bessie Pittman watched him and listened. Not for nothing was she known throughout the neighborhood as curious and bright, not to mention fearless, determined, naughty, and garrulous.

The man entered the house at the bidding of Bessie's father, Ira Pittman, a carpenter with the lumber company. Ira, 44, and his wife, Mollie Grant Pittman, 36, had five children, all living at home and most of whose names the census taker misspelled, writing Josfie (for Joseph Edward), 16; Henery (for Henry Bryan), 13; and Money (for Mary Elbertie), 12. But he got Myrtle (Maybelle Myrtle), 7, and Bessie, 4, right.[2] Their father said that the three older children had been born in Alabama, the younger two in Muscogee—Myrtle in 1903 and Bessie in 1906.[3]

The Pittmans also housed three boarders in their sparsely furnished house that lacked both a bathroom and a toilet. The walls were unplastered and the windows were paneless; the windows had to be covered with paper in the winter to keep out the cold. Their boarders were Walter Meafie, 36, William Meafie, 26, and Arthur May, 22. All three were also Southern State employees.[4] Ira paid the rent—one dollar a room—but the census taker did not note how many rooms there were, certainly not enough for ten people.

Although his wife and three older children could read and write, Ira Pittman himself was illiterate. Despite this handicap, he had for the last decade been a foreman for Southern State in a logging camp near Gateswood, Alabama, where his first three children were born. There, he and his crews ratcheted cut lumber onto high-wheeled, ox-driven carts, drove the carts to a rail spur, then unloaded and reloaded the logs onto freight cars for delivery to the Muscogee mill twelve miles across the Perdido River into Florida.[5]

At Muscogee, almost half of whose 700 inhabitants were Southern State employees, Ira worked twelve-hour days, seven days a week for $1.25 a day. His son Joseph earned a dollar a day when work was available, and his younger son, Henry, born with a deformed foot, stacked slabs of wood for shingles for sixty cents a day. The workers were paid in chips that could be redeemed for cash, most of which were spent at the company commissary for food, clothing, and household goods.[6]

Still, the Pittmans did not think of themselves as desperately poor. Like their neighbors, they were "getting by," moving from one logging camp to another, one mill town to another. They had enough to eat from their garden and the commissary, and they raised chickens as well.[7]

Adventurous, hot-tempered, and willful, Bessie was eager to learn anything new and always looked for recognition. Not from her mother, however, whom she regarded with contempt mingled with fear and thought of as slovenly, lazy, and mean—a woman who whipped her children "when she was in a mood." Once when Bessie's brother Henry was ill and she was sent to the store for ice to cool his fever, the ice melted on the way home. When her mother tried to whip her, Bessie picked up a piece of firewood, "and we talked things out with my eyes flashing fire. She knew I meant what I said and she retreated, never touched me again."[8]

Writing of this period in an autobiography published years later when she was known as Jacqueline Cochran, world-famous aviator, Bessie said that at the age of six years she overheard her mother tell a friend "that I was not one of the family." Early in her career, news stories, both under her own name[9] and written by others,[10] began to appear, claiming flatly but offering no details that Bessie had been "orphaned at the age of 4." These seemed to the Pittman and Grant families pure fictions, dreamed up by Bessie to further dramatize the Cinderella theme of her biography. Indeed, according to Bessie's niece, Billie Ayers, Mollie recorded Bessie's name in the Grant family Bible after her birth on May 11, 1906, and a neighbor, Erma Peagler, had witnessed the delivery.[11]

Ira died in 1928 before his daughter learned to fly and the "orphan" stories appeared. Ayers said that even though Mollie may have been hurt by the stories, no one in the family wanted to embarrass the flier by disputing her claims. "We were proud of her and knew she was only trying to better herself."[12]

Too young to enter the combined grade school and high school and with both parents working, Bessie was left to explore the woods around Pine Barren or to roam the unpaved streets of the company-owned town of Muscogee. She was not interested in the company office, a two-story building with a hall on the second floor for public meetings and social functions. Nor did she find the church or post office worth more than a glance through the open doors. But the railroad depot and its roundhouse were worth observing. There, she could watch endlessly the connecting and rerouting of cars from the Louisville and Nashville and the Alabama and Tennessee railroads.

The commissary offered a view of counters filled with groceries, clothing, shoes, hardware, and, best of all, toys. She couldn't buy them, but she could look. At the barber shop, one of the few privately owned businesses in town, she could peer through the street window into the gas-lit interior and watch the men laughing and talking. A sign over the door that someone read aloud to her said, "In God we trust. All others pay cash," but she didn't know why it made people laugh.

In an area abounding in freshwater springs, she drank from the artesian well in the center of town, a place where all travelers stopped for water and gossip. Best of all were the days when the meat wagon arrived. She ran to greet the three Waters brothers who owned it—Verner, Jordan, and Tom. They let her climb on the back near the scales, where huge chunks of meat were surrounded by chipped ice and stored under canvas. There, she watched while the brothers cut and weighed the orders, placing them in the enamel basins and plates brought by their customers.[13]

Untutored and alone, Bessie wandered her various sawmill towns and camps, a child in an adult world, some of it frightening and ugly. One day, walking near her home, she saw a crowd of men dragging a black man into the woods. She followed until they stopped at a clearing. There they tied their prisoner to a tree and burned him alive. "I was too young then to have any great feeling about the injustice or loss of life but I took away from that scene the very bad memory of burning flesh."[14]

On another occasion, hearing the squeals of a pig being slaughtered, she rushed to the far side of the camp hoping that she might be given some of the meat. But after watching the small intestines being removed, cleaned in running branch water, cut into small pieces, and thrown into a huge kettle of boiling water, she found the stench so revolting that she was never again able to eat the inner organs of any animal.[15]

As one after another forested area was cleared and the sawmills shut down, Ira Pittman moved his family to wherever he could find work. Before Bessie was eight, she had lived in Gateswood and Samson in Alabama and Muscogee, Bagdad, and Millview, all in the Pensacola area of Florida.

Bessie was still six when the family moved to Bagdad, a port dominated by the Bagdad Land and Lumber Company. Founded in 1840, it was located on East Bay, about twelve miles east of Pensacola. There, Bessie saw her first seagoing freighters being loaded with lumber cut from land lying north of the

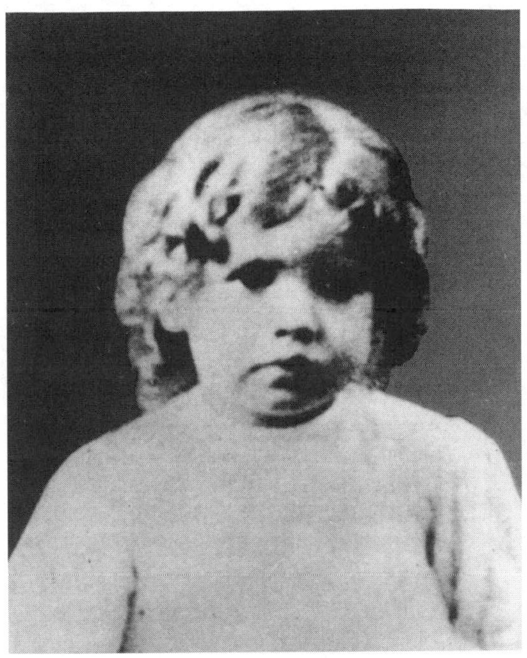

1.1. A childhood portrait of Jackie Cochran (then Bessie Pittman), in the second grade at Bagdad Elementary School, Florida. (Courtesy Dwight D. Eisenhower Library. Photographer unknown.)

city and all the way to the Alabama border. She walked through wire grass under long-leaf yellow pine trees towering 100 feet over her head and watched the company-owned Florida and Alabama Railroad cars carry lumber to the mills in town. Housing with electricity was provided for its 1,000 employees by the company, but laborers like Ira were paid only thirty or thirty-five dollars a month.[16] The first day in her new home, Bessie climbed onto a chair to reach the light cord that turned on the bare bulb hanging from the ceiling, a new experience.

Bessie started school in Bagdad but ran out the door on the third day when her teacher struck her with a ruler. "Why, I don't remember," she is quoted as saying, adding, "I was always a feisty, independent child. Perhaps that was it. But because of the child I was and the woman I would become, it wouldn't have been like me not to hit back under such circumstances."[17] Bessie herself was to write years later about the teacher: "Anna Thompson. I'll never forget her . . . didn't get the chance of a second slap because I struck back and then took off at top speed through the door. . . ."[18] Since "there was no one around to make me go to school—least of all my 'parents,'"[19] she then ventured out alone into what seemed to be a vast metropolis.

Everywhere she looked, she saw something that she had never seen before. Automobiles drove by on paved streets. She herself walked on cement sidewalks. During her joyous exploration of this new world, she passed by the shipyard and the lumber mills, a newspaper office, a post office, a grocery store, and a livery stable. She learned her ABCs from letters painted on the sides of passing boxcars. She watched children playing outside the public school from which she had fled—not like the one-room wooden shack she was used to but rather a brick building with a classroom for each grade. There were seven churches, two hotels, and a boarding house. But most interesting of all was the window of a millinery shop displaying huge hats trimmed in feathers or fur.

When night came, the child extended her exploration of this new and exotic environment by climbing and perching atop a tree to witness a "chitlin party" held by black laborers who danced and played wonderful music.[20] When the circus came to town, she tried to join the troupe but was left behind when she fell asleep during the night. A second attempt to see the world beyond Bagdad, this time with a band of gypsies, also failed when they refused to take her.

Despite these frustrated attempts, Bessie still found much more to see and hear in Bagdad. She sat for hours, enchanted by the fables and stories told by "Aunt" Jennie Smart, an old, toothless, black woman. And once, when the old woman dozed off open-mouthed during her narration, Bessie impishly fed her a dry soda cracker just so that she could watch in amusement as Aunt Jennie blew cracker crumbs in all directions. She listened, too, to "Grandpa Whiskers," another town character, who had a white beard and drove a team of horses and a wagon for hire. From him she learned that she had a navel because, when she was very little, an Indian shot her in the stomach with an arrow. Grandpa Whiskers further explained that "in my excitement over this bow and arrow affair I had sat down suddenly on an ax and as punishment for this carelessness had become a girl."[21]

The company doctor offered to help Bessie when she told him that her second teeth were growing in crooked and crowded. He pulled two of them and told her to press the others with her thumb to straighten them. She followed his directions diligently, which resulted in a set of straight, white teeth, enabling her to escape looking like most of the men and women in the camp, whose teeth were snaggled and stained by tobacco and snuff.

Although Ira and Mollie were not Catholics, they urged Bessie to attend Mass when an itinerant priest came to town, presumably hoping that he might exert a calming influence on their adventurous daughter. Bessie guessed that her "real" parents had been Catholics, and this was Mollie's way of keeping her original promise to the child's biological mother. Nevertheless, the child became friends with the priest who came monthly to Bagdad, and she attended his Mass regularly. From him, she learned far better lessons than those of the town storytellers and years later became a convert to the Church.

The following year when the truant officer was checking for missing students, Bessie returned to school to find a new teacher, Miss Bostwick from Cincinnati. "She was the most beautifully dressed woman I had ever seen," Bessie was to write years later. She spoke with a different accent and was very severe, cracking knuckles with a ruler. "But she was fair."[22] That first week, her new teacher showed Bessie the boarding house where she lived and offered her ten cents a week to bring her firewood for the small stove in her room. The room looked like a palace to the child and soon she began daily visits.

From a small pot on the stove, the teacher gave her the first prunes that she had ever tasted and taught her table manners and the necessity of personal hygiene. As a result, Bessie used a twig from a sweet gum tree to brush her teeth and took a daily bath, dragging a tin tub to the back porch and filling it with buckets of cold water from the well. Her mother and sisters thought daily bathing ridiculous, but it marked the beginning of a lifelong obsession with cleanliness so extreme that a friend said years later, "You know that Jackie was nuts about cleanliness."[23]

Miss Bostwick also gave her a comb, a hair ribbon, and a new dress to replace the one made from a flour sack, one in which "I could hold my head up with the other children from the right side of the tracks." She also helped her to read and gave her a copy of *David Copperfield*. It was slow going for a child who had just learned to read, but she finished it, writing down every unfamiliar word. After school, Bessie went to the teacher's room, where each word was explained—the meaning of the words and how they were pronounced. Miss Bostwick's departure from Bagdad after a second year at the school marked the end of Bessie's formal education.

The Pittmans' next move was to Millville, an all-day-and-into-the-night train ride east along the Gulf coast. They traveled in the caboose and, whenever the train needed fuel, were expected to help the crew gather discarded pine knots left alongside the tracks by lumber crews for just such an emergency.

Cold and hungry, her only cover a piece of cloth torn from an old blanket, Bessie watched the peddlers who came aboard selling fried chicken. Ira had no money. Years later, Bessie could still recall the aroma of the chicken and the longing that she felt when another peddler came aboard hawking little glass pistols filled with tiny, colored, candy balls.

From the train station in Panama City, Bessie waded three miles ankle deep in sand bogs to reach Millville. On arrival, she immediately explored a nearby farm where she saw sweet potatoes being boiled to feed the farmer's pigs. She stole two for her first meal. In the forest behind the house assigned to Ira, a shack on stilts, Bessie found and ate pine mast, small nuts that fell from pine cones onto the forest floor. Two days later on the waterfront, she was given a pan of mullet by a fisherman. From the farmer whose potatoes she had stolen, she borrowed a cup of lard to fry the fish, making the first hot meal that the whole family had eaten in a week.

The ramshackle house in Millville, like the one in Muscogee, was sparsely furnished. Bessie slept on a "St. George" bed, a wooden platform suspended from the wall. She spent her days outdoors searching for food to supplement her diet of rice, beans, and mullet. She fished, crabbed, and waded out to sandbars to gather oysters. With a piece of corn tied to a string, she lured the neighbors' chickens to their demise.

October was the best month for collecting oysters. Accompanied by other youngsters from the camp, she brought her catch ashore, shucking it with her bare hands—hands unusually large and strong for a child—and piled the oysters on the coals that she had prepared for the feast. Sometimes the chicken caught with her corn lure was added to the menu along with corn on the cob and squash from nearby vegetable patches.[24]

Not long after their arrival in Millville, the Pittmans moved from the shack to a company house furnished with a table, rickety chairs, beds with mattresses and with a vegetable garden at the side of the house. To keep the neighbor's cow out of the garden, Bessie borrowed a shotgun and put salt in the shell. The gun was so heavy that she could hardly lift it, but she fired it, the recoil knocking her flat "for a count of ten." The cow never came back.[25]

At the beach one day, Bessie waded out past the sandbars with two little girls. Her companions floundered in the deep water and drowned. "We stayed out all night and the next day while they searched for the girls' bodies. They found them—all eaten up." From this she suffered a lifelong fear of water.[26] Years later, commenting on Millville in a letter to a friend, Bessie wrote: "I think the whole thing should be given back to the Indians."[27]

No longer in school, Bessie began to work helping expectant mothers before and after childbirth. She cleaned their houses, drew well water, cooked, and watched the other children. On one occasion, while caring for a pregnant eighteen-year-old during a violent rainstorm and with no other help to be had, Bessie herself acted as midwife with the teenager giving directions.[28]

As the Christmas season neared, her employers owed her a total of four dollars but hadn't yet paid her. She took on more work for other women, enough to earn fifty cents because she already knew what she wanted for Christmas. Displayed in the company store was the most beautiful doll she had ever seen. Her head was of china and her blue eyes closed when she was laid down. Her cheeks were pink, her hair yellow ringlets that fell to her shoulders, and she wore a dress of silk and lace. The doll cost more than Bessie could ever earn, but it was being raffled. For every twenty-five cents' worth of toys purchased, a chance to win was offered. So Bessie took on even more jobs, drawing water from the wells until her hands bled. After two weeks, she had earned fifty cents, which she spent on toys that she didn't want so as to get two tickets. On Christmas Eve she won. But when she brought the prize home, her mother said that she was too old for dolls and forced her to give it to Willie Mae, the two-year-old child of her older sister, Mary Elbertie, known as "Mamie." To Bessie, this was an injustice that she would never forget. Her fists clenched and eyes shining with tears, she walked away with one thought. Someday she would own that doll—not one just like it, but the one Willie Mae now held in her grubby little hands.[29]

In 1914, after the pine forests near Millville, where Ira Pittman cut timber, had been cleared, he was again unemployed. Hearing that a cotton mill in Columbus, Georgia, was hiring, he moved his family there. To reach Columbus, they rode the train to Milton, Alabama, where, cold and hungry, they waited for their connection in a station without benches. Bessie was wearing a thin cotton dress and had no stockings or shoes. Her mother cut a blanket in half and gave her one piece to cover herself.

They arrived in Bibb City after dark and moved into housing provided by the Bibb City Cotton Mill at the corner of 32nd Street and Riverside Drive. Bessie's new home, like the one in Bagdad, had electric lights and an additional luxury new to her—a bathroom with a tub and a flush toilet. She would no longer need to carry water from the pump to the iron tub on the back porch. The next day, her father gave her the fare for her first ride on a streetcar, up the main thoroughfare, Broad Street.

The following day, eight-year-old Bessie went to work in the mill with the rest of her family. She worked a twelve-hour shift for six cents an hour. Pushing a cart up and down the aisles in her bare feet on the rough cement floor, she delivered bobbin spools to the weavers, who could run as many as six looms at once. Hurrying up and down the aisles, she was so small that she had to push the spools on her cart from one side to the other just to see where she was going.

Whole families worked in a suffocating mist of cotton dust that filled the poorly ventilated and badly lighted mill. There was no place to rest. To relieve themselves, the workers had only filthy outhouses built out over the river. At midnight, after her first six hours of work, Bessie was given a half hour to eat the lunch that she had brought in a paper bag. She ate quickly, then crawled into her cart for a brief nap.

She hid in the cart to avoid "the kind of men you found in cotton mills." "It was one long, continuous fight in which many little girls suffered many things that shouldn't happen to little girls. I knew exactly what to do with my feet when anyone began molesting me."[30] When one attacker, a foreman, surprised her, "pinching me in a way no little girls should be pinched," she struck him in the nose so hard that he jumped back. He never touched her again.[31]

At the close of the first week, her mother took her wages of $4.50, but by the following week Bessie assumed command, handing Mollie $3 and keeping the rest for herself. The next day, she bought from a peddler what she claimed to be her first pair of shoes, though years later, her niece Billie Ayers insisted that all the Pittman children had shoes. They were red pumps with high heels.[32] Teetering down the street, she realized that she could not work in them, and the next week she bought a pair of tennis shoes. On Sundays, she strolled down Broad Street window-shopping, but she returned to the peddler to buy a black wool skirt and georgette blouse. "I must have looked like a midget clown parading along in my costume," she said.[33]

After two months at the mill, she was assigned to repair warp, a job that brought her a raise of $1 a week. A few months later, she was again promoted, this time to the inspection room, where she checked cloth for small flaws that could be combed out, while rejecting material with major flaws that had to be removed by cutting and splicing. Before her ninth birthday, a third promotion placed her in charge of other children, teaching them how to inspect cloth.

Soon after, Bessie suffered "perforated acute purulent appendicitis with diffuse peritonitis."[34] For a small fee, the appendix was removed by a young doctor who, she said, knew enough to put talcum powder on his rubber gloves but put on so much that "a large part of it stayed inside me and formed . . . little barnacles . . . " with the result that "other surgeons in later years started mining me for talcum."[35]

In 1916, the mill workers formed a union and went on strike. With time on her hands when she was not walking the picket line or throwing bricks at the strikebreakers, Bessie read books at home, a dictionary at her side. Reading only increased the scope of her dreams, dreams of being clean, well mannered, and dressed in fashionable clothing. Still a child, she told her fellow workers that she meant to be rich and have a big automobile.

Before the three-month strike failed, Bessie was advised by an older woman among the strikers to get out of mill work and apply for a job that she had seen advertised, for work at a beauty shop in Columbus. By the time Ira and Mollie returned to Florida, Bessie was already employed by Mattie and Charles Ryckley, who owned three beauty shops and ran a hair-goods store at 1146½ Broad Street.[36]

Mattie Ryckley, a small, dark, Jewish woman, offered Bessie her room, board, and $1.50 a week to work as a domestic and to help out at one of the shops. Bessie slept in a small room in back of the kitchen, rose at five o'clock to make breakfast for the Ryckleys and their six children, then washed the dishes and cleaned the house. On Saturdays, she did all the cooking after her employer taught her how to prepare kosher food. The ten-year-old child worked fourteen to sixteen hours a day. After cleaning the house, she went to one of the Ryckleys' shops, where she worked in a small, windowless room making wigs, switches (tresses of false hair), and mixtures to be used in the shop. She also helped with permanent waves, gave shampoos, and ran errands. Before long, she augmented her wages by $8 to $10 a week at what in effect became an apprenticeship, helping other operators who were working on commission. She sent half her earnings to Ira and Mollie, who were in Paxton, Florida, where Ira worked in a sawmill.[37]

The Ryckleys' customers included a number of local prostitutes, one of them the madam of a house. A beautifully dressed and well-spoken woman, Bessie's new friend corrected her grammar, directed her reading, and warned her "of men and their ways."[38] Worried that the young girl would be tempted by a life that seemed to bring the material things that she longed for, her new advisor repeatedly told her of the degradation that this entailed. She advised Bessie to "get where she was going the hard way" by earning a living. Bessie would follow her advice and never forgot the stories of beautiful cities and lovely clothes. Years later she wrote: "My foundation in ethics, honesty and morality came to me not from my foster mother but from Miss Bostwick, a priest and a prostitute. They all taught the same lessons."[39]

Armed with her newly learned skills as a beautician, Bessie began looking for an opportunity to escape cleaning house for the Ryckleys and to work as a full-time operator. That opportunity came when Mrs. Ryckley told an inspector from the labor office that she employed no one under the legal licensing age of sixteen. She explained Bessie's presence by claiming that she was the girl's legal guardian and that the child was not working at the shop. As soon as the inspector left, Bessie demanded room, board, and a job as an operator at $35 a week. If refused, she said that she would tell the inspector that Mrs. Ryckley had lied.[40] Asked if she thought that she had driven a hard bargain with Mrs. Ryckley, she said: "I don't. . . . At the end of three years I was a full-fledged, competent operator and felt that it was about time I earned some salary."[41]

But Bessie was not to remain with the Ryckleys for long. A few months later, she overheard a salesman tell her employer that he could have sold a permanent waving machine to a department store in Montgomery, Alabama, but there was no one there who could operate it. Bessie decided to apply for the job. Years later, working on a manuscript for a second autobiography that was never published, she wrote that after close to three years with the Ryckleys, she moved to Montgomery and was hired by the department store. "When one crowds two years of a previous book into a few pages," she added, "much of the sordidness of growing up must be left out."[42] One of the things left out was a liaison with a man named Robert H. Cochran. She was fourteen and pregnant.

Two

Becoming Jackie

Bessie wrote in her autobiography that she left Columbus, Georgia, for the job in Montgomery, Alabama, but she didn't. She went straight to DeFuniak Springs, Florida, where Ira and Mollie Pittman had settled.[1] There, on February 21, 1921—three months and one week after her marriage—she gave birth to a son, Robert H. Cochran, Jr.[2]

Little is known about the marriage except that it took place somewhere in Georgia on or about November 14, 1920.[3] Even less is known about the father, a twenty-year-old salesman.[4] At any rate, Bessie's eyes were fixed firmly on the future. Several months after giving birth, she left her son in DeFuniak Springs with Ira and Mollie and headed for Montgomery, where she moved into a boarding house and was hired to operate the permanent-wave machine in the beauty shop of the Nachman and Meertief department store. In her autobiography, Bessie places her residence at "12 South Anne [*sic*] Street" and says, "I will never forget it" because it was the first "really nice house" she had ever lived in. She may not have forgotten it, but she did misplace it; 12 South Ann was to be her residence in Mobile several years later.[5]

Attractive, intelligent, and apparently single, the new beautician flourished in the heady urban atmosphere of Montgomery. At work, she was befriended by an older colleague and floor manager, Mrs. Sarah Suzanne Lurton, who rapidly took the place of the earlier Miss Bostwick. Though openly skeptical of Bessie's claim to be seventeen, Lurton was taken by her protégé's quick intelligence and skills with the permanent-wave machine and guided her in sewing, cooking, and reading while introducing her to people her own age.[6]

Given this entry into the Montgomery social scene, Bessie took a few dancing lessons and, working on commission, soon saved enough money to buy a Model T Ford, a purchase that would have ramifications reaching far into her later life. Unable to read well enough to understand the car's repair manual but unwilling to pay for its maintenance, she made a careful study of the motor and within weeks was able to complete such complicated tasks as grinding the valves.[7] Thus, her first car marked the beginning of a lifelong ability to understand the mechanical function of the most sophisticated aircraft. Whenever baffled by engineering texts and diagrams, she would simply ask someone to explain them, then memorize the information.

The pretty blonde with the Model T became a sought-after guest at dances and parties. The jazz age that followed World War I was well under way, with youth defying the mores of their elders and favoring short-skirted flappers, drinking bathtub gin and, for some, uninhibited sexual behavior. Montgomery's best-known exponents of dancing, drinking, and making merry at the time were novelist F. Scott Fitzgerald and his wife, Zelda. It is unlikely that the former shoeless, eight-year-old mill hand and twelve-year-old hairdresser's apprentice ever met the Fitzgeralds, but she was at last beginning to enjoy the social life that she had always wanted. Quelling her natural loquaciousness to watch and listen to her new friends, she was an adept and eager student of proper dress, table manners, and conversational skills.

A year after Bessie arrived in Montgomery, her friend Mrs. Lurton suggested that she was not fulfilling her potential by working as a beautician and urged her to consider the nursing profession. When Bessie protested that with only two years of elementary school she could hardly pass the entrance examination, Mrs. Lurton persuaded the director of training at St. Margaret's Hospital to accept her as a student.[8]

Bessie embraced the new profession with her customary energy and curiosity. She memorized the arrangement of instruments for surgery and was required to assist during operations, one of the "most interesting" of which she considered to be a Caesarian performed on a midget from the Miller Brothers Carnival, which was wintering in Montgomery. Sights in the surgical theater did not repel her. But once, when a woman patient asked her to clean her false teeth, she did refuse. When the head nurse insisted, the fastidious student brought a pan and a pair of tongs to the bedside, thus ensuring that the dentifrice would be cleaned "untouched by human hands"—at least not by hers![9]

On her day off, she gave haircuts to patients in the wards and learned how to shave the men with a straight razor. Off duty, she napped in a dumbwaiter that she pulled up and out of sight between floors. But at the end of three years of training, she did not take the examination required for the registered nurse's degree. "I knew I could nurse," she said, "but I would never get away with a written document."[10] (Bessie's name is not recorded in the hospital archives, but her training is confirmed by a letter from an admirer who recalled knowing her as a student nurse in Montgomery.[11])

Just as she finished her training, Bessie's happy years in Montgomery ended abruptly with the horrifying news from Florida that her four-year-old son, Robert, had been fatally burned in a "yard fire" on May 19, 1925.[12] She hurried back to DeFuniak Springs for the funeral. Bewildered and depressed, she remained in the area for several weeks, staying with her parents and for a time with her favorite brother, Joseph, and his wife, Ethel. But the grieving mother could not afford to be out of work for long. So, without a degree but with three years of experience and hospital training, she found a job as a company nurse in Bonifay, Florida,[13] right back on Sawdust Road, her own name for the scruffy mill towns, clay streets, and ramshackle houses of her childhood.

A letter written some twenty years later by an admirer who had just read a summary of her autobiography in *Life* magazine provides a glimpse of what life was like for her in Bonifay. The writer notes that "at the time Mrs. Odlum was assistant to the mill doctor at Bonifay," he "was rooming at a typical sawmill boarding house run by the doctor's sister, a Mrs. Odis Lowery. For sake of appearances it was called 'The Central Hotel' and boasted a telephone."

The letter goes on: "I wonder if Mrs. Odlum remembers the night that the star boarder went uptown to see a girl, possibly her, fell outdoors and caved in his derby hat.

"As a nurse, Mrs. Odlum must remember that the old mill at Bonifay was a wreck and skinned up quite a few people, including the sawyer who hit himself with a log. I do not know if she were [*sic*] the one who patched up Bill Griggs or not. My wife became angry because I timed an old motorcycle for a friend one Sunday and [she] wished it would kill the next one who rode it. Bill was the first and her wish got results. He was badly bruised on the clay street, the only kind Bonifay had at that time except sand. Old man Donald was police and had a son named Earl, who caused him more trouble than the bunch from the mill. . . .

"I am relating this to let Mrs. Odlum know I was there and I would have written in sooner but, as stated before, I am still on 'The Sawdust Road' . . . working at a mill deep in the Florida Everglades where *Life* is seldom seen. Only when I went home last week and I found the story did I think of the old town."[14]

The new nurse was appalled to find that the doctor's office was filthy and his instruments "dirty and rusty and unsterile."[15] For wages of $3 a day, she set to work cleaning the office and the instruments. Before the week was up, she accompanied the doctor on a call to a site fifteen miles from town. They went to the area on a logging train to treat a man whose leg had been crushed by a tree. Bessie filled an old tub with water, built a fire, and boiled the surgical instruments, including a bone saw, then assisted the doctor in amputating the leg. For the next four days she stayed with the patient, enlisting his fellow workers to awaken her at four-hour intervals to check on his condition.[16]

Another night when the doctor was away—"he always seemed to be away"—Bessie was called to a shack to deliver a baby. Her only light came from a "mojo," a glass bottle filled with oil holding a hollowed-out ear of corn with a rag for a wick. The mother was on a St. George bed. Her three children slept on pallets on the floor during the delivery. With the newborn in her arms, Bessie discovered that there were no clothes for the infant or even a blanket. Suddenly she was overwhelmed by the similarity between this shack and the ones that she had lived in as a child and decided that she "had had quite enough of being a mill-town nurse. I had neither the strength nor the money to do the smallest fraction of what had to be done for these people and I determined that, if I was going to do anything for myself or others, I had to get away and make money. So I struck out for Pensacola."[17]

Bessie did not go to Pensacola, however. Still depressed by the death of her son, she went back to DeFuniak Springs to stay with her parents for several months before moving on to Mobile, Alabama, and a job at Pearson's Beauty Shoppe in the downtown part of the city. She had given up the idea of nursing when she realized that without a license the only work she would find would be in lumber towns. But there was money to be made in the beauty business and she intended to make some. In Mobile, she lived with her mother's brother, W. Jefferson Grant, and his wife, Bessie, at 222 Williams Street. Grant was a hostler, a maintenance engineer servicing locomotives for the Louisville and Nashville Railroad.[18]

While she was still at the Grants' and working at Pearson's, Bessie's husband, Robert H. Cochran, sought a divorce, accusing his wife of adultery with a person "unknown" on or about November 20, 1924. Cochran offered as evidence a letter and a telegram sent to his wife on or about March 7, 1926.[19]

Cochran's first application was dismissed on March 1, 1926, on the ground that it was impossible to find the witnesses upon whose testimony the case rested.[20] But in a second appeal made in January 1927, Cochran produced the required witness, Richard J. McCain, and the court granted him a divorce on February 5, 1927.[21]

According to court records, the adultery took place during a time when Bessie, though apparently a single student nurse, was still legally married to a husband with whom she had lived only briefly. She was developing into a person whom male pilots did not think of as a woman when she was flying or talking about flying, but she "could be very soft, very feminine."[22] She did not fight the case.

Within months of her divorce, Bessie left the Grants for a room of her own. To find it, she walked through some of the better neighborhoods until she saw a house that she liked. When the owner, Mrs. Beaulah Higgins, a widow,[23] answered the door, she discovered a pretty young blond woman who said she had never lived in such a nice house before and pleaded to be taken in as a boarder. Mrs. Higgins said that she had never thought of renting a room or taking in a stranger. But Bessie persisted until the woman agreed to rent her the room in the pretty house at 12 South Ann Street.[24]

A year later, Bessie heard that her whole family was gravely ill with influenza. For someone who claimed to be a foster child, disliked her mother, and disapproved of the rest of the family (except for her older brother Joseph), Bessie displayed unusual concern and hurried to DeFuniak Springs to look after them. Myrtle and Mamie survived, but her father died. "Because there was no undertaker [or they couldn't afford one] I laid him out in his only suit in a cheap coffin."[25] Before she returned to Mobile, she did the same for two of her family's neighbors.

Late in 1928, she moved to Pensacola, Florida. Each move from mill towns to Columbus and Montgomery, to Bonifay and Mobile, occurred after she had reached the limits of advancement in work skills and income. She broke the pattern only for the birth and death of her son and to nurse the parents and sisters whom she claimed were not her own. This time, she chose Pensacola because it was the nearest big city and certain to have beauty parlors. Within days, she found work at Le Jeanne Beaute Shoppe in the Blount Building at 22 East Gregory Street. The owner, whose name—M. Jeanne Stickley—was as affected as the one she gave her business, advertised the "Frederick's and Eugene Methods of Permanent Waving."[26]

Bessie rented a room on the ground floor of a private home. One hot summer night, after working late and returning home in a taxi, she opened the windows of her room and went to bed, only to be awakened by a man standing over her bed, his arm raised, holding something that looked like a knife. He whispered that he would kill her if she made a sound. "I screamed at the top of my voice," she said. He dropped his weapon and bolted through the window, leaving behind an ice pick from the ice box on the back porch. "I moved upstairs the next day."[27] Bessie was a brave woman but not a foolish one.

M. Stickley did not pay a salary, only a commission, but Bessie, who thought her employer "a morose woman" with very little business sense, invested her own savings in better equipment and soon became a partner.[28]

Before long, the talkative blonde with the Model T was dating a number of student pilots at the Pensacola Navy base. Among them was Ted Marshall, a handsome young ensign who became her frequent escort and would play an important part in her later career. They may have been in love, but Marshall was intent on pursuing his own career in the Navy, while Bessie was determined to move on to bigger and better positions in the beauty business.

Always impatient with anyone she thought knew less than she did, Bessie left the partnership three times. The first time, she found work as a traveling saleslady of dress patterns and material. On the road, she improved her spelling by reading road signs, and at night in motels she read books with a dictionary at her side.[29] She also gleaned a fund of information from the many hitchhikers whom she picked up, a habit that she continued for years.[30]

The second time that she left the Le Jeanne Beaute Shoppe she took over the management of a salon at the Edgewater Beach Hotel in Biloxi, Mississippi. After a hurricane destroyed the winter resort, she returned to her partnership until she saw an advertisement in a trade magazine for refresher courses at a beauty school in Philadelphia. "I figured if I went to Philadelphia and took a course—then returned to Pensacola—all the people in Pensacola would think I had the latest [styles] from the North."[31]

Bessie enrolled at the Philadelphia beauty school and was immediately convinced that she "knew more than the school did about most branches of beauty work."[32] The school itself more or less agreed, calling her in after only one day and offering her a job as an instructor for sixty dollars a week and half of every five-dollar private lesson she gave. Despite her conviction that the school was "taking money under false pretenses,"[33] Bessie agreed. But in a further display of her lifelong impatience and irritation with anything less than perfection, she called her Philadelphia experience "my first exposure to how stupid people can be. The school high-pressured and sold these courses to people who had neither the personal appearance nor the ability or intelligence ever to be beauty operators."[34]

Bessie stayed nine months, long enough to set aside savings for her next venture. Then she returned to Pensacola to find that after another three months, "I just couldn't take it any longer."[35] With Stickley unable to raise the $3,000 for her half of the partnership, Bessie agreed to payment at a later date, sold her car, and took a train to New York City.[36]

It had taken her nearly two decades of hard work to leave behind the red-dust lanes and the dirty, crowded shacks and smelly kitchens of Sawdust Road. They had been years of scrabbling to escape a world of tobacco-chewing men in overalls, of women in housedresses and slippers, of grubby children clinging to teenage mothers. But the woman who was to write years later that she "might have been born in a hovel but I determined to travel with the wind and the stars"[37] was finally on her way. For years, she had used a remark overheard as a six-year-old—"I was not one of the family"—as a means of tearing down a past that she had hated and rebuilding it into the future that she desired.

She boarded the train in Pensacola as Bessie Pittman. But from the day she stepped off it at Grand Central station—and forever after—she was Jacqueline "Jackie" Cochran. Although "Cochran" was the surname of the man who had divorced her for adultery, she told everyone she had picked both her names out of a telephone book.[38] Even as close a friend as Yvonne Smith, coexecutor of her will, said, "That's the story she told me. She created it herself."[39] When questioned about it by an editor of her never-published revised autobiography, she wrote back testily: "About the name 'Cochran' it was not the name of my foster family and I don't care to make any further comment."[40]

On a warm summer day in 1929, Jacqueline Cochran walked into the New York offices of Charles of the Ritz, a man known nationally both for his elegant cosmetic products and his expensive beauty salon. The receptionist who looked up saw a young blond woman, her face an oval with a wide forehead, a chin a little too prominent, and a nose a little too long. But her fair skin, colored by the sun, was flawless and her large brown eyes redeemed any other shortcomings. She was very young and very pretty. Wearing a simple dress, low-waisted with a hem above the knee in the fashion of that year, she revealed a good figure and shapely legs. Her hands were unusually large but drew little attention because she wore colorless nail polish and her fingers were bare of rings.

On hearing the blonde speak, the receptionist's smile faded. The request was made in the twanging drawl of the Florida panhandle. A hillbilly expected a job from Mr. Charles? Yet under the steady gaze of the stranger's brown eyes the woman behind the desk sensed a threat to the prevailing calm of the deeply carpeted office. She picked up the telephone and muttered into it. A few minutes later, she ushered Jackie into the great man's office.

From behind a huge desk, Charles waved her to a chair before he asked, "Little girl, what can you do?"

"I can do everything," she replied. "Hire me."

"You're too young," he countered.[41]

Finding the man both irritating and egotistical, Jackie told him that everything he could do she could do as well if not better and that she expected a fifty-percent commission on all her work.

Amused by her unabashed confidence, Charles told her that if he were to hire her, she would have to cut her long, curly hair. Saying that that was out of the question, Jackie rose from her chair and walked out. The next day, Charles called her and offered her a job, assuring her that she would not have to cut her hair, but she refused his offer. She would remember that day twenty-five years later when she observed, "Two of the most competitive lines of cosmetics in the market today are Jacqueline Cochran and Charles of the Ritz."[42]

Jackie's next application was made to Charles's rival, the equally famous Antoine, whose salon was in the Saks Fifth Avenue department store. "Antoine was a dreamer," she said, "an artist by nature with a flare for publicity. He was a bigger name at the time than Charles of the Ritz."[43] Jackie was starting at the top, a mode that she would follow all of her life.

On leaving Antoine's, Jackie walked over to Broadway and the corner of 79th Street, where she had rented a room in the back of a restaurant. The entrance was through the kitchen, but for $3 a week she was assured of privacy. Light came from two windows that offered a glimpse of a small park. There was a closet for her meager wardrobe, and a small bathroom. She had already scrubbed everything in the bathroom with disinfectant, washed the windows, lined the closet shelves, and dusted the bedstead and her one chair.

To keep out odors from the kitchen, she lined her door with felt tape. For the first time in her life, she could keep a place as clean as she wanted.[44]

That night, she treated herself to dinner in the restaurant. With every table occupied, the headwaiter asked her if she would share hers with two young men. One of them was Mike Rosen, who was to become a lifelong friend.

"She was fascinating," he said of that first meeting. "I had never heard a woman talk the way she could talk. What a storyteller!"[45]

Hoping to see her again, Rosen kept returning to the restaurant. They had several dinners together before he asked her for a date. She told him that as a beginner at Antoine's her hours were uncertain and she could not make any definite plans because, in addition to her daytime work, she was already investing in several small beauty shops as part-owner. And when she had no appointments at Antoine's, she supervised the operators, who were all recent beauty-school graduates.

Mike persisted in his pursuit of Jackie, eventually stopping at Antoine's salon, where Jackie took the time to introduce him to everyone on the staff. A few weeks later, Mike invited her to dinner and took her to meet his mother. But Jackie was not looking for a boyfriend. She continued to see him occasionally until the winter months when she began to work at Antoine's salon in Miami Beach. On her return from the first winter there, she rented an apartment at 40 East Tenth Street in Greenwich Village and resumed her dinner dates with Mike. Together, they bought a little Chevrolet coupe, splitting the cost, but only after he agreed to her request that a priest in the Village be allowed to use it during the day.[46]

The following winter, Jackie took the car to Miami, driving nonstop to give herself an extra day there before going to work. She spent that day driving around a Florida that she had never known, a Florida of resort hotels and palm trees instead of pine forests; of shining, high-rise buildings, not wood and tar-paper shacks. Women in outfits called "beach pajamas" strolled to cabanas along the white, sandy shore. Men in white suits played tennis and golf. Along rows of private docks, pleasure boats bobbed in the blue waters. This was the world that the "madam" whose hair she had curled at Mrs. Ryckley's had described. This was the world that she was determined to enter.

Three

Floyd

When Jacqueline Cochran returned to Miami for her second winter season at Antoine's, she intended to be more than an observer of the wealthy at play. At work, she was a tireless perfectionist with a growing clientele. She was also a gregarious, loquacious lover of parties, drinking, dancing, and the company of men. Several of her women clients began to invite her to be a partner to unaccompanied men at their endless round of dinners, dances, and gambling. Among these women, Molly Hemphill, with her husband, Cliff, took over most of Jackie's evenings. They invited her to join them four or five nights a week. Hemphill, a partner in a New York brokerage firm, liked to gamble and always gave Jackie $20 whenever they were at the gaming tables. If she won, she returned the original sum. If she lost, she would not accept more. While paying only $50 a month for an apartment that winter, she accumulated almost $8,000 from her wages, tips, and gambling, an impressive income during a nationwide depression, when 25 percent of the workforce was unemployed and the average annual income was about $2,000.

On one of the evenings with the Hemphills, Jackie was standing at the bar in the Surf Club waiting for the arrival of their host, Stanton Griffis, a broker colleague of Cliff's and former ambassador to Spain. Jackie was watching the door when she saw a slender man enter and turn toward the cloakroom. He wore a business suit instead of the customary white dinner jacket. His face was long, his forehead high, his fair skin freckled by the Florida sun, and he wore horn-rimmed spectacles. A plain man, neither handsome nor ugly, he was looking at her when Jackie said to Molly, "Why don't you ever invite men like him to your parties? He looks like he does something with his life besides gambling. That I could go for!"[1]

"Could you?" Molly asked, stepping forward to greet the newcomer. Taking his arm, she whispered, "She's a little working girl—quite ignorant—not too pretty. She *is* unusual looking, has a beautiful figure and all the boys like her. Even Cliff, I think, is slightly on the make for her. Come and meet her."[2]

Molly didn't know that the man who interested Jackie had accepted Griffis's dinner invitation only after being told that one of the guests was a pretty and interesting woman who worked for a living. It would be nice, he said, to talk to "someone down to earth." He was tired of meaningless conversation about films, sports, and celebrities.[3]

Jackie was introduced to the man, whose name was Floyd—she didn't catch the last name—and he sat on the arm of her chair in the lounge before dinner. She saw that his eyes were blue, and a lock of sandy hair fell over his forehead. He seemed to like her because he also sat next to her at dinner and listened attentively while she told him about her work at Antoine's. When he asked her more about her profession—for that is what he called it—she told him about her part ownership in cheap beauty parlors in New York, how she had once gone on the road selling dress patterns, and how she now wanted to travel again, selling cosmetics and perhaps even starting a company of her own. Floyd countered, "There's a depression on, Jackie. . . . If you're going to cover the territory you need to cover in order to make money in this kind of economic climate, you'll need wings. Get your pilot's license."[4]

After dinner, when the party moved to the casino, Floyd bought $100 worth of chips and gave Jackie $20. She lost the twenty and rose to leave. He asked her to stay on while they played some more. Breaking her rule of losing no more than twenty dollars, she accepted and lost nearly $300 before quitting. Deciding that the "quiet, serious man" that she had been with all evening "didn't look and act at all like the tycoons [she] had seen around the club all winter" and "probably . . . was a clerk in a bank," Jackie began to worry about his losing more than he could afford.[5]

She needn't have. The man she had taken for a bank clerk was Floyd Bostwick Odlum, a forty-year-old millionaire financier industrialist who had turned the stock market crash into a bonanza for himself and would soon be labeled by *Time* magazine "Depression's No. One Phenomenon."[6]

Like Jackie, Floyd Odlum began life poor. Born in Union City, Michigan, he was the fifth child of an itinerant Methodist minister. Like Jackie, he had worked as a child and an adolescent, picking berries, digging ditches, spraying vegetables, and selling clothing from a cart. In 1907, the fifteen-year-old found a job at an amusement park in Grand Rapids, riding an ostrich in a race with a horse. He kept the job until the day he was thrown into the grandstand by his unruly steed.[7]

A year later, his family moved to Boulder, Colorado, where he talked his way into enrollment at the University of Colorado by convincing the registrar that he would pay all of his tuition fees as soon as he graduated. Odlum achieved his undergraduate degree in Humanities in three years, working for both the local daily and the *Denver Post*, as an assistant librarian at the college, and in the summer months operating four fraternity houses as tourist lodgings. He also managed the drama club, the Women's League Opera, the student newspaper, and debated on the university team, for which he won an oratorical prize. In the class yearbook of 1912, the caption under his photograph read: "Manages to get his hands on everything that makes money."[8]

After graduation, Odlum entered the University of Colorado Law School, passing the state law examination in 1913 with the highest mark of any entrant and earning his law degree the next year summa cum laude.[9] Once admitted to the bar, he moved to Salt Lake City, where he was hired for $50 a month by the Utah Power and Light Company, an affiliate of the Electric Bond and Share Company, which had offices in New York.

In 1916, Odlum was transferred to New York to work in the law firm of Simpson, Thatcher, and Bartlett, handling the affairs of Electric Bond and Share. A few months later, he moved to the main office of that company to work on domestic utility consolidations until 1924, when he was promoted to vice president and chief buyer of utilities properties in Europe and South America. In the next three years, he bought for the firm gas- and water-powered properties worth 200 million dollars.

In 1923, while working for Electric Bond and Share, Odlum and his friend George H. Howard pooled $40,000 to found a venture capital firm—Odlum called it "a private speculating company"—that bought struggling businesses (that is, mainly power companies at first), reorganized their finances and management, and then sold them for a profit.[10]

By 1929, the new business went public as Atlas Corporation and was worth $6 million, inspiring a popular Wall Street ditty: "Little investment trust, don't you cry; Atlas will save you by and by."[11] Floyd was widely known as "Fifty-Percent" Odlum for buying "everything at 50 cents on the dollar."[12] Atlas itself had burgeoned by 1931 into the lodestar of the street, eventually controlling or managing such diverse businesses as bus lines (Greyhound), motion picture studios (RKO and Paramount), hotels (Hilton), women's apparel (Bonwit Teller, Franklin Simon), and uranium mines—plus an occasional bank, office building, or oil company.[13]

Odlum's financial success had been phenomenal. Asked how he had converted $40,000 into $150 million, Odlum said: "By concentrating all our investments in buying up troubled investment trust companies. Most of them were in deep trouble, unable to do a thing because of financial and management problems. So say one of these investment trusts, or holding companies as you might call them, was selling for $5 a share you could pay $7. Why, you could just turn around and sell off parts of the portfolio and make $10. We would buy one portfolio at a time, selling it for an automatic profit, then use the cash to repeat the operation over and over again."[14]

Although investment trusts like his were among the hardest hit by the worsening world economic situation, Odlum was a canny surveyor of the market and viewed the depression as "an ideal period in which to get rich."[15] In the summer of 1929, he sold more than 80 percent of Atlas's $6 million holdings, then raised $9 million more by issuing new stock just a month before the market crashed in October. Instead of cashing in his profits, he boldly invested all the money in the market, "buying up investment trusts" and industries "at considerably less than their assets were actually worth,"[16] then repairing, refurbishing, and reselling them for considerably more.

Odlum liked working in shirtsleeves. He played squash, collected paintings, made puns, wrote letters in longhand, and attended informal parties. He disliked coffee, liquor, red meat, swanky parties, dictating to a stenographer, and hurting people's feelings.[17] He also hated being called a "Wall Street man" and insisted he that had been in the Stock Exchange only once, and then as "a visitor in the gallery."[18]

From the moment that he met Molly Hemphill's "Little Nobody," Floyd Odlum was fascinated by her. Syndicated columnist Adela Rogers St. John described her as "the prettiest woman I have ever seen, the big, soft brown eyes, the shimmering golden hair, the lovely clear skin . . . so little, so very, very feminine. As you talk to her you notice the square jaw, the fire in the brown eyes, the steel poise of her body."[19]

A decade later, Helen LeMay, wife of retired General Curtis LeMay, said, "She had the most beautiful skin I've ever seen. It was like the loveliest whipped cream, and her big brown eyes were wonderful."[20]

Within two hours of their first meeting, Floyd must have known that he had discovered his alter ego—a woman who shared his unlimited ambition, to whom success was a virtue. Jackie in turn shared his impatience with anything less than all-out efforts and for settling for any place except first in any competition. Floyd's blue eyes narrowed with interest as she told him how she had saved money to leave Antoine's, the first step in her plan to go into business for herself.

In all of her gregarious party chatter, Jackie had never told anyone of her carefully made plans to achieve a specific goal. As she talked, she felt comfortable with this man who answered her questions in terms that she understood. She was talking to someone who had arrived in New York carrying a straw suitcase and wearing yellow, high-laced shoes and a sombrero. His attire had changed, but his jealous competitors on Wall Street still called him "The Farmer."

Two nights after Floyd and Jackie met, he gave a dinner party at the Indian Creek Golf Club. She was the guest of honor, seated at his right. Yet the next day, he left for New York without saying good-bye. Jackie returned to New York and Antoine's, where operators were not allowed personal calls. But Jackie insisted they make an exception for a call from a man named Floyd Odlum.

Floyd had not forgotten her. Never one to act on impulse, he was giving careful thought to any relationship that he might enter with this woman whose basic desires were so like his. He was alone when he came to Miami, but he was a married man—and had been for almost twenty years. He had met his wife, the former Hortense McQuarrie, a freshman at Brigham Young University, shortly after arriving in Salt Lake City. Red-haired, freckle-faced, impetuous, and intelligent, Hortense was the third of six children in the family of a Mormon church elder. Although she had never known the level of poverty experienced by Jackie, she had sold eggs from chickens that she raised to pay for everything but the necessities provided by her father.

The day that Hortense arrived in New York with Floyd and their three-month-old son, Stanley, Floyd was late for an appointment, so he left her and the child in the New York Central railroad station waiting room with a ham sandwich and a bottle of milk. He expected her to look after herself and the child, and she did. On Floyd's income of $100 a month—Utah Power and Light doubled his salary after six months—she managed to cover expenses, first in an apartment in New Jersey, then in another in Brooklyn, and finally, as they became wealthy, in a house in Forest Hills, Long Island.[21]

When Floyd met Jackie in Miami, he had left Hortense at home with their two sons, Stanley, sixteen, and Bruce, eight. He was alone because he was already considering a separation from Hortense. He dreaded hurting her and disliked the publicity that was inevitable with a divorce. Until then, he had no reason to consider a second marriage. He had already told Hortense that he was thinking of buying a controlling interest in Bonwit Teller, an upper-bracket women's clothing store in Manhattan. He needed her, he told her, to make an informal investigation of the store. His intent was to give Hortense the management of the enterprise, a responsibility that might ease the hurt that she would feel over the separation that he wanted. When the deal finally took place, Hortense approached her assignment as she did everything—or, as she herself put it, with "a complete inability to take things lightly or do things by halves."[22]

Floyd's hasty departure from Miami may have been caused by the theft from his Long Island home of four paintings in his extensive collection, two of them by Watteau and Gainsborough. The thieves were a newly hired butler and his wife, the cook. The couple said that they had acted in revenge when Hortense fired them on New Year's Eve, ten days after they were hired.[23]

Not until May, two months after their Miami meeting, did Floyd make up his mind about Jackie. He called her at Antoine's in New York and asked her to have dinner with him on a night of her choosing. She picked May 11, her twenty-sixth birthday. That night, he gave her a twenty-dollar gold piece as a keepsake, a token that she kept for the remainder of her life. Their affair had begun discreetly because, Jackie said, "he didn't want to hurt his sons." But, she added, "His first marriage to Hortense McQuarrie was over except on paper when we met."[24]

For the next four years, a commitment without marriage suited both Jackie and Floyd. She pursued her own plans with advice and financial support from him as she required. He continued to see Jackie but protected his wife and sons from the publicity of a public separation and divorce. It seemed a strange relationship—the uneducated, extroverted beautician and the quiet, retiring financier—but they were a perfect match, if not one made in heaven then at least ideal for earthly purposes. They were differently motivated. He enjoyed money but enjoyed making the deal more. He was already successful but wanted success for her, too. She was striving for acclaim and authority in her own right. Whether side by side or continents apart, they steadfastly pursued the fame, power, and fortune that they both so highly prized.

Four

Airborne

On July 23, 1932, at Roosevelt Field on Long Island, pilot-instructor Husky Llewllyn escorted his latest prospective student, a good-looking blonde, to a small plane. She was entitled to a thirty-minute sample flight at no charge before she signed a contract for $495, nonrefundable even if she could not solo by the time her training was completed. The plane was a Fleet trainer with dual controls and a sixty-horsepower engine. Llewllyn told his new student to get in the front cockpit and to watch the stick, but to keep her hands off it while he circled the field. At the end of the half hour, he told her to take the stick and try to land. She did—perfectly. As the plane rolled to a stop, Jacqueline Cochran knew that she was going to be a pilot.[1]

On that Saturday, the beginning of six weeks of vacation from Antoine's—her first in three years—she took a train from Penn Station to Mineola, the stop nearest to Roosevelt Field. The idea of her learning to fly was not a new one. It had begun four years before in Pensacola as she listened to the naval cadets that she dated talk endlessly about flying as if nothing else could be as wonderful. And Floyd, too, had suggested that she learn. A woman pilot selling cosmetics could cover a lot more territory, he said, and gain free publicity by doing it. When she told him that she intended to get a license during the first three weeks of her vacation, he said that she couldn't do it in six weeks, let alone three, and bet her the price of the lessons that she would need more time.[2]

Floyd was not the only doubter. Llewllyn said that she couldn't do it in less than two or three months, but he took her money for the twenty hours of lessons. He was glad to get it. The country was in the depths of a depression. In Washington, 20,000 men—jobless and poverty-stricken veterans of World War I—sought payment of the bonus that Congress in the boom year of 1924 had promised to pay them in 1925. The veterans, many accompanied by wives and children, were camped on the Capitol Mall and in parks and empty buildings throughout the city. Before the week was up, the "Bonus

Army" was driven from Washington by Army infantrymen equipped with tear gas canisters, and cavalrymen wielding swords. In Manhattan that same week, 10,000 people gathered in Union Square for a Communist Party rally.[3] The flying business, like most others, was slow, and Llewllyn needed work.

The morning after her first flight—a Sunday—Jackie was at the field by seven o'clock and had to wait two hours before Llewllyn arrived. She walked around looking at planes in the hangars and at a large mural of famous fliers on one wall. Originally a clearing for forced landings, Roosevelt Field had been expanded as early as 1910. Among the pioneer pilots who had used it were John and Matilde Moisant, Harriet Quimby, Blanche Stuart, Charles Hamilton, Clifford B. Harmon, Henry "Hap" Arnold, Charles Willard, and Major Alexander Seversky. The field was named for President Theodore Roosevelt's son Quentin, who had trained there as an Army pilot before being killed in combat over France.

Jackie's logbook shows that from July 24 to July 31 she flew with Llewllyn for a total of seven hours and five minutes. On one of those days he gave her what he called a lesson in aerobatics. In a deliberate attempt to make her sick, he spun, dived, rolled, and looped until Jackie turned and pointed to the field, indicating that she wanted to land. When the plane rolled to a stop, she got out, grinned at him and walked to the field restaurant, where he watched her scarf down a hot dog and soda.[4]

On August 1, her ninth day of lessons, Jackie soloed. A few minutes after she took off, the engine stopped. The novice aviator banked over the field and glided in for a perfect dead-stick landing.[5] That night at dinner, friends asked her what kind of plane she had been flying.

"I don't know," she replied.

"Was it a monoplane or a biplane?"

"It had four wings," she said. She counted four because the two wings on the biplane were separated by the fuselage.[6]

On the third, fifth, and sixth of August, Jackie returned to the field to fly, both with her instructor and alone for another five hours and twenty minutes. On August 8 and August 11, she passed her test flights supervised by O. P. "Dome" Harwood from the aeronautics branch of the Department of Commerce.[7] She also collected $495 from Floyd, having passed all of her flight tests in seventeen days, less than the three weeks that he had set as the deadline.

But there still remained the written examination. Fearless in the air, Jackie, who was terrified if she had to express herself in writing, persuaded the examiner to let her take it orally and asked her friend Mike Rosen to help her prepare. "I didn't think she could pass the examination because I knew how limited her schooling had been. She couldn't write at all," Rosen said.[8] Every evening when she returned from the field, Mike came to her apartment to read the questions to her and explain them, then gave her the correct answer. She memorized the material, passed the test, and received private pilot's license No. 1498, dated August 17, 1932.[9]

Instead of returning to Antoine's, the now-credentialed aviator signed up for a flight to Montreal for the fourth annual Canadian Air Pageant on August 20. Fifty other fliers at Roosevelt also registered to be guests at the Montreal Light Airplane Club. All were promised grandstand seats at St. Hubert Airport, a hotel room, breakfast, transport to the field, and a full fuel tank for the return trip to Roosevelt Field.[10]

For the "Good Will Caravan" flight, Jackie rented a Fairchild 22 from M. E. Grevenberg ("whom I came to know as 'Grevy' and a gypsy of the air if there ever was one")[11] and put up its full when-new value of $2,000 as security. After buying some maps, she asked an old-timer at Roosevelt Field to explain them to her. Instead, he told her to follow the Hudson River until she was over Lake Champlain, then to follow the eastern bank of the lake to Burlington, Vermont where she could land, clear customs, and ask for directions to Montreal.[12]

As she flew north on August 20, a beautiful day, she discovered that she had veered off from the river to a canal and had to fly back to find the river again. Finally reaching Burlington and clearing customs, she asked an airport attendant for directions to Montreal. The attendant thought that she was joking. When he realized that she wasn't, he told her the compass course and distance, at which Jackie confessed that she didn't know how to use a compass. The flabbergasted attendant rounded up some volunteers who gamely embarked on an impromptu lesson in navigation. They pushed the plane first in one direction, then another until it had turned a full circle while Jackie, back in the cockpit, carefully studied her compass. Back in the air again and halfway to her destination, Jackie sighted two huge silos that the men had told her to watch for. With one eye on the compass, she circled the silos to see if she had understood the lesson at Burlington. She had. When she landed at

St. Hubert Airport near Montreal, she discovered that she "was something of a heroine . . . because my first flight away from an airport had been a fairly long distance [350 miles] and across an international border."[13]

Even before she arrived at midday, all roads leading to the airport were jammed with traffic. Thousands of spectators at the field struggled to get good seats for an air show that included stunts by Navy pilot Captain Al Williams and Major Alexander Seversky, the Russian plane designer and pilot who had lost a leg when shot down by a German battleship in 1915 while flying patrol for the Russian Navy.[14]

On August 23, one month after her first lesson, Jackie's picture, with another woman pilot, appeared in the *Toronto Star*. The caption read: "Two society fliers at Roosevelt Field where they took off recently in their plane for a Montreal meet. Mrs. John T. Remy (left) and Miss Jacqueline Cochran." Mrs. John T. "Peggy" Remy did not fly in the same plane with Jackie, and Jackie was not a "society" flier, but it was a good start toward the public recognition that she longed for.

For that recognition, she faced some serious competition at home. Before the end of the month, Louise McPhetridge Thaden and Frances Harrell Marsallis set an endurance record, spending eight days, four hours, and five minutes aloft. Amelia Earhart, too, set two more records. Flying from Los Angeles to Newark on August 25, she became the only woman to fly nonstop from coast to coast and broke the previous women's distance mark by more than 500 miles.[15] These three and a dozen other women were already known for their skill and daring, while Jackie Cochran had only just learned to read a compass. She knew that she needed more lessons.

The previous January, the Bureau of Aeronautics showed that only 57 of 588 women fliers held transport licenses. Jackie wanted to be one of them, too. A month after the Montreal meet, she drove from New York to the west coast in six days to enroll at the Ryan School of Aeronautics in San Diego. On the way, she feared that she might have forgotten how to fly, so she stopped off at Salt Lake City and rented a pusher plane, an old Curtiss-Wright with the engine in the back. She flew over the Wasatch Mountains to see the autumn leaves already dusted with snow, and on the way back, she dived low to chase buffalo on an island in the middle of the Great Salt Lake, feeling like "a modern Indian turning loose a stampede."[16]

The Ryan school on the shore of San Diego Bay proved a disappointment to Jackie. Its founder, T. Claude Ryan, who had built the plane that Lindbergh flew on his historic trans-Atlantic flight in 1927, placed a strong emphasis on classroom lessons. Although she did get some time practicing vertical spins, figure eights, and landings in a tiny Great Lakes biplane, Jackie fretted that there was too much class work and not enough air time. "I unlearned the little bit I had been taught," she complained. "There were thirty-seven of us with only one instructor who did ground school instructions and sat around in the afternoon shooting craps."[17]

Fortunately for Jackie, however, the Ryan school was right across San Diego Bay from North Island, where naval pilots did their advanced training. When the school got too much for her, she fled to the island, where she soon found herself united with several friends whom she had known as cadets when in Pensacola. One of them was Ted Marshall, the handsome ensign that she had regularly dated who was now a lieutenant-commander and air officer aboard the battleship USS *West Virginia.* Marshall and a friend, Naval Reserve officer Paul Adams, invited her to parties and dances aboard the ship. At those parties, the topic of conversation was generally their mutual vocation, flying.

One day when she was feeling particularly depressed and "needed a shoulder to cry on," Jackie wrote, "I started weeping [to Marshall] about my lack of training, and [how] I had paid all this money in and was not learning anything."[18] Marshall proposed a deal: if Jackie would buy her own plane, he and his friends would teach her to fly "the Navy Way," giving her flight instructions whenever his ship was in port. His friend Paul Adams would fill in for him when Marshall was at sea.

Cochran bought a fifth-hand Travel Air trainer for $1,200, hired a mathematics tutor, and the lessons began. When the *West Virginia* was transferred up the coast from San Diego to Long Beach, Jackie quit the Ryan School (with 101 flying hours to her credit) and also moved to Long Beach to continue her "Navy Way" crash course with Marshall,[19] which she described as six months in which "I experienced ten years' worth of trial-and-error flying."[20]

The first time that Cochran took the Travel Air up, the engine quit on her and she made her second dead-stick landing. It was but the first of fifty-three such landings in the same plane. "The valves kept falling out and reseating valves was very expensive," she said.[21]

Forced landings at the time were not all that unusual. "When I learned to fly," she recalled, "we usually guessed our speed by the whirr of the wind in

4.1. Jackie Cochran at the Ryan Flying School at San Diego in 1933. Her instructor, Bob Kerlinger, is in the cockpit of the Great Lakes 2T-1E. (National Air and Space Museum, Smithsonian Institution, SI 2006–280. Courtesy Ryan Aeronautical Library.)

the wire struts and judged our let-down and approach by the position of the lap of the engine with respect to the horizon. One eye had to be kept constantly on an unstable pasture or beach for landing" because "engine trouble and forced landings were almost the rule rather than the exception."[22] Soon, she was flying as far as Palm Springs and Los Angeles. "There were always fields where you could get a stalled small plane down."[23]

On one occasion, taking off from Grant Central Airport in Glendale, her engine failed and she crashed through a metal fence, crossed the highway, and smashed into a parked car. "The car belonged to a traffic judge," she said, "and he fined me $25 for unlawful parking."[24]

Jackie was not injured, but her much-used Travel Air suffered considerable damage. In the crowd that gathered around the wreck were two strangers from the airport who offered suggestions for repairing the aircraft. One was Jack Northrop, the aircraft designer who had left Lockheed to go into business for himself, and the other was Al Menasco from the Douglas engine factory. "As Jack studied the damage, Jackie gushed confidently, 'Someday

I'll be flying one of your planes!' Preoccupied, the designer replied with a thoughtful nod, 'Of course you will!'

"Tactfully, he suggested that perhaps Miss Cochran could profit from a bit more instruction, little thinking that within a year she would indeed be flying one of his airplanes."[25]

Menasco fixed the engine, and Northrop repaired the plane. "It was the kindness of these two who kept up Jackie's faith in aviation."[26]

During the months that she spent at Long Beach, not all danger stemmed from her errant Travel Air. On March 10, 1933, while she was with Marshall having cocktails at the apartment of Captain Gaid Mitchell and Mrs. Mitchell, Long Beach was rocked by an earthquake that caused thirty-six deaths and hundreds of injuries.[27] The front of the apartment building fell away, and the sofa on which Jackie was sitting landed against the wall across the room. For the next few days, the former nurse worked as a volunteer at the local hospital and slept and prepared her meals in the back yard of her apartment.[28]

At Long Beach, Jackie logged another sixty-five hours in the air and spent more hours on ground-school lessons with Marshall, Adams, and her math tutor. She missed Floyd, but her evenings were not spent alone. In addition to dinners with Marshall and his mother, who had their own Long Beach apartment, she went to parties given by naval officers also stationed there. In 1954, one of her escorts, by then a retired captain, reminisced: "1932 doesn't seem so long ago—Long Beach airport, USS *Saratoga*, Coconut Grove and Phil Harris, Paul Adams, but twenty years have gone by all too swiftly."[29]

After her lessons with Marshall and Adams, she flew to the Grand Canyon where she practiced altitude flying, take-offs, and landings from one to three hours daily.[30] She was doing everything demanded of U.S. Navy flight cadets, and in June, she received her limited commercial license from Jimmy Knoll at San Diego, but only after her Travel Air oil line broke and the engine failed again, which caused a forced landing.[31]

That same month, Marshall was transferred to the naval station at Honolulu. But before he left, he and Jackie made plans to enter the MacRobertson Race, an international competition from England to Australia, in the fall of 1934.

Before she returned to New York, Cochran went to see Marshall's brother, George, at his Coachella Valley ranch in southern California, and commissioned him to buy twenty acres of land for her. Two weeks later, when Floyd was on the west coast for a business meeting, she told him to look at the area that she called "the desert fairyland of Southern California." Floyd agreed and asked Marshall to buy land for him, too, adjacent to Jackie's.[32]

Before she left California, Jackie sold her Travel Air for a little more than she had paid for it.[33] Then she drove her Chevrolet back to New York with a limited commercial pilot's rating in her purse. But there was one more rating that she wanted—transport pilot.

Five

Transport Pilot

When Jackie returned to New York in June 1933, she had logged more than 300 hours in the air in less than a year. For the additional training, she needed to upgrade her commercial rating to transport, so she bought her first new plane, a green WACO. Trimmed in bright orange, the commercial aircraft had a 210-horsepower engine and a closed cabin with seats for the pilot and three passengers. It cost $3,200, which she covered with the money raised by selling both her Travel Air and her car.[1]

Brimming with confidence over her aerial achievements, she had an overwhelming desire to show the Pittmans their new Bessie—already being identified by the press as Jacqueline Cochran, New York society pilot. Before beginning her next round of lessons with Llewllyn, she loaded her WACO with a new wardrobe and a cargo of other gifts and flew to DeFuniak Springs and the family that she would not publicly acknowledge but still refused to abandon.

Two of that family, in fact—her eldest sister, Mary Elbertie (Mamie), and her daughter Willie Mae—were already living with her in her East 10th Street New York apartment.[2] Broke and jobless, Mamie had come to her sister for help and Jackie gave it, but on the sole condition that she return the beautiful blonde doll that Jackie had won in the Christmas lottery twenty years before, but was forced to give to her baby niece, Willie Mae. Mamie and Willie Mae were given shelter, and the doll was repaired and redressed, to remain with Jackie until her death. Jackie could forgive, but she never forgot. "[The doll] was one of the very first prizes of my life. And no one should have been able to take that away from me. No one."[3]

At DeFuniak Springs, Jackie gave an entire new wardrobe to her mother, Mollie Pittman, but she stayed with her favorite brother, Joe, and his wife Ethel and their five children. In an effort to extend her help to Joe's family, too, Jackie suggested adopting his five-year-old daughter, Billie, a suggestion that outraged her brother.[4] She apologized to Joe and gave him a picture of herself in her flying costume, signing it: "To Ethel and Joe with love."[5]

The visit was cut short when Jackie learned that her friend and teacher, Ted Marshall, had been killed in an air crash off the coast of Oahu on August 9. Marshall and four other Navy men were aboard a plane that crashed into the sea after both the vertical and horizontal controls of the aircraft collapsed.[6]

Jackie's first thought was of Ted's mother, Mary, whom she had promised to accompany to Honolulu for a visit with Ted the next winter. She knew that Marshall had been reluctant to leave his mother in Long Beach and had tried to provide for her in the event of his death.

Back when he was an ensign, Marshall had allocated a large part of his salary to a bank to be invested in stocks. But the market crash left him with only $1,500, which he gave to Jackie after she said that she had a friend who could invest it profitably for him. The "friend," of course, was Floyd, whose complete trust of Jackie seems to have prompted him to befriend her former boyfriends as well. He also hired Mike Rosen as a troubleshooter for his New York interests, which included assisting Hortense as she took over the management of Bonwit Teller.[7] Odlum not only looked after Marshall's $1,500—increasing it to $80,000 in the next few years—but, undoubtedly with Jackie's future in mind, corresponded regularly with the Navy man on aviation matters. Only eight days before his death, Marshall wrote Floyd assuring him that a motor could run long enough for a round-the-world trip if the plane were refueled in flight and further offering to write friends in the Navy's Bureau of Aeronautics "for study and review of any specific plan that might be presented to you."[8]

To console Ted's bereaved mother, Jackie decided to fly from DeFuniak Springs to Long Beach in time to attend the memorial service for Marshall, taking Joe's twelve-year-old daughter Gwen with her for company.[9]

Flying in 1933 was more like hopping. From Florida, they stopped at Memphis; St. Louis; Omaha and North Platt, Nebraska; and Cheyenne and Rock Springs, both in Wyoming. Taking off from Rock Springs on August 15, her radio was not properly shielded from the motor and pulled the compass off about twenty degrees, causing her to try to cross the mountains nearly 100 miles south of her true course. Forced down by a downdraft, she landed at sixty miles an hour, hit an irrigation ditch in the middle of an alfalfa field, and ground looped, tearing off the left wing of her new WACO.[10]

In her logbook, Jackie identified the nearest town as Linwood, Utah. But a letter written by Mrs. Rex Terry in 1955 described the incident as having taken place "in a pretty green and orange plane on my dad's ranch . . . near Manila, a little town in Utah [near the Wyoming border]. You had a young girl about 14 with you and I will never forget how badly I wanted to be her."[11]

Mrs. Terry's letter was accompanied by a check for a copy of Jackie's autobiography published the year before. She wanted to give the book to her father and asked Jackie to sign it. Jackie destroyed the check and sent the book along with a note saying: "You might be interested to know that the 11-year-old girl [Gwen says she was twelve] who was with me is now married and has a family."[12]

An hour after the crash landing, Jackie borrowed a Ford from Mrs. Terry's father and drove 110 miles to Salt Lake City, where she left Gwen in a hotel room. She found a mechanic and drove him back to the ranch that same night to inspect the plane, then returned to Salt Lake City with him. He promised to order a new wing and install it for her at the ranch. The next day, she and Gwen boarded a commercial airliner at Salt Lake City and reached Long Beach in time to accompany Mary Marshall to her son's memorial service. "She had been wonderful to me," Jackie said, and Jackie never forgot anyone who was "wonderful to her."[13] "Aunt Jackie was fun to be with," Gwen recalled. "She bought me several pretty outfits," and after the funeral they stayed at the Ambassador Hotel in Los Angeles "and I remember sitting in the lobby watching all the movie stars go by. That was pretty heady stuff for a twelve-year-old girl from the country."[14]

As soon as Jackie received word that the repairs to her WACO had been made, she booked seats for the two of them on a commercial airliner to return to Salt Lake City, then hired a car to take them back to the ranch. She took off from the same field where she crashed, heading east on a trip that took two weeks. Forced down at Kerney, Wyoming, by bad weather, she was again delayed at Ottumwa, Iowa, by motor trouble. In Dubuque, she picked up "a precious passenger," undoubtedly Floyd. Again, after landing in a forty-five-mile-an-hour wind in Chicago, she wrote in her logbook: "Had the most precious person in the world for a passenger."[15]

Back at Roosevelt Field on October 8, Cochran entered an all-woman pylon race, part of a charity air pageant. She called the flying "high, wide and handsome," but she was still no match for experienced pilot Edna Gardner, who won the race, also in a WACO. Jackie could only comment: "It was the only all-woman race I ever entered."[16] At ease with male pilots, most of whom liked her and were generous with their advice, she chose to remain outside the circle and camaraderie of women pilots, most of whom were members of the Ninety-Nines, organized with help from Amelia Earhart. Jackie did not like the company of women—and she hated to lose.

After the race, she flew Floyd, who had a bad cold, to Florida for a weekend in the sun. Caught in heavy weather over the Carolinas, she dared not turn back because she didn't yet know how to fly "blind." For the next forty minutes, she flew straight ahead. Floyd, who said he was going to take a nap, saw her cross herself before she emerged from the clouds. Only then did he tell her that his throat was dry, whether from his cold or from fear he didn't say. She landed in a cow pasture near a house to get him a drink of water, then took off again as the skies cleared. They made it to Florida, but Jackie vowed that she would never carry a passenger again until she knew how to fly using instruments only.[17]

She spent the next month practicing for her transport license. Ever fearful of written tests with their problems in higher math, Cochran won the sympathy and help of a number of pilots at the field. Sandy Willetts, the examiner, put her in a room by herself "so she could be quite comfortable and concentrate"—and perhaps also to prevent eager male advisors from helping her. Passing the flight test under Harwood and the written test under Willetts, Jackie—sixteen months after her first-ever flying lesson—became a full-fledged transport pilot in the first week of December.[18]

A week later, Jackie flew to Florida again, this time with a student pilot, Montgomery Jason Chumbley. She had not forgotten her vow to learn blind flying and had already read a book on the subject. During the flight, she covered her portion of the hood with a black curtain and had Chumbley, seated outside the curtain and beside her, "tell me if I was about to run into another plane or fly upside down."[19] This flight by the attractive blonde who seemed to know everybody at Roosevelt Field was reported in the *New York Journal-American*, accompanied by a photograph and detailed description of her flying suit—trousers and jacket of imported tweed, a soft sports shirt, silk scarf, and camel-hair coat. Jackie was dressing the part.[20]

Jackie stayed in Miami over Christmas, probably with Floyd, although they were both careful to avoid publicity about their affair. She returned to New York by way of Charleston on December 29, but flew back to Miami for the Sixth Annual All-American Air Races on January 9. The just-licensed transport pilot did not compete, but undoubtedly managed to meet and talk with some of the country's leading pilots, among them Al Williams, Alex Seversky, Frank Hawks, Jimmy Doolittle, E. E. Aldrin, and Wiley Post. She returned to New York by way of Jacksonville and Washington.

Always angling for more flight time, Jackie wheedled permission from airline pilots to board their aircraft, which carried passengers, but no flight attendants. In exchange for serving meals, a task the copilot hated, she was allowed to fly the plane after the passengers were asleep. This could not go into her logbook, but she estimated such unofficial flight time at about 300 hours and "the finest sort of training."[21]

Dissatisfied with her makeshift lessons under Chumbley, Jackie began in February to contact airline pilots who were grounded when the Postal Service withdrew mail contracts from commercial aviation firms and gave the job to the Army. On April 1 at Newark Airport, she was introduced to Wesley L. Smith, a veteran flier with Transcontinental and Western Air, a man who had trained many pilots. Smith agreed to teach Jackie instrument flying. He was a gruff, outspoken man who both impressed and intimidated Jackie, but not for long. After a few hours of listening to him barking orders at the top of his lungs, she lost her temper and yelled back at him: "Shut up! Don't you ever shout at me like that!"[22] Smith apologized, explaining that he was partially deaf and his shouting was habitual. With her part of the cockpit blacked out, Jackie flew back and forth across the country for four months accompanied by Smith while she learned to interpret maps and logged 400 hours on instruments and radio beacons.

Flying west with Smith in late June, she doubled over in agony with stomach cramps. They landed in Long Beach, where a doctor who came to the hotel told her that she had an abdominal obstruction that required emergency surgery. Jackie submitted to this operation, the second since her early botched appendectomy. With her customary impatience, a week later before the stitches were removed, she signed herself out of the hospital, took a taxi to the airport, and flew the WACO to Los Angeles because she had promised to lend it on that date to her friend Mabel Walker Willebrandt.[23]

She was to pay with pain for her premature departure, but Jackie did not break promises—certainly not to someone like Mabel. Along with Earhart, Mabel became one of Jackie's few close women friends.[24] A popular assistant attorney general in both the Coolidge and Hoover administrations,

Willebrandt was the first woman lawyer to plead a case before the Supreme Court.[25]

After delivering the WACO and returning for follow-up care, Jackie resumed her instrument training although she now weighed only 104 pounds, twenty pounds below normal.[26]

Back in January, Floyd had written in her logbook: "All good fortune to America's future air queen."[27] But Jackie faced stiff competition for that crown. In the preceding twelve months, Laura Ingalls soloed across the Andes from Santiago to Buenos Aires and won the Clifford B. Harmon Trophy as the outstanding woman pilot of 1934. Anne Lindbergh flew 8,000 miles with her famous husband, providing material for her book *North to the Orient.* Amy Johnson Mollison, with her husband, Captain James Mollison, as copilot, flew nonstop from England to the United States. Frances Marsallis and Helen Richey stayed airborne for nine days, twenty-one hours, and forty-three minutes—a new endurance record—and French aviator Maryse Hilsz made a round-trip flight from Paris to Tokyo and back in five days, nine hours, and three minutes.

All these record holders did not intimidate Cochran, the rookie pilot. Floyd's "future air queen" had already set for herself three goals to be reached before the end of 1934. She wanted to win the Bendix Trophy, set a cross-country speed record in the United States, and win the MacRobertson International Race from England to Australia.

Six

Three-Time Loser

After months of private study and flying under the stern tutelage of "Nothing was ever good enough for Wesley," Cochran figured that she had mastered the intricacies of blind flying, air-to-ground communications, radio, and the Morse code and was ready to attack her year-end goals. When Smith himself said: "Jackie . . . you sure can read a map even if you do hold it upside down," and added, "If you keep it up you may even be able to fly straight someday," she recognized it as a compliment and knew that she was ready for sure.[1] Her first objective was winning the September opening event of the National Air Races, the Los Angeles-to-Cleveland race sponsored by Aviation Corporation president Vincent Bendix. Next, while continuing on to New York, she intended to set the transcontinental speed record. Then, in October, she planned to compete in her first international race from England to Australia, the one that she had originally planned to make with the late Ted Marshall.

For all these flights, Jackie needed the best plane that money could buy, and, though not yet ready to publicly acknowledge the mistress he so loved, Floyd Odlum was determined that she would have it. Four months before the Bendix, he wrote directly to the Chief of the Army Air Corps and, identifying himself initially as Director of the International Section of the Chamber of Commerce, proposed that the Army lend Jackie one of its four P-30 pursuit planes in exchange for which he would post bond indemnifying the government against all loss or damage. Stressing particularly the benefits that Jackie's flying an American plane in the prestigious MacRobertson might bring to U.S. foreign trade and the prestige of the American air industry abroad, he concluded his request, somewhat superfluously: "I shall be glad if need be to submit proof of my financial capacity. I am in business and my chief position is that of President and Chief executive of Atlas Corporation (an investment Trust having assets of about $140,000,000 measured by market values). I am also a Director of United Fruit Company, a Director of American & Foreign

Power Company, a Director of Home Insurance Company and President of American Arbitration Association."[2]

When the Army failed to reply to his proposal, Floyd turned to Granville, Miller, and DeLackner, builder of the Gee Bee, a high-speed, low-winged monoplane named for its designers, Z. D. Granville and his four brothers. From eleven available models he chose the Q.E.D., *Quod Erat Demonstrandum*, with an 800–horsepower Wasp Super Sportster, and also demanded for Jackie future production rights to the plane.[3]

Actually, Jackie looked on the relatively new and untested Gee Bee as simply a backup for the plane she really wanted, a Northrop Gamma 2G. Ironically, she placed an order for the Gamma just a year from the day when Jack Northrop had surveyed the wreck of her old Travel Air and suggested that she take some more flying lessons.[4] The Gamma 2G was powered by a liquid-cooled, Curtiss-Wright engine, the SVC-1570–F4, called the Conqueror. But it was enhanced by a special turbo-supercharger, the only one of its kind, designed to reach 750 horsepower.[5]

Jackie's flight in the Bendix Race in September and her following attempt to break the transcontinental speed record would be an excellent test of the Gamma for what she considered the most important contest of all, the MacRobertson Race, starting on October 20. Also known as the Melbourne Centenary Air Race, its prize money was put up by an Australian, Sir Macpherson Robertson, head of the MacRobertson Chocolate Company and co-owner of the MacRobertson-Miller Aviation Company.[6] Robertson said that his objective in sponsoring the race was "To deliver Australia from its isolation, which can only be effected by airplanes; to prove that a fast communication between Australia and England is possible; and to get people to dig up their atlases in order to find out where Melbourne is situated on our planet."[7]

Expenses for the race were unusually high, since entrants not only had to hire one or more copilots, but also had to position ground crews along the route for maintenance and refueling. Most of the entrants were backed by suppliers of aircraft parts and flight equipment as well as fuel. But Jackie was not well-known enough to receive such corporate support. She borrowed some money from her lawyer friend and fellow pilot Mabel Willebrandt. But the bulk of her backing—not to mention "infusions of cash, credit and worldwide connections"—came from Floyd Odlum and his Atlas Corporation.[8]

Jackie needed two copilots, one for the first half of the race as far as India and a second from India to Australia. She hired Wesley Smith, her trainer, for the first half, and his Transcontinental and Western colleague, Royal Leonard, for the second, described at the time as "two of the best air mail pilots in the United States."[9] Before the race, both men scouted their portions of the route, setting up service depots with spare parts and fuel and even making arrangements with amateur radio operators "rather than . . . depend entirely on the official stations."[10]

Five more men were hired that summer. All of them studied plane repair at the Northrop plant in California and engine maintenance at the Wright plant in Ohio and were then dispatched to the five mandatory stop points—Fred McLeod to Allahabad, India; George W. Just to Baghdad; Louis Werner to Hong Kong; Gilbert Clark to Darwin; and Joseph Maier to Charleville, Australia. Two more men, Sid Everett and Fred Entrekin, were hired to accompany Jackie and her aircraft aboard ship to London.[11]

Despite the most thorough pre-flight preparations of the twenty entrants that finally made it to the starting point at Mildenhall Aerodrome, England,[12] Jackie's carefully structured plans—made with the help of Floyd and Willebrandt—began to fall apart in August. On August 28, George Just, the man assigned to Baghdad, got only as far as Paris where a confidence man swindled him out of the $1,800 that Jackie had given him.[13] At the Northrop plant in Inglewood, the General Electric turbo-supercharger on the Gamma's 16-cylinder engine blew up on the test stand.[14] At Dayton, the supercharger on Curtiss-Wright's new Conqueror engine blew up too,[15] leaving Jackie with no plane for either the Bendix or the MacRobertson.

Unwilling to give up on the Gamma, Jackie had Northrop install a third engine—this one without a supercharger. The plane was approved for licensing on September 29, and the next day Jackie left from Inglewood for New York with Royal Leonard as her copilot. She was in a hurry. Only ten days remained before she and Leonard were to sail from New York to England on the S.S. *Berengaria*.[16]

Two hours out and 15,000 feet over Arizona, the Gamma's heater malfunctioned and the engine sputtered, spewing oil out over the canopy. Leonard considered bailing out until he saw that Jackie was losing consciousness from the leaking carbon monoxide that filled the cockpit. He spotted an emergency airfield near Ashford, Arizona, and landed safely.[17]

After ordering replacement parts from Northrop, Jackie took the next TWA flight to New York while Leonard stayed with the plane to make the necessary repairs. The repairs made, Leonard took off once more, only to be forced down yet again at Tucumcari, New Mexico, by another engine failure. He crashed in an irrigation ditch, shattering one wing and the lower part of the fuselage. Exhausted, Leonard telephoned his report to Cochran in New York. "Give up, Jackie," he sighed. "I don't think so," she replied.[18]

The Gamma was out of the race, but Jackie was not. Figuring "any plane was better than no plane," she immediately thought of the Gee Bee, which she still owned, but whose MacRobertson entry rights she had transferred to Clyde Pangborn, another American contestant, after she bought the Northrop Gamma. Meanwhile, Pangborn himself abandoned the Gee Bee and accepted a more enticing offer to copilot a Boeing transport entered by Roscoe Turner. But he infuriated Jackie by demanding payment for an entry that he no longer needed. She said later that if she had been a man she would have asked him to step behind the hangar for a real fight. She did not say whether she had paid Pangborn or not, but she did secure entry in time for the race.[19]

She left all arrangements for moving the Gee Bee and getting it to London to Mabel Willebrandt, who was acting not only as Cochran's sponsor, but also as her lawyer and press spokesperson. While Cochran was aboard the S.S. *Berengaria*, Willebrandt sent a three-page letter to Jackie's London representative, Maurice Turner, detailing a mound of difficulties to be overcome.[20]

Leonard and Smith were exhausted after flying through fog and bad weather from Los Angeles to pick up the Gee Bee in Newark, but there was no time for Leonard to test fly the new plane because within hours he had to board a ship leaving for India, where he was to replace Smith halfway through the race.

Furthermore, Leonard could not leave the country until he gave a statement to the Department of Commerce's Bureau of Aeronautics describing the Gamma's engine failure and crash landing. Willebrandt's aide, Vera Mankinen, took Leonard's statement while bundling him on the boat about two minutes before it sailed.

An otherwise unidentified Mr. Taylor refused to fly the Gee Bee from Newark back to the Springfield, Massachusetts, factory for a day and night of tests by an aeronautics inspector, "saying that he had six children and was not willing to fly it any more." Though claiming to reserve judgment, he nevertheless added that the Gee Bee "was just a little too fast and too rich" for his blood.[21]

Smith himself flew the Gee Bee to Massachusetts for the tests, which were still not completed when the plane was loaded aboard a Cunard liner along with Smith, the government inspector, and the plane's designer, Z. D. Granville. Willebrandt reported that the plane was "in a very good position" in the ship's hold,[22] but for most of a very rough crossing, the three men were too seasick to work.[23]

Though undaunted by the prospect of long flights over the ocean, Jackie had never lost her fear of assault learned in the dark corners of the textile factory and her nighttime encounter with a thief in Pensacola. She asked Mabel to get her a permit to carry a handgun on her return alone from Australia, but Mabel was unable to do this.

After the ship docked at Southampton, the Gee Bee was moved to a nearby airfield where Jackie met Smith hours before the start of the MacRobertson. With Smith taking the controls and Jackie sitting on a wooden cracker box in the back cockpit because the rear seat had not yet been installed, they flew to Mildenhall Aerodrome, the Royal Air Force base. They arrived at dusk in a landing so hard that they both thought a wing had been damaged. Fearing that newspaper reporters would see the damage, they left the plane on the field only to discover the next morning that no damage had been done. However, Jackie noted that the wheels of the aircraft were too close together, making it impossible to roll straight down the runway. By then, she had decided the Gee Bee was a very unreliable aircraft.[24]

Since her arrival in England, Jackie had avoided the press, probably because she was with Floyd. But at Mildenhall, she and Smith were met by a crowd of curious spectators eager to see the American dubbed "the mystery woman" by the press.[25] The following day, she was interviewed with the English pilot, Amy Johnson, who had entered the race with her husband, Jim Mollison. Both women complained that they lacked experience with their respective planes with only twenty-four hours left to practice. Jackie also said that her leather flying suit and boots made it hard to appear feminine enough "when the only things you can wear while flying are man-like." Never one to neglect her business interests, she added that she would carry her compact and powder her nose before each landing.[26]

On the morning of October 20, 20,000 spectators were at Mildenhall to watch the contestants take off. The Mollisons left first; Jackie and Smith were fourth.[27] Mechanics had worked on the Gee Bee all through the night, but Jackie's doubts were quickly confirmed. "As soon as we were airborne, the plane sort of staggered, dipped slightly and we knew we were in for a real ride. Neither of us knew that Gee Bee well enough. . . . Noise. God, that plane was noisy. . . . There was no insulation to hold down the racket or keep out the cold. We were freezing and flying at 14,000 feet with no oxygen."[28]

Nearing the Bucharest airfield, they attempted a landing, but one flap was stuck and the other limited in movement. Pulling up, they made a second attempt, and again the flaps did not respond. "By that time, we had loosened my canopy and agreed that if we failed on the third attempt to land, there was nothing left but a jump. Finally, we got both flaps back in flying position and came in very fast. It was a good long field and luckily so—we used it all—and our race ended right there."[29]

A Romanian reporter for whom English was a second and poorly understood language wrote:

> The aviatrix landed . . . where the ground is proper and were [*sic*] Mr. [Radu] Irimescu, Under-Secretar [*sic*] of State [Romania's Air Minister and later a business associate of Floyd's and a U.S. citizen], was waiting for her.[30]
>
> As soon as she arrived the presents [*sic*] took the ship to be provided with necessary gas and oil.
>
> But immediately the aviatrix told Mr. Irimescu . . . that she is going to abandon the race, because the ship motor was deranged.[31]

However, true to her promise, after eight hours of blind flying and a life-threatening landing, Jackie did not forget to powder her nose.

The Romanian reporter added:

> Anxious to take a picture of the aviatrix in her caracteristic [*sic*] suit, she protested, in asking us to permit her to take off her coat and to arrange her face.
>
> Regardless of her fatiqued [*sic*] of 8 hours of flying, the aviatrix arranged herself with the aid of a comb, powder and rouge and presented herself like you see her in the above picture.[32]

Jackie left Smith behind to repair the Gee Bee. In Bucharest for only a few hours, she bought a coat to cover her flying costume and then boarded the Orient Express for Paris.[33]

That night, as her train approached the border of Hungary, officials opened the door of her compartment and asked for her passport. It lacked a visa for Romania because she had not planned to enter the country, only to land at Bucharest and continue on from there. The officials could not speak English, but their gestures clearly indicated that they wanted her to leave the train.

As Jackie wrote later: "I backed into the far corner of my compartment with a water bottle in my hand prepared to fight it out physically, if necessary. Suddenly I thought of the Bucharest evening paper in my handbag with a front page picture of myself and the Air Minister. I showed it to them and then pointed to my flying clothes. The officials backed away and left me in peace." Next morning, however, the conductor told her that she answered the description of a jewel smuggler.[34]

Wesley Smith shipped the Gee Bee to Newark after repairing and test flying it.[35] Back at Newark, Jackie tried to sell the plane to a South American delegation after hiring test pilot Lee Gelbach to demonstrate it. Gelbach ground looped it. Over the next three years, she loaned the plane to two different pilots to use in Bendix races, but was never able to sell it. Eventually, she used it as a trade-in on a new Beechcraft.[36]

In a scathing assessment of the Gee Bee, she wrote: "It was a no good ship and will come to a bad end. How it managed even with numerous rebuildings to stay in the air this long is a mystery. Its characteristics on the ground are terrible. It will ground loop without the slightest provocation."[37] Later, she wrote: "I think I am one of the three human beings who survived flying a GB—myself, General Doolittle and Wesley Smith."[38]

As Jackie had predicted, the Gee Bee did indeed come to a bad end. Answering a letter to an inquirer years later, Floyd Odlum wrote in her absence that Jackie and Wesley Smith took off in the MacRobertson "in an untried and not entirely finished (so far as cockpit and instruments were concerned) plane. No wonder they found fuel cocks marked off when they should have been marked on. No wonder only one flap worked when they tried to land. That Gee Bee was a tricky, dangerous plane. Captain Serabia of Mexico got killed in it while taking off on a record attempt from Washington to Mexico City."[39]

Jackie had gambled for high stakes and lost. Making flying her priority for the preceding two years had come at a high price. Expenses included hiring the two pilots and seven mechanics for the stops en route. She had paid

$23,000 for the Northrop Gamma and $17,000 for the Gee Bee, much of the money provided by Floyd. Curtiss-Wright did reimburse her for all expenses resulting from the failure of the supercharger, including her trip to England and refueling equipment at the stopping points along the MacRobertson route.[40]

A week before Christmas, Jackie was hospitalized again, this time for a serious sinus infection.[41] On the last day of the year, Z. D. Granville wrote Jackie that he was sorry to hear that she was ill.[42] She could have answered that it was his fault—that flying his Gee Bee at the icy altitude of 15,000 feet without oxygen had caused her sinusitis—but she did not. Nor did she spend time fretting about her losses. She was too busy making plans for the new year.

Seven

In a Holding Pattern

During the more than two years that Jackie had spent learning to fly and honing her skills to break records, she never forgot her initial purpose in becoming an aviator: to sell cosmetics made by her own company and to reach distributors of her products throughout the country by flying her own plane. The pretty blonde who held eager photographers at bay in Bucharest while she powdered her nose was an unabashed user of and believer in women's need for cosmetics. She claimed that she had known women who spent more on cosmetics than on food, "And they looked better for it in two ways. Most people eat too much anyway."[1] She also said that the proper use of cosmetics would take only fifteen minutes a day to fulfill a "woman's right, indeed her duty, to be . . . presentable."[2]

For her office, she leased space on the thirty-fifth floor of a building at 630 Fifth Avenue near Rockefeller Center. She ordered stationery for the Jacqueline Cochran Cosmetics Company with the logo "Wings to Beauty" and hired away Antoine's office manager, Genevieve Crowley, to run the office.[3] Floyd arranged the lease of a laboratory at 1203 Chandler Avenue in Roselle, New Jersey, and Jackie hired a cosmetic chemist and a perfume consultant to teach her the characteristics and availability of the ingredients that she would need. Although her formal education was limited to two years of grammar school, Jackie had already proved that she was extremely intelligent and very determined in her pursuit of fame and fortune.

To test the market for her product, she opened a salon in Chicago at 700 North Michigan Avenue and recruited another of Antoine's employees, hairdresser Peter Rivoli.[4] To Rivoli, she sent makeup, hair dyes, moisturizing cream, and nail polish in plain jars and bottles with typewritten labels for trial before investing in expensive packaging. By going "on the road and in the air," she tested and tried to sell her products all around the country. She found her first two distributors, the department stores of Pogues in Cincinnati and Halle Brothers in Cleveland.[5]

7.1. The president of Jacqueline Cochran Cosmetics, "Wings of Beauty," Jackie wore Parisian designer clothing, mink coats, and expensive jewelry but rarely rings such as the one pictured here. She disliked drawing attention to her very large, muscular hands. (National Air and Space Museum, Smithsonian Institution, SI 78–15317.)

Floyd probably provided most of the capital for the new firm, but Jackie knew every aspect of the business that she had learned over the years as a beautician in Montgomery and Pensacola, teaching in Philadelphia, and working for Antoine in New York while moonlighting by managing cheap shops at night. Seeking a wider market for her products, she flew to Los Angeles where she planned to open a second salon the following year.[6]

Los Angeles also provided the base for a second project, building a house for herself and Floyd, a beautiful house to take the place of all the unpainted shacks, rented rooms, and tiny apartments that she had occupied in the past. The site that was to become the Cochran-Odlum ranch was a combination of the twenty acres that she bought when she visited Ted Marshall's brother, George, and the 712 acres that Floyd purchased soon after.[7] The property was near the village of Indio in the Coachella Valley, twenty miles east of Palm Springs. "The valley is about 30 miles long and 20 miles wide at the northern end of the Salton Sea. I truly believe this valley is one of the most beautiful places I have ever seen," [8] she wrote.

"Spring with its multicolored carpet of verbena, Spanish bayonets, trumpet vine and night-blooming primrose cannot be bettered any time. The perfume of these native blossoms mingled with the fragrance of the flowers of the man-planted tangerine and grapefruit can be detected in the air a mile high. During April I can shut my eyes while flying and tell when I am over our ranch."[9]

In the two decades following the spring of 1935, the ranch grew to include a main house, five guest houses with a total of ten bedrooms, a heated swimming pool, a nine-hole golf course, tennis courts, a skeet range, and stables for riding horses. The long drive to the main house was lined with date palms, grapefruit, and tangerine trees as well as flower and vegetable gardens.[10]

To build the first house on the property, Jackie summoned the siblings that she would not acknowledge publicly as her family, the Pittmans. She sent money to her brother, Joe, to buy a truck and asked him to drive it to Indio, bringing with him her two brothers-in-law, Jess Hydle and William Alford, the husbands of sisters Mamie and Myrtle.[11] Then she rented a special traincar to bring her two sisters and their children along with their household goods from Florida to Indio. They were to live in nearby housing that Jackie had rented for them. Staying at the construction site all day, Jackie would drive at night to her apartment in Los Angeles, often bringing along her favorite niece, Joe's eight-year-old daughter, Billie.[12]

Jackie asked Joe, a former house painter, carpenter, millwright, and engineer, to assist the local foreman, Charles Shibata. She recalled working with them herself as "a part-time bricklayer, carpenter and plumber. We leveled, enlarged, landscaped. I laid tile down on my hands and knees. I worked like a dog on it and it took me a year and a half to finish. I remember fighting with the damned mason about the fireplace. I wanted a certain look and he wouldn't give it to me."[13] The mason was Charlie White, the local blacksmith.[14]

Jackie realized that she would need an overseer to supervise continuing expansion of the facilities as well as employees for the house and ranch. When she asked a young Los Angeles woman, Vi Strauss, to take the job, Strauss declined, saying the summer heat was unbearable and she did not like the desert. But with the persistence of a used-car salesman, Jackie assured Strauss that the job was seasonal, from October to May, and she would not have to be at the ranch in the summer. In spite of the young woman's misgivings, she was persuaded to take the position.[15]

On the last day of the following September, Jackie called Strauss to say that she was in Los Angeles and would pick up her new property manager the next day. As they stood in the living room of the newly completed house, Jackie gave Strauss her first assignment. She was to buy furniture for the empty room. Strauss refused to take the responsibility until Jackie gave her a written promise that whatever Strauss chose would be acceptable. The new household manager was to hold that position for almost thirty years.[16]

In spite of continuing health problems, Jackie was a tireless worker endowed with boundless energy. While juggling both her new business and the building of the desert home at Indio, she turned her attention to the two planes that she now owned. With no buyers for the Gee Bee after it crashed at Newark, she hired Wesley Smith to supervise repairs. When these were completed, Smith arranged a rental of the aircraft to Hollywood pilot Lee Miles for $30 per flight along with a $1,000 minimum charge and a $2,000 deposit against damage.[17]

That left her with Northrop's troublesome Gamma. After Leonard's crash landing in Tucumcari, New Mexico, caused Jackie to switch to the Gee Bee for the MacRobertson Race, the Gamma was returned to Northrop's factory.

Repairs were made to a wing and the lower fuselage, and a new experimental engine was installed—a Pratt & Whitney Wasp, Jr., the Sai-G with 400 horsepower and a controllable pitch propeller. The plane was approved for licensing as a single-cockpit aircraft for racing on August 28, just two days before Jackie was to compete in the Bendix Race on August 30.[18]

Jackie later claimed that it was she who opened the Bendix Race to women contestants. But the groundwork had already been done by Amelia Earhart and Ruth Nichols after the 1933 race from New York to Los Angeles, when Nichols dropped out at Wichita, Kansas, and Earhart came in last. The following year, Earhart and four other women pilots boycotted the race after being refused entry on an equal basis with men.[19] The only other woman entering the 1935 Bendix was Earhart. But it was Jackie who insisted that the Bendix admit women without restrictions.[20]

For several weeks before the race, Jackie went to bed an hour earlier each night until she was retiring at noon in preparation for the scheduled starting time a few hours after midnight. She also increased her consumption of meat to build muscle and exercised to strengthen her arms and shoulders.

Cochran was prepared for the Bendix, but her Gamma was not. During test flights, the rebuilt plane developed a bad vibration. Unable to correct it in time, the day before the race, both Northrop and Pratt & Whitney representatives asked her to withdraw the Gamma. Yet when she asked if they were willing to say that the plane was malfunctioning, they refused.[21] Jackie's response was that she had no choice but to fly because if she didn't, probably no other woman would be allowed to enter the race again.[22] This was hyperbole. Her primary interest in the Bendix was not opening it for other women, but winning.

Hours before the race on August 30, a second attempt to keep her from flying in the Bendix was made at a meeting called by the male pilots after weather reports of approaching fog and rain. "One or two of them got up and said the weather was bad and I should be prevented from taking off," she recalled. But she was defended by her friend Ben Howard, who said: "She probably knows more about instrument flying than any man in the room."[23]

At midnight, 10,000 people were lined up along the fences bordering the Union Air Terminal at Burbank to see the planes of the nine competitors roll away from the parking ramp. A fog crept in from the sea after Earhart, accompanied by Paul Mantz and Al Menasco, took off. Earhart said later that she flew while the two men played poker in the back of her Vega.[24]

More than an hour passed before the fog cleared enough for the remaining competitors to see the flares marking the end of the runway. Takeoffs resumed at 2:03 A.M. when Roy Hunt roared down the runway, followed at short intervals by Ben Howard, Royal Leonard, Roscoe Turner, Russell Thaw, and Earl Ortman. Jackie's Gamma was the next to last at 4:22, followed by Cecil Allen in a Gee Bee. His little plane careened down the runway and disappeared in the fog. Two minutes later, Allen crashed and died in a potato patch two miles from the airfield.[25]

Twenty-five years later, Jackie, who was not averse to bending the truth in the interest of her reputation as a pilot, told a different story, one in which she said she took off after Allen. In her first account of Allen's crash, she said that she drove to the wreckage.[26] In a second account, she said that a policeman drove her to the wreckage, where she saw that Allen had been decapitated. She also claimed that on returning, she was asked to drop out of the race—this time by Pratt & Whitney's Bill Gwinn. "Are you willing to say to the public that the motor is malfunctioning?" she asked. "I can't afford to say that," he replied. "Then," Jackie said, "I can't afford not to take off." She also claimed that a Northrop representative repeated the request to drop out, but when he refused to say that the plane was malfunctioning, she gave him the same answer—that she would not withdraw.[27]

When she climbed into the cockpit, the Gamma was surrounded by photographers whose flash guns blinded her. Fog covered the field obscuring the hangars along the side of the runway. Assailed by doubt, she got out of the plane and telephoned Floyd, who had gone ahead to Cleveland. When she asked him if she should drop out, he told her that she must decide for herself. She did, climbing back into the cockpit and gunning the motor for takeoff.[28]

With a full load of fuel, the Gamma lumbered down the field, its engine failing to give her the power that she needed. As she barely cleared the fence marking the end of the field, her trailing antenna was torn off. She headed westward from the runway, flying so low that she was forced to fly out over the Pacific and into the fog before she dared to make a shallow turn on instruments and head east.[29]

The rear of the plane, where the cockpit was located, was vibrating violently, and the engine began overheating. At sunrise, as she neared the Grand Canyon, she saw a violent electrical storm ahead. Rather than risk battling through it, she jettisoned fuel through valves that had never been tested.

Some of the escaping gasoline was sucked back into the cockpit, forcing her to open the canopy to breathe. With the wind tearing at her face, she looked for an airfield and found one, coming down at Kingston, Arizona. On landing, she leaped from the cockpit, her clothing soaked in fuel and a potential torch for a single spark. Running into the airport restroom, she stripped off her clothes, drew a sinkful of water, and began to wash. Someone came in and gave her an overcoat as a temporary cover while another person went into town to buy her a shirt and trousers.[30]

At the close of 1935, six other woman pilots had set new records, but Cochran was not one of them. Earhart claimed two for flights from Honolulu to Oakland and Mexico City to Newark. Laura Ingalls also set two speed records for flights from the east coast to the west coast and back. Jean Batten from New Zealand broke Amy Johnson Mollison's record in a round trip from England to Australia and then became the first woman to solo across the south Atlantic. France's Maryse Hilsz set an altitude record of more than 38,000 feet, and German flier Elly Beinhorn flew from Germany to Turkey and back in a single day—2,230 miles.

As a pilot Jackie was now best known for dropping out of two air races, the MacRobertson and the Bendix. And by failing to complete the Bendix she could not fly on from Cleveland to New York to set the cross-country speed record she coveted. She was a long way from being acknowledged as America's Queen of the Air.

Eight

Pygmalion and Galatea—with Wings

Five weeks after Jackie dropped out of the 1935 Bendix Race, Hortense McQuarrie Odlum ended her twenty-two-year marriage to Floyd. The divorce was granted on October 7 at Reno on the grounds of cruelty,[1] but Floyd's fears that Hortense would name Jackie as corespondent proved unfounded. Although he was too well known as a millionaire and financial wizard to escape press coverage of the divorce, Cochran's name was never mentioned.

To guide Hortense in her new responsibilities as president of Bonwit Teller, Floyd continued to employ Jackie's former boyfriend, Mike Rosen, as her advisor at the store.[2] Six months after her divorce, Hortense married Dr. Porfilio Donminici of Santo Domingo.[3]

Floyd, who had always regarded his relationship with Jackie as a permanent one, was now ready to marry her. But the self-proclaimed orphan felt that her husband-to-be should know the truth about her "unknown parentage," so before the marriage, Jackie said in her autobiography, she "went south and got sealed letters from the two people then living who might know the facts. I gave them to Floyd and he handed them back to me, still sealed, and they still rest that way in my lock box. I do not know what is in them. Having gone through my early years without knowing why my own parents were not around looking after me, I decided when I reached maturity that I did not want to know. But I thought Floyd had a right to know."[4]

Later, she told a different story, saying that she hired a detective who gave her a written report, one that would remain unopened in her vault. Her close friend and air force colleague Brigadier General Charles E. ("Chuck") Yeager said in his autobiography that the still-sealed envelope was burned when Cochran died.[5]

"Floyd wasn't interested in her background. He wasn't that kind of snob," said his daughter-in-law, Judith Odlum. "It didn't matter where she had been. He was creating this character. What went before wasn't important. He knew what he had and where he wanted to go."[6]

What he had would have daunted most men. Years later, the pretty blonde with the big brown eyes and flawless complexion was described by a friend as "quick to make dramatic decisions. She also had a need to be in charge, to take over, to do something. Her threshold for boredom was very low indeed."[7] Pilot and mentor Chuck Yeager called Jackie "a tiger," someone "who expected to get her own way in everything and, if you ever crossed her, you'd better duck."[8]

Yeager's wife, Glennis, said, "Jackie couldn't stand tranquility," and added that "Floyd just doted on her. His day was made if Jackie gave him a hug or kiss. Each of them lived in separate worlds. Jackie was always off and running somewhere and Floyd was deeply involved in his business dealing."[9]

Jackie didn't always get her own way with Floyd, but he delighted in the attention that she aroused. "He idolized her," a friend in Indio said. "He couldn't fly the way she could. In return she idolized him. You could see it when they were together, when they were discussing a project, disagreeing, testing each other."[10]

Jackie and Floyd were married by a justice of the peace in Kingman, Arizona, on her thirtieth birthday on May 11, 1936.[11] The witnesses were George Marshall and his wife, Freda.[12] That same weekend, Floyd's twenty-two-year-old son, Stanley, announced his engagement to, then eloped with, a Forest Hills woman, Beverly Klahr. The bride was a graduate of fashionable Finch School; Stanley had dropped out of Dartmouth and was living with his mother. His rush to the altar may have been a gesture of defiance over his father's remarriage.

When Floyd and Jackie married, the bridegroom was one of the wealthiest men in the United States. As head of Atlas Corporation, he had closed out the first phase of merging and liquidating twenty-two companies before creating Atlas as a new instrument of corporate reorganization and financing. He began by underwriting the newly issued common and preferred stock of Paramount Pictures for $6,000,000.[13] The canny trader with the long face, horn-rimmed spectacles, and freckled, balding head might have seemed a bit drab to others, but to Jackie, he was a knight in shining armor. More than his wealth and power, what impressed Jackie most about Floyd was his lack of pretentiousness, his dry wit, his kindness to friends, and his rapt interest in and shrewd guidance of her own activities.

Floyd was neither intimidated nor embarrassed by Jackie's brash egotism, unlimited energy, and boundless ambition. Disliking publicity about himself, he loved seeing her picture in the newspapers and reading about her career, one in which she continued to be known not as Mrs. Floyd Odlum but as Jacqueline Cochran.

Judith Odlum saw her in-laws as a sort of Pygmalion and Galatea. "There was a symbiotic relationship there that was truly hard to figure out. They were totally dependent on each other," she observed. "She needed his support. He really adored her admiration."[14]

At the time Jackie and Floyd were married, the newlyweds were staying at the ranch in Indio, but for their respective businesses they needed a base in New York. Floyd found it in River House, an apartment building at 435 East 52nd Street, overlooking the East River. A private elevator to the twelfth floor opened onto the entrance hall. "I had a balcony that you could have a ball on," Jackie said, "a living room larger than my living room [at the ranch] and two bedrooms and a kitchen with hotel service to boot."[15] Within the next decade, they would also have a house in Stamford, Connecticut, on the shore of Long Island Sound and a cottage near Sands Point, Long Island, where Jackie played golf. In addition, they kept a suite at the Mayflower Hotel in Washington and another at the Ambassador Hotel in Los Angeles.[16]

Jackie said that although she and Floyd were temperamentally different, "when it came to knowing what we wanted out of life—security, power and a certain kind of fame—we were very much alike. And work. Hard work was always a tie that bound us together. When it came to schemes and dreams Floyd had as many as I did."[17]

While Floyd continued restructuring Atlas Corporation, Jackie returned to her pursuit of the next Bendix Trophy to be awarded in the fall of 1936. After the 1935 race, she had leased the Northrop Gamma to Howard Hughes, the handsome, eccentric millionaire and the world's largest manufacturer of oil-drilling machinery. Hughes was also the producer of three successful Hollywood films—*Hell's Angels*, *Scarface*, and *The Front Page*. A frequent dinner guest at the ranch, Hughes astounded other guests on one occasion by appearing at the table wearing tennis shoes and ugly, oversized trousers belted with a rope. He proudly announced that he had purchased three pairs of the pants for only one dollar.[18]

In spite of his odd behavior, he was a brilliant aircraft designer and a skilled pilot. He replaced the Gamma's engine with a special 950-horsepower

Wright Cyclone and set a record in it on January 13, 1936, flying from Los Angeles to New York in nine hours, twenty-seven minutes, and ten seconds. It was the record that eluded Jackie when the plane failed her in 1934 and 1935. By the following May, Hughes had flown it to two more records—Miami to New York in four hours, twenty-one minutes, and thirty-two seconds and from Chicago to Los Angeles in eight hours, ten minutes, and twenty-three seconds.[19]

Hughes had rented the plane from Jackie with an option to buy. But when the lease was up, he was in Chicago and too busy to return it, so he bought the plane from Jackie, then sold it back to her for less than it had originally cost her. Considering that Hughes's final payments amounted to more than the Gamma had cost her in the first place, plus all her repair costs, Jackie concluded that for all the trouble, money, and worry that the plane had cost her, the Gamma "paid me back in spades."[20]

However, Cochran mistrusted Hughes's Cyclone engine, the same as the one that failed her in 1935, and replaced it with a Pratt & Whitney Twin Wasp, Jr. But she figured that if Hughes could set three records in it, the Gamma surely would be her ticket to the 1936 Bendix Trophy.

She figured wrong. Flying from Los Angeles to New York where the race was to begin, she was planning to stop for the night at Columbus, Ohio, when smoke suddenly billowed from beneath the cowling. Turning back to Indianapolis, she headed the nose down to keep the smoke from masking the cockpit. A local paper reported: "She landed the plane travelling almost 125 miles an hour, did a ground loop which damaged her landing gear and climbed out of the cabin without any sign of hysteria."[21] But before she left the burning aircraft, she looked for and found her purse because her lipstick was in it.[22]

A week later, she returned to Indianapolis to pick up the repaired Gamma. But shortly after taking off, she discovered that the radio was not working and, with bad weather ahead, decided to return to the airport, where she narrowly missed an incoming TWA plane. Describing this second crash in her autobiography years later, Cochran said that she was "coming in for a landing with the flaps down, [when] the engine quit and the flap mechanism broke so I could not raise the flaps and stretch my glide. I hit hard on the runway, so hard it broke the metal plane in two. The two parts bounced in the air several feet and collided. Although I was covered with gas and oil I was not injured and refused to go to the hospital for a checkup and within twenty minutes was on a commercial plane bound for New York.[23] At another time, she added that the two pieces collided "with me in one of them but [the plane] didn't burn and I landed right side up. It's a mishap if you can walk away from it."[24]

Immediately after the incident, however, the *Indianapolis Star* gave slightly different details, quoting Cochran as saying: "I was circling at a low altitude preparing to land. I saw the airliner at about one thousand feet altitude and thought I had plenty of time to land ahead of it. I headed for the long east-west runway. I began losing altitude rapidly and tried to gun the motor but it failed to respond."[25]

Jackie had to give up on the Gamma. "The pieces of that plane and another Northrop Gamma that Russell Thaw [another Bendix contestant] had cracked up a few weeks before were shipped to the factory" and made into a single plane, which she later sold to health magazine publisher Bernarr MacFadden.[26]

But she refused to give up on the Bendix. With the September 4 New York starting date rapidly approaching, she hurried back to Los Angeles and leased a high-powered monoplane from aircraft designer Vance Breese.

Three other woman competitors were considered serious contenders—Amelia Earhart, Laura Ingalls, and Louise Thaden. Earhart was flying her new Lockheed Electra, the plane that she intended to fly around the world the following April. Her copilot was Helen Richey, then the only woman flier carrying mail on a scheduled airliner. Ingalls was going to fly solo in her Lockheed Orion, a plane in which she had wrested the women's cross-country speed record from Earhart. Thaden, like Richey and Earhart, was a member of the woman pilots' association, the Ninety-Nines. With Blanche Noyes, another Ninety-Niner, as her copilot, she entered a Beechcraft, a standard owner-operated model. The top three male contestants were Roscoe Turner, Ben Howard, and Joe Jacobson.[27]

A week before the race, the plane that Breese had leased to Jackie crashed during a test flight when the retractable landing gear collapsed. Not only was she out of the Bendix again, but also three of the first five places were won by women: Thaden/Noyes were first, Ingalls second, and Earhart/Richey fifth. William Gulick of New York and George Pomeroy of Washington, D.C., finished third and fourth.

Among the male pilots, all three main contenders failed. Turner never even reached the starting point, crash landing at the Zuni Indian reservation in New Mexico while en route to New York. The other two started, but never finished. Jacobson bailed out when his Gamma blew up in midair. Howard (with his wife Maxine, commonly known as Mike) crashed in a forced landing in New Mexico. Both Howards suffered compound fractures of both legs and a surgeon was forced to remove one of Ben's feet.[28]

Jackie had again missed her third chance to win the Bendix Trophy, but she gained two lifelong friends. When the Howards left the hospital, Jackie invited them to the ranch where they stayed several months recuperating from their injuries. Ben Howard had already recognized in Jackie the potential of a great pilot—intelligence, courage, determination, and eagerness to learn. That she was a woman did not lessen his assessment, his own wife Mike also being, like Jackie, beautiful, charming, and a gifted pilot. During the convalescence, Jackie, who until then had had little rapport with other women, came to count on Mike as a trusted confidante.

Before long, she would find a second woman friend—Amelia Earhart.

Nine

Jackie and Amelia

By 1935, ambitious, manipulative Jackie aided by Floyd could rely on the assistance of a hundred or more influential acquaintances in her dogged pursuit of fame as an aviator. But they remained acquaintances, not friends. Floyd and the Howards were her only close friends until November, when she first met Amelia Earhart, the nation's most famous woman pilot.

Back in 1932, when Jackie was learning to fly at Roosevelt Field, Earhart's husband, publisher and publicist George Palmer Putnam, had introduced himself to her. "Well, little girl," Putnam asked, "what is your ambition in flying?" "To put your wife in the shade," Jackie snapped.[1]

Since then, she had seen Earhart at the National Air Races and at Roosevelt Field but had never been introduced to her until pilot Paul Hammond and his wife, Susie, asked her to dine with Earhart at their Manhattan apartment. Within minutes of that first meeting, the woman whom Jackie had vowed to overshadow became her second woman friend.[2] The two women could not have been more different. Tall, slim, elegant Amelia was a shy, quiet woman who had learned to address the public from a stage, but feared adoring fans closing in on her, clutching at her clothing and reaching for her hand. Blonde, full-figured Jackie, eight years Earhart's junior, was a compulsive talker, exuding a kind of untamed energy. She would have welcomed the devotion of avid fans—fans that she did not as yet have.

Educated at a finishing school and at university, Amelia was a social worker until her transatlantic flight in 1928, when she became the first woman to cross the ocean in an airplane. At the insistence of Putnam, Earhart had already written a book about that first crossing—*The Fun of It*. Jackie, whose intelligence quotient was probably as high if not higher than Amelia's, had had only two years of elementary education. Her speech was frequently ungrammatical, her spelling that of an eight-year-old. Growing up in lumber towns, she had been as poor and grubby as the tenement children that Earhart once taught at a settlement house in Boston.[3]

A staunch pacifist, Amelia supported the Equal Rights Amendment proposed by the National Women's Party and was a founding member of the Ninety-Nines.[4] Jackie joined no women's groups. When asked what she thought of women she said, "I don't think much of 'em. I'd rather spend an evening with a man any time than a woman."[5]

A few days after the dinner at the Hammonds, Amelia asked Jackie to fly with her to California in her new Lockheed Electra. She told Cochran that on its initial "shakedown cruise" for the Bendix Race, the Electra's navigator's hatch flew open and the fuel system ran erratically, convincing Earhart that she needed more flight time in the aircraft before attempting to fly it around the world.[6] With bad weather grounding them for four days in St. Louis and another three in Amarillo, it took Jackie and Amelia two weeks to fly to California.[7] During that time, they discussed politics, business, science, religion, and aviation. Amelia, who customarily avoided revealing anything about her personal life, opened up to Jackie, describing her childhood, her parents, and her sister.[8] The garrulous Jackie became a good listener who later recalled: "Those first few days with Amelia gave me an opportunity—even more than in the months that followed—to get to know her well and to know her was to love her."[9]

A few days after they arrived in Burbank, Amelia went to the ranch in Indio for the first of frequent visits. Among the interests she shared with Jackie and Floyd was that of extrasensory perception. Prompted by Floyd, Jackie had already experimented with "automatic writing." With her eyes masked by a handkerchief, she put a pencil to paper and started "writing uncontrollably" messages that she thought must have come from her subconscious.[10] On another occasion, she had concentrated on a telephone call that she wanted from Floyd until, she claimed, he actually made one at the time and place that she had chosen.

During that first week that Amelia spent at the ranch, the two women heard that a passenger plane had disappeared en route from Los Angeles to Salt Lake City. Amelia asked Jackie to locate it. Jackie named mountain peaks, described roads, transmission lines, and even a pile of telephone poles on a site near Salt Lake City. Amelia called Paul Mantz, her advisor for her world flight, in Los Angeles and asked him to use Jackie's description to locate the place on an aviation map. After he did so, Earhart drove to Los Angeles that night and took off in her Electra at dawn. She searched the area for three days

9.1. Jackie and Amelia Earhart at the Cochran-Odlum ranch in Indio, after Earhart cracked up the Electra 10 in her first attempt to fly around the world. (Coachella Valley Historical Society, Indio, California. Photographer unknown.)

before giving up, but that spring when the snow melted, the plane was found within two miles of where Jackie said it would be.[11]

On December 27, when a United Airlines plane was lost outside of Burbank, Jackie told Amelia where to look and Earhart found the wreckage. Again, on January 12, 1937, with guidance from Jackie, Amelia located a second lost plane. Columnists Drew Pearson and Robert Allen wrote that Amelia had a psychic gift.[12] They failed to mention Jackie, a slight that she would never have tolerated if it had been anyone except Amelia.

When Amelia suggested that Jackie might locate her if she were forced down on her future world flight, the two women decided to test that possibility on an upcoming flight from New York to Burbank that Amelia was to make with Putnam. She would record her location on the hour while Jackie did the same back in New York. Jackie forgot to do so until the third day, when she wrote that Amelia had landed on the previous night at Blackwell,

Oklahoma, fifty miles off course and had taken off the next day at nine o'clock, stopping at Winslow, Arizona, for fuel.[13]

After Putnam read the report, he wrote to Jackie that they were not off course when they stopped at Blackwell and that they took off at seven the next morning, not nine, but they did stop at Winslow. Jackie told him that seven o'clock in Blackwell was nine in New York, and that she had never heard of Blackwell before she wrote the name in her report. As for his denying that they were lost, Jackie quoted a favorite expression of old-time barnstormers: "I ain't lost but I don't know where I am."[14]

A frequent guest at the ranch, Amelia usually came without Putnam. She stayed in one of the five guest houses that had been completed, along with the main house, a swimming pool, and stables for Floyd's horses. When Jackie was working in New York, she occupied Jackie's bedroom—the only guest ever invited to use it. Earhart spent her days alone, riding across the desert, taking long walks, and swimming in the pool.[15] At dinner, she joined the other guests at the ranch, guests invited from a list that spanned a wide spectrum of aviators, industrialists, financiers, film stars, and neighbors. Jackie's nine-year-old niece, Billie Pittman, who was visiting at the ranch, never forgot the evening when her aunt introduced her to Amelia and her escort, aviator and film producer Howard Hughes.[16]

Although Jackie regarded Earhart as her dearest friend, her initial dislike of Putnam increased over time. She thought that he pushed Amelia into her record-setting flights like the one that she was about to make.[17] Floyd said that "she was his meal ticket. He was the advance publicity agent and she would run around so he could write stories about her and get her picture in the paper." Odlum thought that Amelia was beginning to realize that her marriage was a mistake, but "she wouldn't do anything about it." Jackie disagreed. "I think she was in love with George and I think he was a bum. First class. She was nuts about him. It was her attitude. Her face would light up when he'd telephone or the way she'd look at him." Cochran couldn't understand it. "He was a complete dope. He was the dullest person I've ever been around."[18]

Her dislike flared on an evening when Amelia and Putnam arrived for a weekend after Earhart had given a lecture in Pasadena. She looked tired. Jackie made a bowl of milk toast for her, and while half-reclining in a big leather chair, Amelia began to eat it. Putnam glared at his wife, muttering, "Nasty! You're dressed like a lady. Why don't you sit up like one?" Jackie picked up an ashtray and threw it at him. "You dirty bum!" she shouted. "If you want to talk to your wife that way get out of here. How dare you speak to your wife like that in my house!" She recalled that Amelia "didn't finish her milk toast and she liked my milk toast."[19]

As the time neared for Amelia's world flight, Jackie became increasingly worried about her friend. Cochran prepared for her own flights with rest, exercise, and by studying detailed maps of her route prepared by experienced pilots. She spent hours making practice takeoffs and landings and she thought that Earhart's preparations were minimal and haphazard. While Putnam was in New York, he left Amelia to supervise the building of their house at Toluca Lake in Hollywood. In addition, Putnam had her sign contracts for the flight on a number of projects, including writing exclusive stories for the *New York Herald-Tribune* at each of her stops. He sold the right to use her name to Bausch & Lomb for sunglasses and a light meter, to Vincent Bendix for a radio-direction finder, to Standard Oil for fuel depots and maintenance along the route, and to Pan American for flight plan assistance.[20] He also scheduled a series of lectures to be given on her return, and signed a book contract.[21]

Putnam spent more time on promoting the flight than on coordinating the maintenance depots that his wife would need at each stop. He hired Paul Mantz as her mentor. As egotistical as Putnam, Mantz resented his employer treating him as a hireling rather than a colleague. He patronized Amelia, too, telling her to "Listen to Papa!"[22] Amelia told Jackie that she was angered by his patronizing manner, but she had to take his instructions for practice flights. Jackie empathized with Amelia because she had never forgotten Mantz's comment about her own withdrawal from the 1936 Bendix. He said that Cochran "never won a race or finished a flight in her life."[23]

Jackie was also concerned about Amelia's choice of navigator, Harry Manning. He had been the captain of an ocean liner before accepting leave to make the flight with her. Cochran told Amelia to take Manning out on a clear night over the Pacific and "see if he could find his way back. She did," Jackie said, "and he didn't."[24]

Informed of Manning's limitations, Putnam hired a second navigator, Fred Noonan. Jackie also disapproved of Noonan, who was known to be highly competent but had been fired by Pan American Airlines amid rumors of alcoholism.

On March 17, Earhart left Oakland for Honolulu with two navigators,

9.2. *Left to right:* Ben and Maxine (Mike) Howard, Jackie, and Amelia Earhart at the Cochran-Odlum ranch in Indio. Amelia was resting after crashing her Electra 10 in her first attempt to fly around the world in 1937. The Howards had sustained injuries in the 1936 Bendix race. (Coachella Valley Historical Society, Indio, California. Photographer unknown.)

Manning and Noonan, and Mantz, who wanted to meet his girlfriend there. Manning was also to leave the flight before the next stop—a tiny atoll in the Pacific, Howland Island. But three days later when taking off from Honolulu, Amelia cracked up the Electra.[25] She returned to California to await repairs to the aircraft. Twenty-four hours after she arrived exhausted and worried, Amelia was back at the Cochran-Odlum ranch to join Jackie and Ben and Mike Howard, who were still recuperating from injuries suffered in the Bendix Race the previous summer. Amelia described the crack-up in detail to Jackie and the Howards, who remained silent when she asked them, "Aren't you going to ask me, 'Are you going to try it again?'" Only Cochran answered. "I hope you don't."[26]

But Amelia tried again, revising her route to circle the globe in the opposite direction. She planned to leave Oakland for Miami and then on to South America, Africa, the Middle East, Asia, Australia, New Guinea, Howland Island, Honolulu, and back to Oakland. When Jackie urged her to abandon the project, she said that too many commitments had been made by Putnam. When he needed money for the Electra's repairs, Floyd, along with Vincent Bendix, Bernard Baruch, and Admiral Richard Byrd gave it to him because they all admired Amelia.[27] Yet Jackie continued to admonish her friend. "I told her she wasn't going to see that damned island [Howland]. I wish you wouldn't go off and commit suicide because that's exactly what you're going to do."[28]

On hearing the news of Earhart's disappearance near Howland Island on July 2, a chastened Putnam went to Jackie's apartment in Los Angeles, hoping that the extrasensory experiment that she had shared with Amelia might help him to locate his missing wife. Jackie told him where Amelia had gone down, an area subsequently searched by the Navy without results. Noonan, Jackie said, had hit his head on the bulwark and was unconscious, but Amelia was alive and the plane still afloat. "I followed the course of her drifting for two days. . . . On the third day I went to the cathedral and lit candles for Amelia's soul which I then knew had taken off on its own long flight."[29]

Soon after Earhart's disappearance, at a memorial for her lost friend, Jackie said, "The Amelia I knew was soft, sweet, educated, refined and a rather shy person—feminine, able and without fear." And in an interview more than forty years later, Cochran declared, "I knew she wasn't strong enough for that trip. I loved her. I still miss her and I can't talk about it any more."[30]

Amelia was gone—on her way to becoming a legend. Her throne as America's queen of the air was empty. Jackie intended to claim it.

Ten

Up, Up, and Away!

That summer, while the newspapers were reporting Earhart's progress in her world flight, Jackie was best known, if at all, for dropping out of races. She cracked up in Bucharest in 1934 and turned back in the Bendix Race of 1935. She failed to enter the Bendix in 1936 after crashing her Gamma twice in eight days at Indianapolis.[1]

To replace the Gamma, Jackie bought a Breese that crashed in a test flight. But the queen of dropouts never flagged in her determination to become the most famous pilot—male or female—in the world. She had formidable competition. Louise Thaden with Blanche Noyes as copilot had won the 1936 Bendix in a Beechcraft cabin biplane with a standard Wright motor. Jackie may have had this in mind when she bought one like it. The new Beechcraft (model D17W, serial no. 164, license NX18562) was delivered to her at Newark by Frank Hawks, former racing champion and one of the nation's most famous test pilots. The plane cost Jackie $20,145.[2]

When Hawks accompanied her on a flight from New York to the west coast, they repeatedly argued over the way in which she landed the Beechcraft. He insisted that she was bringing it in too fast, and if she continued to do so she would kill herself. Jackie told him that she would bring roses to his funeral. Ironically, she did so only a few months later after he was killed flying into a power line.[3]

Like Mantz, Hawks had doubts about the ability of women pilots. After his cross-country trip with Jackie, he wrote to Floyd Odlum: "I have written a half-dozen letters regarding Jackie's status in flying and subsequently destroyed them. Her instruction has been exceedingly spotty and is inadequate for the task she is ambitious to complete this fall."[4] Adopting Mantz's "Listen to Papa" attitude, Hawks insisted that "new and stringent arrangements" be made regarding Jackie's instruction. He also told Floyd that Mantz no longer wished to be her advisor.[5]

If Hawks or Mantz thought that Floyd would interfere in Jackie's plans, they were mistaken. Six weeks after she took possession of the new Beechcraft, Jackie set two women's international speed records. On July 26, three and a half weeks after Earhart's disappearance, she flew a 1,000-kilometer course from Los Angeles to San Francisco at an average of 200.71 miles an hour. Two days later, she flew a 100-kilometer course between Inglewood Air Center and Garden Grove in California. Her average speed was 203.895 miles an hour.[6] In the same model plane as Thaden had used a year earlier, Jackie flew four miles an hour faster than Thaden's record as well as besting Earhart's mark of 1930 by 200 miles an hour.[7] Telling reporters that her aim was to replace Earhart as America's leading woman pilot, she said that she would enter her Beechcraft in the 1937 Bendix Race the following month.[8]

Although the Beechcraft was good enough for setting two records, Jackie thought that it could be better. She had the 450-horsepower motor replaced by a special, 600-horsepower Pratt & Whitney motor after testing it for fuel consumption.[9] Two weeks later, she entered the Bendix. As the only woman contestant, she knew that she could win a special prize that Vincent Bendix was offering for the first woman to finish the race—$2,500. All she had to do was finish, but she aimed to place third among the male contestants.[10]

She was the first to take off from Los Angeles on September 3, gunning the Beechcraft through a dark, overcast night for the first five hours with only a compass and a few radio checkpoints to guide her.[11] She did place third as she had hoped, spanning the course to Cleveland in ten hours, twenty-eight minutes, and eight seconds. In addition to the women's prize, she won $3,000 for third place.[12] She had at last finished in a Bendix and done it in a plane that Paul Mantz and Frank Hawks said that she could not handle.

Certain that she was ready to fly something faster than the Beechcraft, Jackie knew what she wanted. She had seen the plane at Roosevelt Field in July when her new Pratt & Whitney engine was being installed in the Beechcraft. The aircraft was the sleek, silvery creation of Major Alexander Seversky, the dashing Russian she had seen stunt flying after her first long flight to Montreal in 1932. As she stood looking at the plane, Seversky approached her and said, "I just wrote you a letter to ask you if you want to fly my P-35."[13]

"Lead me to it," she replied. "Why don't you let me fly it in the Bendix?"[14]

Seversky said that he had already promised the plane to another pilot, Frank Fuller, who won the Bendix in it. But two days after the National Air Races, he flew Jackie to the Army base at Wright Field in Dayton to demonstrate the P-35 to the Army. With Seversky flying the single-seat plane, Jackie sat on a metal ring in the baggage space without a safety belt while he proved the aircraft's maneuverability by "looping the loop." "Each loop pressed the ring into my sitting apparatus for almost a permanent imprint and each loop threw some talcum powder out of Seversky's wooden leg on back into the space where I was confined with not too good air at the best," she said.[15]

Doubting her ability just as Hawks and Mantz had, the field's medical officer, Captain Harry Armstrong, told Jackie that she could not handle the plane. "You have no business flying this airplane," he said. "It is a killer. We have cracked up more than 20 of them."[16] She replied, "Every airplane can be flown. If you can fly a Gee Bee you can fly anything."[17]

Jackie soon discovered that the military was about to cancel further orders for the plane because it could not reach a required speed of 300 miles an hour and because it was considered a dangerous aircraft after a number of earlier deliveries had crashed, killing several pilots. The shrewd Seversky had asked her to fly it because he thought that if the military authorities knew that a woman could fly it—one without previous training in a pursuit plane—then the plane would be viewed as safe.[18]

Early the next morning, Seversky took Jackie out to the field where the P-35 was parked. Unlike every other plane that she had mastered, there were no dual controls on this one for airborne lessons. Only after he had described the functions of the instruments in the cockpit did Jackie realize that she had no paper and pencil to make notes. There was no radio that she could use to ask advice once she was airborne. "Don't do anything," the anxious designer told her. "Just take it up and fly it around. Don't play with it. Just come down and land it."[19]

"There was an all-grass field and a low ceiling," Jackie recalled. "I wanted to put the flight off because I wanted to be able to get up high enough to play with the airplane a little bit, to get the feel of it."[20] However, aware that the ramp was lined with watching Army officers, she did as she was told, flying for twenty-five minutes before coming in for a landing as slowly as she thought possible short of stalling out.

When she dropped the landing gear the rudder pedals began to vibrate violently. Seversky had warned her that the vibration indicated that the wheels were not down and locked.[21] Pulling up and circling the field again, she remembered that Seversky had cracked up one of these planes on the day

10.1. Jackie with Maj. Alexander Seversky, designer of the Seversky Pursuit, in which she set a new women's speed record in September 1937. That December she broke all speed records between New York and Miami in a Seversky plane. (Coachella Valley Historical Society, Indio, California. Photographer unknown.)

before the Bendix, landing at Floyd Bennett Field. He had approached the runway in a perfect glide, but as the wheels touched down, the nose came up, the left tire blew, the tail wobbled, the brakes jammed, and the landing gear collapsed.[22] What if it happened to her? She pulled up.

On her second approach, the pedals vibrated again. "By then I was satisfied that I would have to make a belly landing, so I cautiously came in with this maneuver in mind. Strangely enough," she said, "the landing gear was down in place and the landing was normal and perfect."[23] Jackie said later that she wasn't afraid to crash, but she was afraid of the blot it might make on her reputation as a pilot.[24]

Seversky was impressed by Jackie's performance at Wright Field. A month later, he invited her to fly his "Executive" model, a double cockpit version of the P-35 with a 1,200-horsepower Twin Wasp engine, at the Detroit air show. He thought that she could set a record in it on a three-kilometer course. On September 20, they spent the morning as teacher and pupil—Seversky in the front seat, Jackie in the back, while he instructed her in approaching the course. She was to climb first to about 1,500 feet, diving and leveling off at between 100 and 150 feet in conformance to the National Air Association rule for the record run. After several flights with Seversky, Jackie made some more runs in her Beechcraft to familiarize herself with the course.[25]

The following day when the weather improved, she took off on a round trip of the course, her first alone in the plane, cruising at 225 miles an hour. Then, with timing officials at their posts, she began the first of six runs, climbing to 1,300 feet, wheeling and diving to 100 feet. Her course was above railroad tracks, their engines belching black smoke, but as one observer noted, "she held the course without losing or gaining more than a yard of altitude."[26] After she made a perfect landing, the NAA official announced her time for the fastest lap as 301.66 miles an hour.[27]

She had gained for the United States the world's unlimited speed record for women formerly held by Helene Boucher of France at 276.5 miles an hour. She also bested the United States speed mark formerly held by Mrs. Mary Haizlip at 252 miles an hour.

Unfortunately, Seversky did not get the Army contract that he wanted. The order went to Curtiss-Wright's P-40 after Army officials noted that although Jackie exceeded the required speed of 301.6 miles an hour over three laps, her average overall was only 292.39—not fast enough—and they remained convinced that the plane had "dangerous characteristics."[28]

Unlike Paul Mantz, Seversky had trusted Jackie as a pilot. While Mantz no longer wanted to be her advisor, he was the hired custodian of her Northrop Gamma, and even in that role she did not trust him. A month before she left for the Miami Air Races in December of 1937, she accused him of padding his bills for the plane's storage and maintenance and of failing to charge enough for renting the plane to motion picture studios.[29] Mantz denied her accusations in a five-page answer. He reminded her that he had helped her to sell the Breese plane—one he considered a man-killer—and that he had advised giving up the Gamma for a Beechcraft, a move that resulted in her breaking her first and second records.[30]

"The general tone of your letter seems to intimate that you have been seriously overcharged and mistreated," he wrote. "In the first place you will recall, Amelia asked me to see if I could assist you in your flying activities as up to that time you had not been successful in any of your undertakings. After listening to your stories at Indio and to the unfortunate treatment and mishaps you had I assured you, and particularly Amelia, that I would do everything I could to help you to at least break some records and accomplish something in aviation." He also reminded her that he had told her that her Gamma was not the kind of ship to fly around pylons and that she seemed "ground shy," implying that she was unable to handle the big ship and afraid to fly too close to the ground at high speed. He also said that he had undertaken to assist her in spite of her reputation for having accidents. "Tying up" his name with Jackie was a risk to his reputation, but Amelia, he said, had told him to help her because "she felt it would more than repay me if I could only break your jinx."[31]

His letter was salt in Jackie's wounds, reminding her of losing a friend that she had loved dearly. It was written three days before Jackie was the principal speaker at a memorial tribute to Earhart. She spoke from a wooden platform at Floyd Bennett Field in Brooklyn to several hundred Earhart fans who shivered in a freezing wind. Jackie said, "Her last flight was endless as in a relay race of progress. She has merely placed the torch in the hands of others to carry on to the next goal and there on and on forever."[32]

Thirteen days later, on December 3, Jackie flew Seversky's Executive nonstop from Floyd Bennett Field in Brooklyn to Miami. Seversky had put extra fuel tanks in the wings and the back compartment. In addition, he replaced the pilot's seat with a 42-gallon fuel tank. Jackie took off in an overweighted plane, sitting on a tank of highly explosive aviation fuel. The aircraft was badly off balance as it left the runway. "When I tried to level out I overcontrolled the other way and started a shallow dive for the ocean," she said. "This porpoising kept up for the first 200 miles during which there was no time even to look at a map."[33]

When she arrived at the Miami airfield, she was told to remain airborne while a squadron of Navy planes was giving an exhibition for the crowd. "My gas was low and when I came down close behind the last Navy plane I had not enough fuel to taxi to the hangar but had to be towed there."[34] But she had set a new record from New York to Miami—four hours, twelve minutes, and seventeen seconds, besting by eight minutes the one set in 1936 by Howard

Hughes flying her Gamma. It was the kind of record that Jackie wanted—a man's record.[35]

While her victory was being announced, she learned that two pilots, Rudy Kling and Frank Harris, had both been killed when their planes crashed in a pylon race. In the confusion that followed, her record was barely noticed as members of the reception committee rushed to the scene of the accidents. Eventually, she was led to the microphone where she said, "I'm happy to be here but I would be much happier if it were not for the crash that just happened."[36]

During the Miami air races, Jackie continued to fly Seversky's plane, setting a women's record of 252.875 miles an hour on December 9 over a 100-kilometer course and breaking her own record of the previous July. On December 13, she repeated the 100-kilometer course, boosting her speed to 255.973 miles an hour, but, while she coasted down the runway after a perfect landing, the plane began jerking. "One wing was pulled off altogether and the landing gear was torn off," she said. "The tail had jumped its lock throwing the plane to one side."[37]

Jackie had paid $2,500 for the use of the aircraft plus $50 an hour in flight time. She was certain that she was not liable for any additional costs from the accident. Mechanical failure, not pilot error had caused the crash, she insisted. Fortunately, she could prove it from pictures taken by a motion picture photographer who had followed her down the runway in a truck during the landing.[38] Seversky was delighted with the $10,000 insurance payment. It would pay for a new plane, a prototype of a newer design with a thinner, faster wing, and a transcontinental range.[39] Jackie asked for a model of the P-35 with a wing span of eighteen inches, the first of many such miniatures that she was to display in the foyer of her River House apartment.[40]

At the close of 1937, Jackie went home to Indio to celebrate the holidays with Floyd and a household full of guests that included Benny and Mike Howard.[41] She had reason to celebrate. After five years of unceasing effort, the first recognition of her as a pilot of note appeared in two different magazines. The first was in the December issue of *National Aeronautics* magazine. In a full-page feature devoted to famous pilots, she was described as "one of the world's outstanding feminine pilots."[42] The article cited her third-place win in the Bendix against male pilots as well as her records for the three 100- and 1,000-kilometer closed courses. No doubt she prompted the writer to conclude with, "She owns beauty salons in Chicago and Los Angeles and a cosmetic laboratory in New Jersey. She will enter the national market with her beauty preparations in 1938, using the most appropriate slogan—'Wings to Beauty.'"[43]

The second article appeared in the January edition of *U.S. Air Services*, a brief biography as she told it—the four-year-old orphan from Pensacola who dreamed of becoming a pilot, the graduate nurse and cosmetician who held a transport license. The three-page article cited her records in a separate column and listed her other accomplishments—her "Wings to Beauty" cosmetics, the salons in Chicago and Los Angeles, her date farm at the ranch, and her sheep ranch in Arizona (Floyd's arrangement with George Marshall). She said that with the profits from all these, she hoped to open an orphanage.[44]

Jackie had taken a giant step toward her goals of being known as a great pilot and a successful businesswoman.

Eleven

First Lady of the Air Lanes

The celebration of Jackie's successes in 1937 came to an abrupt halt during the holidays when she suffered a severe attack of sinusitis. In intense pain, she left the ranch for New York City on a chartered plane, accompanied by a doctor and a nurse.[1] For the following three months, she was bedridden much of the time. Her principal correspondent, in addition to Floyd, was Mike Howard.[2] Mike had stayed on at the ranch after Ben, his foot replaced by a prosthesis, went back to work as a research pilot for United Airlines.

In late January when Mike was able to walk again without crutches, she went to Los Angeles where she visited Jackie's salon and reported that business was thriving under the management of Peter Rivoli, who had opened the Chicago salon. She also went to Mantz's United Air Services at Burbank to check on the care of Jackie's Gamma and her Beechcraft that was being used by Frenchman Max Constant, a flight instrument specialist whom Jackie had befriended.[3]

Jackie's morale was given a major boost on February 17 when she was named a winner of the Clifford B. Harmon Trophy for outstanding achievement in 1937, one of the most coveted aviation awards given by the International League of Aviators. She was cited for her speed records set at Detroit and her New York to Miami flight.[4] Other winners of the Harmon Trophy were Howard Hughes for a transatlantic speed record; Dick Merrill, another American transatlantic flier; and a New Zealand woman, Jean Batten, for her Australia to England flight.[5]

Two days later, Jackie left her sickbed to receive the General William E. Mitchell Memorial Award for the greatest contribution to aviation in 1937.[6] That night, she covered her face, pale from weeks of illness, with "Wings to Beauty" makeup, donned a designer dress that hid her weight loss of nearly fifteen pounds, and went to the annual Aviation Ball at the Roosevelt Hotel in New York. Captain Edward Vernon "Eddie" Rickenbacker made the presentation to a smiling Jackie.[7] The next morning, she was back in the hospital for extensive surgery on her infected sinuses. Her secretary, Mary Nicholson, reported to Mike Howard, "Jackie Cochran feels miserable but her condition is good."[8]

Her misery did not prevent Jackie from planning for her future. On March 12, she signed an agreement with Alexander Seversky for the use of a new, improved model of his P-35, called the AP-7.[9] In it, she intended to set three new records for 100- and 1,000-kilometer closed-circuit courses and for a flight from San Diego to Jacksonville, Florida.[10] Advised by Floyd, Jackie agreed to pay $30,000 for rent of the plane and to be responsible for any damage. If the aircraft was not ready for the Bendix Race in September, Seversky agreed to substitute one of his other models, the AP-1 or AP-2, and if she had to use either substitute, he would refund $10,000. If she did not fly in the Bendix, she would refund the $30,000 to Seversky. There was also a provision that if, within three weeks of signing the agreement, she found a buyer for $100,000 worth of Seversky's company stock at market value, but at nothing less than $2 a share, she would not have to pay him the $30,000.[11]

At the time Jackie signed the agreement, she was able to get up for brief periods of time, but was still in pain. She wrote to Mike, "Your nice letter came just a little while ago and I am so blue I could just jump out the window. . . . The doctor just gave me another treatment a little while ago and got the right side of my nose bleeding again, plus hurting like hell."[12]

To hasten her recuperation, Jackie spent the last week of March in Florida before going to Washington on April 4, when Eleanor Roosevelt presented her with the winged Harmon Trophy. The former barefoot child from Muscogee had become the woman honored at an intimate gathering arranged by the first lady. Among the twelve guests were Seversky and his wife, Evelyn, and Floyd Odlum, who must have been ecstatic at seeing the woman he loved seated next to the president's wife.[13]

After the luncheon, Mrs. Roosevelt took Jackie aside to discuss the disappearance of Amelia Earhart. Amelia, who had been an overnight guest at the White House on several occasions, was a favorite of Eleanor's and the subject more than once in the first lady's syndicated newspaper column, "My Day."[14] She asked Jackie for a memorandum on Earhart's disappearance with all known data on the flight. Jackie passed on the request to Paul Mantz, admonishing him to tell no one about Mrs. Roosevelt's request.[15]

Never one to neglect her own interests, Jackie added in the same letter a

11.1. Jackie sitting at the controls of a Douglas DC4–E, with copilot and dear friend Maxine "Mike" Howard, wife of another record-setting aviator, Bennie Howard. (National Air and Space Museum, Smithsonian Institution, SI 2006–281, and Ralph Morgan, Newark Airport, New Jersey.)

lengthy complaint about Mantz's failure to sell the rebuilt Gamma. She was willing to lower the asking price if Mantz produced a firm offer, but he had not done so; Floyd had already told her that Mantz's sole prospective buyer had changed his mind and bought a Stinson. "If so," she taunted Mantz, "he is undoubtedly off the list of prospects."[16]

Later that summer, it was Floyd who sold the Gamma to Bernarr MacFadden, the magazine publisher whose promise to turn 98-pound weaklings into strong men had made him a fortune. Before the sale, Floyd gave MacFadden a complete history of the plane. Odlum cited the records set in it by Howard Hughes and Frank Hawks; he also told of the changes of motors and rebuilding of the aircraft by Northrop who combined a fuselage from a damaged Gamma owned by Mrs. Edmund Guggenheim with the usable parts from Jackie's Gamma after her two crash landings at Indianapolis in 1936.[17]

A week after her luncheon at the White House, Jackie was still under a doctor's care and enduring extensive dental work, but she was not too sick to accept an invitation for an interview on WMCA, a New York radio station. Asked if there was a place for women in aviation, she said there was, but not in commercial aviation. How women pilots were supposed to fly without being paid for it or without a rich husband to foot the bills, she did not say. When the interviewer declared that Jackie had done more for aviation than any other woman, she proved her lasting affection for Amelia by replying: "No, I think Amelia Earhart has done more than any other woman."[18] She followed the modest disclaimer with a sales pitch for "Wings to Beauty," stating that she had personally designed a complete line of products and hoped to soon have them on the market.[19]

Three days later, Jackie was back in the hospital for more surgery. When she came home from the second operation, Floyd celebrated her return with the gift of an elephant ride in Ringling Brothers' Circus on opening night at Madison Square Garden. A major stockholder of the Garden, Floyd remembered Jackie's story of trying to run away from home with the circus, and he arranged for her to lead the parade, seated on an elephant. She wore a spangled frock, silvery knee boots, and a two-foot-high turban that swayed gently as the huge beast lumbered around the ring. Other elephants followed, each with a woman rider. Once backstage, Jackie watched the other women dismount. As two men approached her with a ladder, she waved them away. "I noticed the other girls were sliding down the snoots of the elephants, so down the snoot I went and in good form."[20] The experience prompted her to suggest that they keep an elephant at the ranch. Floyd refused, claiming that it would be destructive and expensive. But she did not give up the idea until she had researched food bills for an elephant.[21]

In spite of recurring headaches, Jackie planned a trip to expand sales of her cosmetics. In addition to her three shops in Chicago, Forest Hills, Illinois, and Los Angeles, she had already placed the products in four department stores—Pogues in Cincinnati, Halle Brothers in Cleveland, Wanamakers in Philadelphia, and Garfinckles in Washington, D.C.[22] For her sales trips, she planned on using her Beechcraft Staggerwing, the plane that was dangerously overpowered with a 600-horsepower engine instead of the standard 400-horsepower one. One of Australia's leading women pilots, Nancy Bird, after a ride in the standard model, said that she experienced a tremendous

11.2. Jackie's childhood wish to join the circus was granted by her husband, Floyd Odlum, a board member of New York's Madison Square Garden, where he arranged for her to ride in the Ringling Brothers elephant parade. (Ann Wood-Kelly Collection, the Woman's Collection, Texas Woman's University, Denton, Texas.)

centrifugal force. "As he [the pilot] went into a deep turn, my tummy was pressed against my backbone."[23]

Jackie loved the Beechcraft. After one of Mantz's pilots crashed in it, Jackie asked Ben Howard to do the repairs and had emblazoned on its sides her slogan, "Wings to Beauty." To promote her products, she flew to Missouri, Alabama, and Indiana, where she was honorary starter for the Indianapolis 500 auto race in late May before going on to Dallas for more sales calls.[24]

On her return from Dallas, she took two weeks off for a trip to England and Europe with Floyd, sailing on the *Normandie* in mid-June.[25] When the ship docked at Southampton, they were met by an emissary of Floyd's friend Lord Beaverbrook, the British newspaper baron. At dinner that night, Jackie was seated between Beaverbrook and Winston Churchill. Beaverbrook, who was the proud holder of a private pilot's license, spoke of a plane crash caused by the absence of oil in one engine. He could not understand why the pilot had not checked his oil gauge. Jackie said that there was no gauge on that aircraft. In fact, she said, a $25,000 prize was offered to anyone who could develop one. Beaverbrook said that she was wrong. She bet him that she wasn't. "I wouldn't tell you how to publish a newspaper," she replied, "but at least I know something about aviation."[26] Floyd hastily changed the subject, but the next day after she returned to Beaverbrook to offer proof, she said, "I thought I saw a gleam of respect in his eye."[27]

If Jackie had Beaverbrook's respect, another dinner guest, Winston Churchill, earned hers. "It was the first time," she wrote years later, "I've ever heard a person talk almost continuously and wished he could talk faster and longer. I have always believed that if Churchill had been in office as prime minister of England in 1938 and 1939 there wouldn't have been World War II."[28]

Back from Europe in early July, Jackie began preparations for the 1938 Bendix, preparations that included a Civil Aeronautics Authority test to renew her transport license. She loathed and feared tests. She began to practice for this one with Max Constant, who had used her Beechcraft while she was in New York. In August, they made an instrument and radio flight check from Burbank to New York.[29] In return for Constant's assistance, Jackie accompanied him to Washington to help him secure citizenship papers so that he could enter the Bendix. She also offered to lend him her Beechcraft for the race, provided that she receive Seversky's new AP-7.[30]

For the CAA test that she still faced, both of the Howards offered help. Ben called examiner Fred Novinger in Boston and asked him to give Jackie the test at Newark, assuring him that she was a very competent pilot. Mike reported to her that Ben had forgotten to tell Novinger that Jackie had "stage fright." "Bennie," she wrote, "said it is much better for Fred to be told that you have the jitters over the test."[31] After Jackie took and passed the test with Novinger at Newark, she wrote to Mike: "Novinger is a grand person but did make me work and no fooling. I am grateful to you and Bennie for getting Fred to give me the test."[32]

Her strategy for the upcoming Bendix was to allow for every possible contingency. She had maps prepared by Constant for four different routes from Los Angeles to Cleveland with beacons and radio beams marked on all of them.[33] Because the race rules dictated a minimum of five hours' flight time in any plane entered, when Seversky's AP-7 was not ready, she went to his factory on Long Island to fly older versions of the aircraft, similar except for a new landing gear that he was designing.[34]

To climb above storm clouds, she would need oxygen. The previous fall when she first flew the P-35 at Wright Field, Captain Armstrong had introduced her to a civilian, Dr. W. Randolph Lovelace, who was working with Armstrong on the use of oxygen for high-altitude flight. For the Bendix, she asked her doctor in New York to write to Lovelace requesting an oxygen mask that the latter had designed for TWA pilots. Lovelace persuaded TWA president Jack Frye to lend her one.[35]

On August 16, Jackie sent her entry information for the Bendix to the man in charge of printed programs, Danton Floyd at the United Air Terminal. Her two-page letter listed every record that she had set, along with the Harmon and Mitchell awards and a notice that her new cosmetics would go on sale that fall. The letter closed with a stern reminder forbidding release of her picture or the program material to the press without her approval.[36] If she won the race, she intended to use the program material for endorsing aviation products, endorsements for which she would be paid.

Five days before the race, Floyd, who was in Jersey City, wired Jackie a list of fifteen numbered instructions. The first nine concerned her equipment. She was to see that turn and bank gauges were calibrated, to have Seversky's "so-called radio tube" installed, to see that the oxygen mask was working, and to think of a way to shield her eyes from the rising sun. She was to have the aircraft waxed to gain speed and to check the balance of the plane on takeoff with the head tank full. Floyd also wanted the frequency and hours of the radio station that would be broadcasting the race.[37]

The remainder of Floyd's list included instructions on refraining from any pilot protest against amateur pilot Bernarr MacFadden entering the race. After all, MacFadden had bought her Gamma. She was to be sure that she crossed the front of the grandstand in Cleveland at a height no greater than 1,000 feet if the field was open, but if crossing at the back of the stand, no higher than 500 feet, and never to fly over the stand. His last three requests were for her to make certain that a time had been arranged for at Floyd Bennett Field if

11.3. Cochran prepares her Seversky AP-7 for the 1938 Bendix Trophy Race. She considered *13* to be her lucky number and insisted that it be on all of the planes that she flew. (National Air and Space Museum, Smithsonian Institution, SI 2006–282. Photo courtesy Fairchild Industries.)

she continued on from Cleveland to New York for a speed record, to provide herself with emergency food, and to get the check for any prize money won by Constant, the money to be divided with him.[38]

Two days later, Floyd sent her another wire. "Your high hairdress in picture appearing in today's newspaper did not look as good as your old hairdress. All my love. Floyd."[39]

Jackie could not follow all of Floyd's instructions. Seversky did not deliver the AP-7 to Los Angeles until three days before the race, when he flew it himself, setting a new east-west record of ten hours, two minutes, and fifty-five seconds.[40] Tex Rankin called the AP-7 "a very much man-size plane to be flown by such a girl-size woman."[41] The girl-size woman had no opportunity to fly it because a leak in the fuel system required extensive repairs, and all planes were impounded for three days prior to takeoff. All she could do while the mechanics worked on it was to sit in the single-seat cockpit memorizing the gauges and dials until she could locate them with her eyes closed.[42]

At midnight on September 2, Jackie was the third of nine contestants to take off from Burbank in the plane that she had never flown. Buffeted by storm clouds as she climbed to 22,000 feet, she discovered that the fuel in the right wing tank would not feed unless she kept that wing higher to draw the gasoline into the left wing and from there to the engine.[43] The primitive oxygen apparatus designed by Lovelace and Dr. Walter Boothby at the Mayo Clinic, along with Captain Armstrong at Wright Field, consisted of an oxygen tank with a rubber tube leading to a corncob pipe stem that she clenched between her teeth. Condensation from the pipe dripped over her chin, freezing there until she wrapped some tissue paper around the stem and fastened it with a rubber band.[44]

A little more than eight hours later, a cheering crowd of 120,000 spectators at Cleveland saw Jackie's silver plane roll past the grandstand and down the runway. She had won the Bendix in eight hours, ten minutes, and 31.4 seconds.[45] One of the judges drove a car out to the end of the field to bring her back to the platform where officials waited to greet her. She kept him waiting while she combed her hair and applied a fresh coat of lipstick before she descended from the cockpit. Among the reporters surrounding the plane, one wrote that she looked "fresh and radiant."[46] Another heard her say to the judge, "Where's Floyd? I want some cigarettes. I've been smoking a pipe—an oxygen pipe—all the way from California and I need a cigarette for a change."[47]

She stayed in Cleveland only long enough to greet Floyd and refuel the plane before flying it on to Floyd Bennett Field in an attempt to set a west-east speed record. She broke the women's record, but not the men's, which was held by Frank Fuller, who had won the previous year's Bendix.[48] Cochran's time was ten hours, two minutes, and thirty-five seconds. Fuller had done it in nine hours and thirty-five minutes.

Jackie left the AP-7 at Floyd Bennett Field and caught a commercial flight back to Cleveland in time for the Aviation Ball, where she was seen "dancing in a pretty dress."[49] Guests of Jackie and Floyd at the ball included Gloria Vanderbilt, Lady Thelma Furness, Max Constant, the Severskys, her former teacher Wesley Smith and his family, and Tex Rankin, famed test pilot and stunt flyer. Jackie had reserved hotel rooms for all of them as well as quarters for her chauffeur, her secretary, and three mechanics.[50]

Three weeks later in the *New York Times Sunday Magazine*, she was called

11.4. Jacqueline Cochran is greeted by Vincent Bendix in 1938 after winning the Bendix Race in a Seversky Pursuit, averaging 249 mph. (National Air and Space Museum, Smithsonian Institution, SI 79–3161.)

11.5. Jackie with the Bendix Trophy after winning the cross-country race in 1938. Vincent Bendix *(left)* sponsored the contest and Seversky *(right)* designed the plane. (National Air and Space Museum, Smithsonian Institution, SI 84–14781.)

11.6. Two 1938 speed champions, Jackie Cochran and Alexander Seversky, stand with Ray Brown, NAA official *(left)*, before the "Lucky 13," the P-35 designed by Seversky. Both fliers used this aircraft—Jackie to win the Bendix Trophy Race from Los Angeles to Cleveland, defeating ten male contestants, and Seversky to set an east–west, cross-continental record. (National Air and Space Museum, Smithsonian Institution, SI 82–13214. Courtesy Institute of Aeronautical Sciences, 79–3161.)

"First Lady of the Air Lanes."[51] In another article, *Popular Aviation* magazine writer Helen Waterhouse called her "the red-haired ace lady bird, a queer combination of real femininity and real business sense—this queen of the skyways. Shrewd and sweet, gracious and a good sport, Jackie Cochran should go far in the coming years in her chosen fields."[52]

The former blonde turned redhead was not waiting for those coming years to reap the benefits of her Bendix victory. After collecting $12,500 in Bendix prize money, she was paid to endorse the products of both the Kendall Oil Company and the General Tire and Rubber Company.[53] For the full-page advertisements, she asked that Seversky's plane be pictured along with a portrait of her. She also suggested to both firms that the text of the advertisement state that she used their products in her own airplane "in which she covers

75,000 miles a year in connection with her cosmetics business." She collected fees from both firms to praise not only their products, but also her own.[54] Taking advantage of the publicity that she received during the week following the National Air Races, she went to Akron, Cincinnati, and Washington, where she appeared in stores selling her "Wings to Beauty" line. To Mike she boasted, "they practically had to close the store in Akron when I was there—had to take twelve policemen from the street to handle the crowd. There were big crowds in Cincinnati too and in Washington and you should have seen the men who came up to speak to me and don't think I didn't sell them some cosmetics for their wives. I am very tired," she admitted, "not having any rest and standing on my feet behind a counter for days."[55] Jackie was tired, although determined to promote not only her business but also her growing reputation as an expert pilot. That fall, she spoke at a celebration of Aviation Day given by the New York Sales Executive Club. She was where she wanted to be, sharing the rostrum with Eddie Rickenbacker, Roscoe Turner, Casey Jones, Seversky, Major Al Williams, and Jimmy Doolittle.[56]

Jackie had been welcomed into the circle of aviation's elite—the aircraft designers and manufacturers, test pilots, airline executives, and military pilots—accepted as a colleague. Clad in designer dresses, she enjoyed playing the feminine role assigned to her by men of that era. But when the conversation turned to informal revelations by pilots of individual flight experiences—"hangar talk"—Jackie was accepted as "one of the boys."[57]

Although Jackie was "one of the boys" to male pilots, she was not, like her beloved friend Earhart, "one of the girls." When she was invited to speak to the Ninety-Nines at a formal banquet, she said she could not get to the dinner but would be glad to speak later in the evening. The club's president, Daisy Kirkpatrick, replied that this would be too awkward because the guest speakers always sat at the head of the table.[58]

A second rebuff came from Olive Beech, chairman of the board and chief executive officer of Beech Aircraft Corporation. After Jackie refused to set a definite date for a speech to the Soroptimist Club of Wichita, Kansas, Olive withdrew the invitation. As strong-willed as Jackie, Beech had already engaged in mild skirmishes by letter with Cochran after the latter kept complaining about bills and service on her Beechcraft.[59]

By late November, Jackie had been a guest speaker for clubs and associations in Chicago, Buffalo, Philadelphia, and Newark. She told her friend Mike that she was exhausted, feeling terrible from a relapse of sinusitis, and that she intended to go to the ranch for a month's rest.[60] But en route to Indio on a commercial airline, she stopped off for three days in Detroit, where she gave one more speech on December 15 to the General Motors Men's Club.[61]

Floyd was waiting for her at the ranch. "Fifty-Percent Odlum" had just reached an out-of-court settlement of a lawsuit filed against him by the ex-president of Utilities Power and Light Company, Harley L. Clark. Clark claimed that Odlum had bought $19 million worth of the company's debentures at less than 50 cents on the dollar and, in addition, $2,844,000 worth of principal and interest notes for only $650,000. After Floyd's offer to settle for $3,200,000 was accepted, *Business Week* asserted that "Odlum Wins Again."[62]

It had been a good year for Jacqueline Cochran and Floyd B. Odlum.

Twelve

Keeping the Crown

On March 12, 1939, Jackie was named a Harmon Trophy winner for a second time—the outstanding woman flier of the world during 1938. (The other Americans winning a second Harmon Trophy were Howard Hughes and Colonel Roscoe Turner.)[1] But the newly crowned Queen of the Air Lanes was already looking for ways to remain on her throne. Earlier in March, she told William Enyart, Secretary of the National Aeronautics Administration, that she wanted to set a new altitude record. Aware that Jackie would claim any record that she could, Enyart denied her assertion that she held the cross-country speed record, limiting her to a woman's record. He wrote that she had stayed too long in Cleveland after winning the Bendix Race before going on to New York, and that Frank Fuller, winner of the 1937 Bendix who reached New York in nine hours and thirty-five minutes, remained the record holder.[2]

On March 20, Enyart wired her that a barograph and official forms were being sent to the NAA contest representative Larry Therkelson, but he complained that previous record reports from Therkelson had been incomplete, causing delay in official recognition. To be certain that Jackie was closely observed, he suggested that she ask for an assistant to Therkelson, appointed by Joe Nikrent, another NAA official on the west coast.[3]

On the same day that her win of the second Harmon Trophy was announced, Jackie took off from Palm Springs Airport in her Beechcraft, a fabric-covered plane with no heating or pressurization systems. Clad in heavy woolen clothing, she used Lovelace's oxygen apparatus—the tank and tube that she had borrowed for the 1938 Bendix.[4] She knew that the crude arrangement was dangerously inadequate above 15,000 feet, but once she had set a definite goal, she ignored all danger to reach it. After ascending in circles for two and a half hours, her ears ached severely and her nose began to bleed after a blood vessel in her sinuses broke. She stopped climbing only when the aircraft would no longer respond to the controls. To escape decompression sickness, she tried to descend as slowly as she had risen, but was so disoriented from lack of oxygen that she leveled off for a landing at 5,000 feet before realizing her mistake.[5]

Landing back at Palm Springs, she saw that her barometer registered 30,052 feet—the record that she sought. The news was promptly released by the public relations firm of H. A. Bruno & Associates. Hired by Floyd for Jackie, Harry Bruno was a friend of aviation's greats—among them Amelia Earhart, Charles Lindbergh, Frank Hawks, Jimmy Doolittle, Eddie Rickenbacker, and Alexander Seversky.[6] Bruno would remain Jackie's publicist for years, although three decades later, she was to insist, "I never had a public relations person. I've never tried to seek it. I never tried to use it in connection with my business."[7] She also claimed at a later date that she had reached 33,000 feet.[8] In an unpublished manuscript, she said a history of the Beech Aircraft Company was mistaken in acknowledging a height of only 30,052 feet when she had actually reached 34,000 feet.[9]

The record-setter failed to impress Bill Enyart. Although he acknowledged her altitude record, two days later, he informed her that the Federation Aeronautique Internationale, arbitrator of world records, had abolished international records for women pilots of light planes, with the exception of long-distance flights and speed for 100, 1,000, 2,000, 5,000, and 10,000 kilometers.[10] Jackie wrote back that if those were the records to be set, then she intended to set them.[11]

She also wanted the records in her own name. When her license renewal notice was addressed to Mrs. Jacqueline Cochran Odlum she told O. P. Harwood of the Civil Aeronautic Authority that she was Miss Jacqueline Cochran in all of her business and flying activities and that she had given no one the authority to change her name on the license.[12]

A week later, she wrote to Enyart requesting the appointment of Max Constant as an official NAA timer. Attempting to have a man who was her employee appointed an official judge of her performance was typical of Jackie as she sought to eliminate all variables from her program for success. Enyart was out of town, but she received a telegram from his office stating that Constant could not be appointed without his taking a written examination. A formal application and the examination papers were sent to Constant under separate cover. Jackie received a pointed reminder that while Constant was on the west coast, official NAA timers were available in New York.[13]

Jackie's aspirations were unlimited. In addition to plans for more record setting and her pursuit of markets for Jacqueline Cochran cosmetics, she was considering possible movie stardom. A guest at the ranch, John Monk Saunders, who had written the scripts for two popular films, *Dawn Patrol* and *Wings*, was working on a script about her for a picture to be filmed in the fall. "I am going to be back out [to the ranch] in two or three weeks," she wrote to a friend, "to have a screen test but I don't want the papers to get hold of this as it might not materialize and it would spoil some of the publicity later on."[14] The movie did not materialize.

Although Jackie had scorned women's records and refused to compete in women's air races, she gave a party in late April for members of the Ninety-Nines. Among the guests were two non-members, Army Air Corps Colonel Charles Wayne Kerwood and his wife, Beatrice. Kerwood was in charge of the Aviation Building at the World's Fair in New York, and a special Aviation Week was scheduled to begin on May 22.[15]

On the following day, the Women's National Aeronautical Association was to give a luncheon honoring Eleanor Roosevelt for her enthusiastic use of air travel. As the WNAA's Woman Pilot of the Year, Jackie was asked to present Mrs. Roosevelt with a plaque.[16]

Eager to enhance her acquaintanceship with the first lady, Jackie wrote to her asking for a private meeting before the luncheon. Mrs. Roosevelt answered, "I could visit you the morning of the 23rd if that would be satisfactory."[17] But a week later, Jackie received on White House stationery an unsigned letter stating that Mrs. Roosevelt would be at the Aviation Building on May 23 at 12:15 and would not need the transportation that Jackie had offered.[18] There was no mention of a morning meeting. The first lady's staff was obviously not as impressed with Jackie as was their boss. Six days before the scheduled luncheon, while Jackie was on another sales trip for her company, Floyd wired her in Chicago that neither he nor Jackie's office manager, Genevieve Crowley, could locate the WNAA luncheon committee, and the World's Fair office said that Aviation Week had been taken off the program.[19]

A perfectionist in scheduling any event from business meetings to dinner parties, Jackie was horrified at the prospect of the president's wife making a special trip to New York for a non-existent ceremony. Somehow, the luncheon was given, but before a small group in a building not yet open to the general public, and Mrs. Roosevelt was presented by Jackie with an engraved plaque from the WNAA.[20] Two days later, she wrote to Mrs. Roosevelt: "It's a pity the WNAA when they found the building unfinished and unopened to the public did not postpone their presentation until a later, propitious time when you would again be at the fair anyway."[21]

Jackie also wrote to Jack Frye, president of Transcontinental & Western Air, stating that the ceremony that should have been good publicity for the airlines was a dismal failure. The building was not open. "Only 40 people were there, no airline representatives," and the plaque was "a rather sorry looking affair. I really felt mortified by the whole thing." She thought that a more suitable gift for the first lady would have been a silver model of the DC-3 and suggested to Frye that she get one and present it to Mrs. Roosevelt the next time that she was in Washington, provided that Frye pay for it.[22] If the first lady was upset, it was not with Jackie. Three weeks later on June 15, she invited Jackie to Washington to present her with her second Harmon Trophy.[23]

That summer, Alex and Evelyn Seversky spent three weeks as house guests of Jackie and Floyd in their New York apartment at River House. Seversky was upset. His return from a visit in Paris was delayed when Evelyn became ill. During his absence, the board of governors of the Seversky Aircraft Corporation refused to re-elect him president. Instead, they appointed him chief designer and changed the name of the firm to Republic Aircraft Corporation.[24] Floyd Odlum was not surprised. Although recognizing Seversky as a brilliant designer, Floyd thought him no match for the business skills of the board. "He was far out of the blue with his ideas and money was going down the drain."[25] But Floyd was also certain that with Seversky's designs, and sound business management from the board, Republic was bound to prosper. He bought $10,000 of the company's stock, eventually making a substantial profit.[26]

During the Severskys' stay at River House, their tactful and gracious host grew tired of hearing Seversky's troubles every night after dinner. "I finally found a way to shut him up at bedtime," Floyd recalled. "He loved playing the accordion. I had an accordion and I would place it on his lap."[27]

Seversky's loss of leadership in his company did not deter Jackie from buying his AP-7, the prototype that eventually evolved into the P-47, an Army Air Corps fighter plane named the Thunderbolt by Republic. On July 18, she accepted the company's offer to have it flown for ten hours of tests at the company's risk before it was turned over to her.[28]

12.1. First Lady Eleanor Roosevelt presenting Jackie with her second Harmon Trophy, awarded for outstanding international achievement in aviation, on June 15, 1939. (Courtesy Dwight D. Eisenhower Library. Photographer unknown.)

While the low-winged monoplane with its 950-horsepower engine was being tested, Jackie set another record in her Beechcraft—one not listed by Enyart at the NAA. After just six hours of instruction, on August 8 she became the first woman to make a "blind landing" at Pittsburgh. Using the radio landing guidance system while under a hood that obliterated her view of the field, she made a perfect landing at the City-County Airport. As witnesses, she took along her instructor Lloyd Santmeyer and Air Corps Reserve Lieutenant Fred Ruch.[29]

When the new AP-7 was turned over to her, she entered it in the 1939 Bendix. Instead of leaving in the early hours of the morning as she had done in previous races, she planned to fly nonstop in daylight with a maximum load of fuel. The night before the race while she slept in her suite at the Ambassador Hotel in Los Angeles, a heavy fog rolled in from the Pacific, blanketing the field. She waited all morning at the end of the runway hoping that the fog would lift. It did not. "The plane had to cross the finish line in Cleveland by not later than five o'clock in the afternoon and when I saw that the time limit could not be made," she said, "I did not want to have the dubious distinction of having the fastest time in the race, but losing the race on a technicality so I rolled the plane back to the hangar and took an airline to Cleveland to see the remainder of the races."[30]

When officials in Cleveland first announced that she was not flying in the Bendix, someone started the rumor that she had overslept and that when she discovered that she could not win, she quit. The criticism was unwarranted. To take off earlier in a dense fog, fuel tanks loaded with highly flammable fuel, was near-suicidal, and to leave too late to win was a waste of time and money.[31]

Without a Bendix win, she hastened to set more speed records. On September 15, she flew a 1,000-kilometer marked course in the AP-7 from Burbank to San Mateo, California, in two hours and two minutes. Her average speed was 305.925 miles an hour. Beating her previous time of 204 miles an hour by more than 100 miles an hour, she bested Frenchwoman Helen Boucher's time of 256 miles an hour for the international record.[32] Rolling to a stop on the runway, she left the plane in her customary manner, keeping photographers waiting while she took off her helmet, shook out her hair, and applied lipstick before climbing down from the cockpit. "Whew!" she exclaimed. "Has anyone got a cigarette?"[33] Two weeks later on September 28, she bested her earlier 100-kilometer speed, reaching an average of 286.418 miles an hour.[34]

Press notices were not all Jackie's on that September day. On the same day, Hortense Odlum celebrated her fifth anniversary as president of Bonwit Teller, her success featured in the *New York Times* the next day, along with Jackie's latest record. In the five years since Floyd Odlum bought control of the failing store and turned it over to Hortense, she had tripled its sales and staff, redecorated it and opened new departments, and installed confidence in her employees who were taught how to develop closer shopping relationships with their customers.[35] Earlier in the year, recognition of her accomplishments extended beyond the business world with the publication of *A Woman's Place: The Autobiography of Hortense Odlum*, published by Charles Scribner's Sons, with excellent reviews.[36]

In the spring of 1940, three photographs appeared across the center of a full-page story in *Time* magazine. From left to right were Jackie, Floyd, and Hortense. Hortense was described as wife No. 1, able president of Bonwit Teller, still Floyd's business associate, and a big Atlas stockholder. Jackie, wife No. 2, was defined as an aviatrix and co-owner of the ranch. No mention was made of her business or her records. The story was Floyd's, headed "Odlum Makes a Deal." On behalf of Atlas, he had engineered a takeover of U.S. Aircraft's Curtiss-Wright Corporation. With a helping hand from Floyd, the two Mrs. Odlums were both celebrities, but if Hortense was willing to rest on her laurels, Jackie was not.

Thirteen

Women and War

On September 28, 1939, the day that Jackie broke her own 100-kilometer record and Hortense celebrated her fifth anniversary at Bonwit Teller, both events were overshadowed by the surrender of Poland to the invading armies of Germany and Russia. Jackie thought of her friend, aviator Ernst Udet, an ace in World War I and by then a general in the Luftwaffe. In 1936, when they were guests at a party, Udet asked her to step out on a balcony where he would not be overheard before he said to her, "You know we are going to war with you." "Oh, no!" she whispered. "You're crazy."[1] Udet told her that the Germans had 100,000 military pilots whose training he described in detail before asking her not to reveal him as a source of this information because he would be executed for treason. "But I love your country and I hate to see this happening," he said. "We are going to go to war and you are going to be involved in it."[2]

Jackie told no one—not even Floyd—before consulting her lawyer friend Mabel Walker Willebrandt. Mabel suggested that they meet in a nearby park when Jackie asked her what she should do about Udet's revelation. With access to most of political Washington, Mabel thought it important enough to arrange a meeting for Jackie with Major General Oscar Westover, chief of the Army Air Corps. After hearing her report, Westover was probably more tactful than Jackie claimed, but she interpreted his comments as, "You're just a little girl and you shouldn't bother your mind with things like this." Furious, Jackie snapped, "I think you are a fool to talk to me like that. I got this from a source that I know is real."[3] However, Jackie refused to reveal Udet as her source because she liked and trusted him. He died two years later, his death officially declared a suicide, but it was whispered on the streets of Germany that he was shot behind closed doors because of his open disapproval of Hitler.[4]

Jackie knew that the training given to American military pilots could not compare with that described by Udet. During the summer of 1936, at the request of Mayor Fiorello LaGuardia of New York City, she had flown to Williamsburg, Virginia, to pick up a display intended for the World's Fair. As she approached the Williamsburg airport, two Air Corps planes closed in on her. She radioed the tower, "I've got a couple of idiots closing in on me. I don't do formation flying and I can see their teeth."[5] She landed, picked up the display, and hurried on to Richmond for a dinner with the governor.

The next day as she prepared to return to New York from Richmond in threatening weather, she was astounded to learn from one of the two pilots who had annoyed her at Williamsburg that he could not take off when she did. "We are not allowed to fly on instruments," he told her. Not long after, she wrote to the man who would succeed Westover as Air Corps commander, Major General Henry Harley "Hap" Arnold: "They [the Air Corps pilots] may fly formation but they are not flying in bad weather. How are they going to fight?" she asked.[6]

If and when the Air Corps was sent to fight the Germans, Jackie was prepared to help. Before sundown on the day that the Polish surrendered, she wrote a long letter to Mrs. Roosevelt, suggesting that a role in national defense be given to women aviators. In the event of war, they could serve as pilots of ambulance, courier, and transport planes to release men for wartime service. "Should there be a call to arms it is not my thought that women pilots go out and engage in combat," she wrote, "but every male pilot will be needed in active service."[7] Proposing some official status be given to the women pilots, Jackie told Mrs. Roosevelt that the nations of Europe had already recognized the potential of women fliers in national defense. Three years earlier, German officials had appointed Hanna Reitsch, a woman whom Jackie knew and admired, to be a captain in the German Air Force, assigned to organize and direct training for a women's air corps. Russia's program for women had already started the previous year. The French and English were also forming women's air auxiliaries for the military.[8]

However, Jackie suggested, the subject did not belong in Mrs. Roosevelt's syndicated newspaper column. "I don't think it is public opinion that must be touched," she wrote, "but rather official Washington, especially the military."[9] Jackie knew that there would be no women's air service without the approval of men—in the military, in Congress, and in the general public.

Jackie was not the originator of this plan. As early as May of 1936, Ninety-Nines member Mrs. Theodore "Teddy" Kenyon had suggested that women could assist in war by ferrying planes.[10] Many of the women needed for an auxiliary force were already licensed pilots—members of the Ninety-Nines, whose air meets and races Jackie had shunned. But five weeks after her letter to the first lady, she was a speaker at a World's Fair program honoring the Ninety-Nines. She praised the recent decision of the Civil Aeronautics Board to open student pilot programs to women—albeit in a ratio of one woman to nine men—and advocated a federal preparedness program for women fliers. But she opposed women becoming combat pilots or competitors with men in commercial aviation.[11]

Unlike Earhart, Jackie claimed that in winning their social and political independence, women had sacrificed the old-fashioned homage to femininity. "There was a time," she said, "when it was quite a thing to be a woman."[12] Jackie would continue to make it "quite a thing." Although she was welcomed as "one of the boys" in "hangar talk," she did that talking in designer clothes, her hair and makeup flawless.

If she assumed that she would be the automatic choice of the Ninety-Nines as the future auxiliary's leader, she was mistaken. Typical of the members as skilled and experienced as Jackie, Edna Gardner Kidd protested vigorously at Jackie's failure to mention her in an article, "Women in Aviation."[13] The operator of a flying school, the irate Edna said that with 4,000 flight hours to her credit, she had placed first in 90 percent of all competitive flying for both men and women during the last fifteen years.[14] In a second letter, she claimed that Earhart had told her, "Edna, aviation's greatest failure lies not with men but with the women[,] for it is . . . the women I hope [who] will one day have charge of the schools. . . . I leave this educational advancement in your charge."[15] Jackie apologized.[16]

Although the Ninety-Nines were less than enthusiastic about her possible leadership of an auxiliary, Jackie had major support from Eleanor Roosevelt and many of the nation's great aviators who, with their families, had been guests at the ranch or the River House apartment in New York. Along with Alexander Seversky, she was named a Harmon Trophy winner for 1939—her third. The announcement was delayed until September of 1940 because the donor, Clifford B. Harmon, was ill.[17] Jackie was a member of the selection committee for the Robert J. Collier Trophy that was awarded annually for the greatest achievement in aeronautics or astronautics in America, the only woman on the 15-person committee that included Major General Arnold, plane builder Donald Douglas, war ace and manager of Eastern Airlines Captain Eddie Rickenbacker, and the NAA's William Enyart.[18]

With Americans opposed to entering the European conflict, Jackie returned to the pursuit of more speed records, aided by two men—Floyd Odlum and Max Constant. As head of the Atlas Corporation and chairman of the board of Curtiss-Wright, Odlum told William W. Kellett, the new president of Republic Aviation Company, that Jackie wanted to know when a new Republic plane would be ready for her next record attempts. She intended to break the men's and women's international record for 2,000 kilometers and the men's and women's national record for 100 kilometers, currently held by Roscoe Turner. In addition, she hoped to best Howard Hughes's cross-country record of seven hours and fifty-two minutes by waiting for fair weather and a 50-mile-an-hour tail wind likely to occur in January of 1940.[19]

Floyd worked out a detailed mathematical analysis of winds, altitude, and fuel consumption.[20] Max Constant wrote to the Department of the Interior for geological surveys of 100-kilometer, 1,000-kilometer, and 2,000-kilometer closed courses at Carlsbad, New Mexico. With them, he drew maps, writing instructions on choices of altitude and fuel consumption on little strips of paper that he affixed to the maps.[21]

Meanwhile, Jackie prepared physically. In spite of sinusitis and intestinal troubles, she established a routine to increase her strength and endurance, listing nourishment and medications. The list included five meals a day with as much fat as possible and plenty of starches plus a quart of milk. Medications included Syntropan and Betalin three times daily before meals, Oleum Persomorpheum and Bemax twice daily, and Glauber's salts in hot water every morning.[22]

On April 6, she flew Seversky's new Republic AP-9 on a 2,000-kilometer course from Mount Wilson to Albuquerque and back at an average of 331.716 miles an hour. The previous record of 311 miles an hour was held by a German, Ernst Seiberg, in a Junkers bomber. On April 30, she did the 100-kilometer course at 292.6 miles an hour, topping Roscoe Turner's record and giving her a lifetime total of seventeen national and international records.[23] These were the records that Jackie wanted—men's not women's.

All of her record flights were dangerous. While running fuel tests on the AP-9, she pushed the plane into a dive over Albuquerque and lost control of the aircraft. "I was just sitting there with the stick flapping . . . sitting in a dishpan—a tin one at that—sliding down a shallow flight of steps."[24] She regained control by lowering the flaps to slow the plane down, but she was shaken by the experience. Returning to Los Angeles, she asked for an explanation from aeronautics authority Dr. Theodore von Karmen at the California Institute of Technology, by then a frequent house guest at the ranch. He told her that she had experienced "compressibility," creating forces greater than the plane could endure and that only by slowing the aircraft down had she prevented it from disintegrating.[25]

The new record holder was not overly modest about her achievements. Given a script for a radio broadcast, she crossed out "one of the world's outstanding women fliers," replacing it with "the officially recognized world's outstanding woman pilot."[26]

Jackie was ambitious, but generous to anyone who helped her. She wrote letters of recommendation for job seekers and invited many to the ranch, where she introduced them to her influential guests. One of the many thank-you notes that she received was from a P-43 mechanic, Erwin Hoenes, who recalled spending a weekend at the ranch "riding, swimming and playing croquet with you and Mrs. Northrop."[27] For those who were ill, she located a suitable doctor and often paid their bills. She recommended Max Constant for a job at Douglas Aircraft. After he was told that the firm did not hire aliens, Jackie asked Mabel Willebrandt to hasten the completion of his citizenship papers.[28] Meanwhile, she paid him to work on her Beechcraft. She also invited Constant to live at the ranch while he gave flying lessons to film star Robert Taylor, who soloed on November 15, a promising pilot.[29]

Jackie helped Constant during a summer and fall when she was undergoing another operation for sinusitis that required follow-up treatments at Johns Hopkins hospital in Baltimore. At the same time, Floyd was at Mayo Clinic in Rochester, Minnesota, for diagnosis and treatment of rheumatoid arthritis.[30]

Neither his illness nor hers kept Jackie from traveling to promote sales of cosmetics or attending meetings of the NAA's Collier Award committee. In another typical display of gratitude to three more of her benefactors, she was determined that the prestigious award for 1939 be given to the designers of the portable oxygen apparatus that she had used in the 1938 Bendix Race. One was Harry Armstrong of the Army Medical Corps, the man who told her on her first visit to Wright Field that Seversky's AP-7 was too dangerous for her to fly. The other two were Dr. W. Randolph Lovelace and Dr. Walter M. Boothby at the Mayo Foundation for Medical Research.

At a Collier committee meeting, Jackie described the work of the three doctors to provide pilots with oxygen at high altitude. "Mr. Douglas here is trying to build an airplane to go to 40,000 feet," but she pointed out that there was no system for pilot survival at that altitude.[31] At the request of the committee, she went to the Mayo Foundation to discuss their work with Boothby and with Lovelace, who had arranged for her to borrow an earlier version of the tank with tube and pipe.

Later at Wright Field, she tested an improved model with a mask over her nose. "The work was pretty crazy," she recalled. "I'd take small animals up in my plane as high as they and I could stand it. The chickens would explode. What a mess!" However, Jackie's true grit was limited. "I'd fly mice," she added, "but I refused to take the billy goat and the snake."[32]

When the three doctors displayed their new portable tank to the committee, Jackie noted, "Arnold had never seen one; Douglas had never heard of one."[33] With Arnold's support, Jackie's candidates won a unanimous vote from the committee.[34] The award was given to U.S. Airlines for their safety record, with special recognition for the three doctors.[35]

That December, Jackie was at the White House when President Roosevelt presented the award. After the ceremony, Roosevelt drew her aside. When he asked, "Are these medical or scientific doctors?" she seized the opportunity to ask for his support, telling him that if he could spare the time, Dr. Boothby would explain. After Boothby's briefing, F.D.R. promised a "large sum" from presidential funds, but when he added that the money would be divided between the Army Air Force and the Navy, fearless Jackie protested. "That's foolish! It should be put in one laboratory and they both should use it."[36] Whether he agreed or not, she didn't say.

On leaving the White House, she went to lunch with Hap Arnold and Clayton Knight, head of recruiting for the British Ferry Command, who needed American pilots to ferry bombers to England, planes provided under the lend-lease program pushed through Congress by Roosevelt. Arnold told her that she should fly one herself to give the recruiting publicity. "This was the opportunity I was looking for," Jackie said. Not only could she become the first woman to fly a bomber across the Atlantic, but also once in England, she could observe the training and assigning of women pilots in the British ferrying service. Both were crucial steps in achieving her goal of founding and leading an American women's flying auxiliary.[37]

For approval of the bomber flight, she presented her pilot's logbook and flight records to the British authorities in Washington and asked for an appointment to be made with their ferry command in Montreal. Her records were approved, but officials stalled, voicing doubts about a woman flying a bomber. While she waited, she gave some thought to the future recruiting of American woman fliers for the auxiliary that she envisioned, concluding that the first, most eligible candidates were members of the Ninety-Nines. With her own status as the outstanding American woman pilot confirmed by her third Harmon Trophy, Jackie invited members of the Ninety-Nines to hold their annual meeting at the Mayflower Hotel suite in Washington that she and Floyd kept as a *pied-à-terre*. At the informal meeting, Jackie repeated the proposal that she had made to Eleanor Roosevelt—that a government-sponsored corps of women aviators serve in national defense by flying non-combat missions. The idea must have appealed to them because when they elected new officers, Jackie became president.[38]

It is not surprising that the Ninety-Nines thought her a fitting president. When a member asked her what planes she had flown, Jackie sent her a list that included the following: Fleet, Fairchild, Great Lakes, Ravel Air, WACO, Stearman, Monocouple, Stinson, Northrop Gamma, Gee Bee, Douglas DC-2, Vultee, Beechcraft, Ryan, Seversky, Howard, Luscome, and Republic. At that point, she left off the Travel Air.[39]

This done, it was time to put pressure on the British Ferry Command in Montreal. Floyd's old friend Lord Beaverbrook had been appointed Britain's wartime director of supplies and procurement. Beaverbrook approved her bomber flight.

Assuming that the men in the Ferry Command would be reluctant to let a woman fly a bomber, Jackie prepared for a flight test by taking a captain's course given to pilots of Eastern Airlines because the airline was already making scheduled flights to Iceland over the route that she would be flying. The course included blind flying at night and flying on instruments while one engine was stopped.[40] She did both satisfactorily and left for Montreal on June 16, 1941.[41]

Fourteen

Testing the Waters

The first day that Jackie walked to the Lockheed Hudson bomber parked on the tarmac in Montreal, she was met by the pilot assigned to test her. When he asked for her experience, she told him that she had 900 hours during the first year that she flew and that she had flown the P-47 and the Gee Bee.

"You're pretty hot, aren't ya?" he snickered.

"I'm good," she answered.[1]

Her surly mentor neither gave her a rundown on the plane nor a chance to check out the cockpit, but she saw that the two-engine aircraft had a hand brake so low on the floor that she would have to bend down too far to see over the cockpit when she pulled it. That night, Jackie telephoned several friends, asking about the Hudson bomber. One said that it was fine while airborne, but "an absolute stinker to land."[2]

For her test flight, the man put her in the back cockpit, and on landing, she had to use the hand brake. "There was a crosswind and trying to get this brake and control at the same time was really rough, but I did it," she said. She recalled making eight, perhaps ten landings, all of them successful, but when she decided that they were enough and began taxiing toward the hangar, he objected. Jackie lost her temper. "I'm going to go in and tell you what I think of you," she shouted, "and you are going to give me a ticket right now on this airplane, or I am going to turn you in and when I get through with you, you'll wish you'd never heard my name."[3]

"Who do you think you are?" he snarled.

"I mean a hell of a lot more to aviation than you do, boy!" was her answer. Then she asked him to make a few landings from the back seat. "He made three," she said, "and damn near cracked up on one of them. He wrote my ticket. He didn't dare not do it."[4]

He wrote the ticket, but added a recommendation that she not be permitted to fly the plane "because of a physical inability to handle the brake in an emergency."[5] He was overruled by the command. Yet another bridge had to be crossed after the navigator, Captain Grafton Carlisle, warned her at dinner that the male pilots at the field had held a meeting and planned to strike. They were afraid, Grafton said, that the success of a woman pilot would lessen their chances for a pay raise that they were going to demand. The command settled the matter by appointing Jackie First Officer, but assigning Carlisle to take off and land the bomber. She was to fly it only while airborne.[6] Once certain that the flight was on, Jackie announced to the press in Montreal that while in England, she would study the role of women in the ferrying service "with reference to possible similar use of women in national defense in the U.S."[7] Jackie later claimed that Carlisle's solution did not satisfy the men who resented her making the flight.

On the day that she was to leave, Jackie discovered that no life raft had been put aboard, and that the wrench for the oxygen system was missing. Spying one in a mechanic's overalls pocket, she gave him ten dollars for it. With Carlisle handing over the controls as soon as they were airborne, Jackie flew as far as Gander, Newfoundland, the first leg of their journey. The next morning as they prepared to leave, she saw that a second oxygen wrench that she had purchased was also missing and a cockpit window had been broken.[8]

When Jackie arrived in London on June 20, a crowd of reporters were there to interview the first woman to deliver an American-built Lockheed to Britain. British officials attempted to enforce their customary policy of silence on ocean ferrying, "But they had never had a flying glamor [*sic*] girl to deal with before," the Associated Press's man reported. "They finally gave up when British and American reporters entered Miss Cochran's room."[9] The glamor girl kept them waiting while she changed and renewed her makeup for the photographers. Interviewed, she called the Lockheed Hudson a "grand" plane and told reporters that her only companion on the crossing was Captain Carlisle. Actually, there was another man, a radio operator. She also gave her age as thirty-two, when she had just celebrated her thirty-fifth birthday.[10]

When news of her flight reached Mobile, reporter Frank Gordy of the *Mobile Register* went looking for Jackie's kinsmen and found "Uncles and aunts, and cousins by the dozens—scattered from Mobile to DeFuniak Springs." Uncle W. J. Grant, in whose home she lived in Mobile, blurted, "Well, I declare, she always was the nerviest thing." Gordy wrote that her mother, Mrs. Ira (nee Mollie Grant) Pittman, who lived with a son on a farm near DeFuniak Springs, was "unavailable for comment."[11] Mollie had chosen to honor her daughter's version of herself as an orphan and foster child.[12]

Other relatives were eager to claim her. Grant said that Jackie was born in or near Muscogee at Gateswood, Alabama. E.W. "Manny" Waters, first cousin of Ira Pittman, recalled that Jackie's father worked for the Southern State Lumber Company, moving frequently, but was not certain where any of Ira's children were born. None of these members of Jackie's family had seen her since she left for New York. They said that they followed her career in the newspapers. Mollie's friend Mrs. C.A. Hobbs told Gordy that Jackie visited her mother at DeFuniak Springs "some time ago" and that Mollie spent her time between DeFuniak Springs and Jackie's home in California.[13]

Meanwhile, Jackie, who remained in England for 10 days, hitched a ride to Montreal on a B-24 bomber with fourteen pilots and a radio man, sharing her cigarettes with all during a rocky ride against headwinds. "At the end of 14 hours we became nervous. Word came back that we were headed for Montreal. Later this was again corrected to Gander. The truth, I'm sure," she said, "is that the pilot was off course and didn't know where we could get in, if at all."[14] They made it to Gander, and the next day to Montreal.

On arriving in New York, Jackie hurried to River House to change from her filthy flight suit before giving an interview to the press. Taking advantage of the publicity, she told reporters that while she was in England, she observed the work of fifty women pilots, members of the Air Transport Command—women who ferried military planes from factories to bases. She said that she planned to write a report with her recommendations for adapting the British system for an American national defense program. She went on to say that from the 2,000 American women with pilot's licenses, 1,000 with two or three months' special training could do what the ATC women were doing.[15]

The next morning, Jackie received a telephone summons from the office of the president, inviting her to Hyde Park for lunch with F.D.R., Eleanor, Princess Martha of Norway, and Sara Roosevelt, the president's mother. After the meal, Roosevelt asked Jackie to give him a detailed description of wartime England.[16] A few days later, she was invited to the White House by Mrs. Roosevelt. Eleanor, along with members of the General Federation of Women's Clubs and the Women's Aeronautical Association, was upset with the War Department decision to close the pilot-training program of the Civil Aviation Authority, replacing it with the War Training Service whose students would be trained for combat. That eliminated women.[17]

At the close of Jackie's meeting with Mrs. Roosevelt, the president sent her to see Robert A. Lovett, Assistant Secretary of War for Air, who in turn sent her to Hap Arnold, by then chief of the newly named Army Air Force. In the chain of command, Arnold passed her along to Lieutenant Colonel Robert Olds, who was forming a Ferrying Command to eventually become the Air Transport Command.[18]

Olds assigned her, as a dollar-a-year volunteer, to collect data on the availability of women pilots to ferry military training planes. He wanted 100 women who had logged 500 flight hours.[19] This was not Jackie's plan for a women's auxiliary. On July 21, she wrote to Olds, "You are thinking in terms of present movement of equipment and I am thinking of shaping up a women's pilot organization for future usefulness in time of war with present ferrying as an initial incident."[20]

Nevertheless, she accepted the assignment to go through 300,000 cards listing pilots registered by the CAA. She worked in the office of Olds's new command in the basement of the Munitions Building with a staff of six officers and one enlisted man. She also brought seven of her own employees from her New York office to aid in a search that resulted in the names of 3,000 women pilots, all graded by Jackie for their experience. Her report to Olds listed 50 with 500 hours, 83 with more than 200, and about 2,000 who would require little training to ferry primary-type airplanes.[21] But Jackie hadn't done the count for Olds—she wanted it for the auxiliary that she intended to create.

In need of more pilots for his Army Air Force Ferrying Command, Olds proposed to Arnold that he hire as civilians the fifty most experienced women for a three-month trial. Arnold turned him down. Jackie, who saw Olds's plan as a foot in the door opening to women, went to Arnold to argue the case, but he told her, "the use of women pilots would serve no military purpose at this time." She interpreted "at this time" as his admission that they might be needed later.[22]

Although Hap Arnold had put Jackie in a holding pattern, he had admired her since witnessing her nonstop effort to secure the Collier Award for the three doctors. Both Arnold and Jackie were driving personalities and both were long-range planners. Because Arnold could not use women pilots for lack of planes, he thought of a friend who could. Air Marshall Sir Arthur T. Harris, head of the Royal Air Force delegation to Washington, was in desperate need for additional pilots for the Air Transport Auxiliary—the British ferrying service employing as civilians both men and women.

In October 1941, two months before Pearl Harbor, Harris received a call from Arnold. "He said he could not spare a single pilot but he was sending me 'the only person who could help me—and don't laugh.' Within a few minutes into my office erupted a blonde bombshell," Harris recalled. He asked her how many pilots she could get. She said, "Maybe six, but I could soon make it sixty and later, six hundred."[23] But she added that he must agree to release her if and when she was asked to return to the U.S. to set up training centers for American women pilots.[24]

While she began looking for eligible recruits listed in the roster that she had already prepared for Olds, Floyd Odlum was working for the government as a "dollar-a-year" man in Washington. "He went to breakfast with Harry Hopkins, stopped at the White House and came out with a job as head of O.P.M.'s Division of Contract Distribution," *Business Week* magazine reported.[25] His job was to prevent shortages of materials from shutting down small firms, with the resulting unemployment for thousands. Within the first two weeks in office, he had arranged for $54,000,000 in defense contracts going to firms in "distressed areas."[26]

Floyd was in Washington, D.C., when the Japanese attacked Pearl Harbor on December 7, 1941. Jackie's flying license had lapsed while she was in Indio recovering from another sinus infection, and she needed both a renewal of the license and a birth certificate for her British identification card.[27] With his access to the higher echelons of government, Floyd persuaded Donald H. Connelly, director of the Civil Aviation Authority, to reinstate her flying license that had expired and to give her a temporary identification card in lieu of the birth certificate that she did not have.[28]

In a new conflict with Olds, by then a Brigadier General, Jackie was on her own. Arnold, promoted to Major General a week after Pearl Harbor, gave Olds permission to hire the fifty women pilots. Jackie immediately wrote to Arnold, "It's terribly confusing to have you say that women won't be needed or used here for many months to come, and have General Olds tell me the next day that there is a shortage of pilots and he is going to use women as a consequence."[29] Arnold answered by sending her letter and a memo to Olds to "make no plans or open negotiations for hiring women pilots until Miss Jacqueline Cochran has completed her present agreement with the British authorities and has returned to the U.S."[30]

On January 23, 1942, Jackie sent a two-page telegram to each of the women whom she wanted for the ATA, explaining that those chosen would first have to pass a flight test and physical examination given by the officials in Montreal and that ranks and pay would be the same as those for British women in the ATA. Those wanting to join were asked to wire her at her New York office.

The day after sending the telegrams, she announced her plans to the press, saying that when she flew the bomber to England the previous June, she first had the idea of forming an American women's unit for the British ATA. "It is apparent," she said, "that at least for months to come there will be no place for women in affiliation with our American fighting force."[31]

Of the forty women whom Jackie recruited for the ATA, twenty-five passed their flight check and physical examination in Montreal. They were to go to England in small groups on ships in convoy, and Jackie was to arrive before them, flying a bomber for the second time. A day before her flight was scheduled, she was admitted to a Montreal hospital, feverish from an ulcerated leg—a severe reaction to two typhoid inoculations. Released two weeks later, she hitched a ride on a British commercial plane from Baltimore via Bermuda and Lisbon.[32]

Although Jackie's friend Air Marshall Harris liked Jackie, many of the British whom she encountered did not. She was too pushy, too bluntly outspoken, and too boastfully American. Soon after her arrival in March, she crossed swords with an English medical officer when he told her that her recruits would have to "strip naked" (Jackie's description) for a physical examination. She refused. "Her girls" would not strip. When he insisted, she appealed first to Pauline Gower, commander of the ATA women pilots, who sympathized, but said that she could do nothing. Jackie appealed next to the commanding officer of the ATA, who kept her waiting for two hours before refusing her request. When she threatened to go to ever higher authorities, he surrendered to the fierce, demanding woman.[33]

One of the recruits, Ann Wood, a twenty-two-year-old college graduate who had learned to fly in the Civilian Pilot's Training Program, arrived in England with the third group on May 25. She missed Jackie's confrontation with the medical officer, but heard it discussed more than once. "Jackie was a prude," Ann said. "She wanted everything to be proper. She was so strict with us. Wanted us to represent the U.S. . . . Above reproach. She could party hard but we had to be good girls. But I went to London every chance I got—to party!"[34] Neither Wood nor any of the twenty-three other women who passed the ATA physical—one failed—could know that the woman who regarded herself as their protector had once been a child who hid in the dark corners of a textile mill to escape sexual attacks from male workers.

A few weeks after Wood's arrival, Jackie began to invite her to parties that she held in her Chelsea house. Wood, like Earhart, was Jackie's opposite. A beautiful woman, tall and slim, well-educated, and at ease with the British, she assessed Jackie critically, but with understanding and, before long, with genuine affection. "She felt inferior to the British and she'd pick fights that were silly sometimes," Wood recalled. "We'd walk into a restaurant—we were in uniform—and Jackie would ask for the best table. Sometimes she was critical of the food and when she lost her cool she was hard to control. She wanted to make something happen all the time and she knew people who could make that possible. She had the uncanny ability to envision where she wanted to be and get there. There was something magical about her."[35]

"Jackie always managed to cause a commotion which generally leaves her a few enemies in its wake," Wood added. "They mocked her for not flying, for her rented Daimler, her mink coat, her lovely house in Chelsea. The British didn't understand. She didn't go there to fly. She wanted to assess our performance and to prove, or disprove the program. Only later, after the Americans had served in the ATA, did they approve."[36]

Given the honorary title of flight captain, Jackie made frequent calls at the Air Ministry. On a day when Ann waited for her in the car, she came out and took a little dictionary from a large purse that she always carried. "Now, Annie," she said, "look up these words." For each word that Ann found, she read the definition to Jackie, pronounced it, and spelled it. "I honestly think her reading ability at that time was so minimal she couldn't even look them up."[37]

Jackie admitted later, "I still regret my lack of schooling. I have never learned to spell well. Finding a new word is like finding a diamond. It immediately starts showing up on my tongue."[38] Wood confirmed this, marveling at how Jackie used a new word on every suitable occasion until it was permanently locked into her ever-expanding vocabulary.[39]

14.1. After flying a bomber to England in the summer of 1941, Jackie joined the British Air Transport Auxiliary as a flight captain. Shown here in her Auxiliary uniform in 1942, she had just been reelected president of the Ninety-Nines, the international organization of women pilots. (National Air and Space Museum, Smithsonian Institution, SI 2003–7208.)

Jackie spent most of her time on administration while the twenty-four Americans moved planes from factory to field, field to field, and the damaged aircraft back to factories for repair. Recalling one of the latter, she said, "It was fabric covered. So we pasted that. One wing was shot off so we sawed the other one to match."[40] The Americans flew unfamiliar aircraft with only a sheaf of handling notes. Their code for a pre-flight check was "Hot-tempered member of Parliament F. G.—hydraulics, trim tabs, mixture, prop, flaps and gills."[41]

When her charges came to London on their days off, Jackie welcomed them in her Chelsea house, cooking ham, grits, and fried chicken for them, much of the ingredients brought by Air Force officers arriving from the United States.

On May 25, almost six months after Pearl Harbor, Arnold arrived on his first trip to England.[42] At a dinner that Lord Beaverbrook gave in his honor, Arnold told Jackie that Air Marshall Harris was giving a stag dinner the following night at the Savoy. She offered Harris the use of her suite for after-dinner conversation, saying that she would leave for her house. He accepted, but insisted that she stay—as she probably intended. During that evening, almost three years after Britain entered the war, Jackie learned that the British had too few planes to provide a fighter escort for bombers. With such a shortage of aircraft, the British were forced to confine air attacks to night raids. Arnold, Harris, and U.S. Admiral John H. Towers decided that the American Eighth Air Force would undertake daylight bombing, and the British, the night attacks.[43]

Later that same night, Arnold told Jackie that it was time for her to return to the United States to form the women's auxiliary. She said that she would have to wait three months for her release by the British.[44] Meanwhile, she was assigned to the Eighth Air Force to devise a plan for its ferrying service. As soon as the English released her from the ATA, she arranged a ride home, but—just before she boarded the plane—a messenger delivered an order from the Eighth Air Force commander, General Anthony Frank, asking her to stay until he conferred with her. She heard nothing more from Frank until three days later, when he invited her to dinner. He thanked her for a report that she had given him, but there was no conferring.[45] Impatient with the delay, she left for home on September 9 to create at last the auxiliary that she envisioned.

Fifteen

Taking Over

On the morning of September 11, 1942, Jackie's first day back in the United States, she opened the pages of the *New York Times* at the breakfast table. Turning them rapidly, she stopped when she saw a picture of a beautiful woman shaking hands with a two-star general. Above the picture was the heading, "She Will Direct the Women Ferry Pilots," and under it the caption, "Mrs. Nancy Harkness Love being congratulated by Maj. Gen. Harold L. George."[1] Arnold had promised her the job. What had happened?

During the five months that Jackie was in England, the Army Air Force had reorganized and expanded. Olds had been replaced by General George as head of the Air Transport Command.[2] George's deputy was Cyrus Rowlette Smith, founder and former president of American Airlines, a Texan who held women in general in low regard and had already had a run-in with Jackie that resulted in his forbidding any mention of her name on the airline's premises.[3] Within the Air Transport Command, the Domestic Ferrying Division was headed by Brigadier General William G. Tunner, a West Point by-the-book man.[4] Tunner and George were in desperate need of pilots. Nancy Love, working in the operations office of the ATC, suggested that the Domestic Ferrying Division employ women. An accomplished pilot herself who knew some of the best women fliers in the nation, Love said that these women could be employed as civilians to deliver small training planes.[5]

When George approached Arnold with the concept, Arnold rejected it, telling him that until there were no more male civilian pilots available, he would not employ women.[6] Arnold was waiting for Jackie to come back with a plan for using women pilots that differed from Love's. Love favored accepting a small number of experienced fliers. Jackie wanted to recruit a much larger number to be taught and assigned not only to ferrying duty but possibly as pilots and copilots towing targets, flying daytime tracking missions, nighttime searchlight missions, and administrative flights.[7]

Seven days before Jackie came home from England, George again sent a memo to Arnold pressing him to reconsider the use of women and to do it within the next twenty-four hours. Arnold was out of town, and George did not wait for his answer. On September 5, he issued an order from Arnold's office stating that women were to be recruited. On the same day, Nancy Love sent out telegrams that she had already prepared to the women whom she wanted as ferrying pilots. While the telegrams were being sent, Jackie was at a British airfield ready to board a plane for home when General Frank's message delayed her departure. Frank was a friend of George. When the announcement by Love and George was made, Jackie was somewhere over the Atlantic and Arnold was out of town. With neither present, George announced the formation of the Women's Auxiliary Ferrying Squadron—the WAF—to the press in the offices of Mrs. Love's friend, Secretary of War Henry Stimson.[8]

A bewildered and angry Jackie telephoned Arnold, who told her to come to his office the next day. That Saturday when she entered his office, the news clipping in her hand, he said that he had asked the Ferrying Division to prepare plans for the activation of a women's group with the understanding that these would be submitted to him first, and through him, to Jackie.[9] Instead, the Ferrying Division had gone around him to Secretary of War Stimson with plans that he had not seen. "He was mad all over," Jackie said, "and when mad, General Arnold could make the fur fly!"[10] Arnold picked up the telephone and ordered General George and C. R. Smith to come to his office. With Jackie present, he told the two men to meet with their staffs and Jackie to work out a program acceptable to her.[11]

In a War Department release three days later, on September 14, Arnold named Jackie Director of the Women's Flying Training Detachment for the Army Air Force. As a civil servant, she was to head a program creating a pool of women pilots trained for non-combat purposes so as to release as many men pilots as possible for combat and other duties.[12] Although Arnold had insisted that hers be the only organization for women pilots, Jackie shrewdly pointed out that the publicity already given to Love's appointment would prompt charges of dissention in his command. Love, she said, should remain head of the WAF, but the women Love hired would be limited to serving in the Ferrying Division.[13]

Arnold agreed to this arrangement, but it marked the beginning of distrust and dislike on the part of both women. Jackie later described the WAF as "Nothing of importance. A bunch of society dames."[14] Actually, this was not true. Many of the WAFs flew bombers—B-24s, B-25s, B-26s, and B-29s in addition to the large cargo C-47 and the pursuit plane, P-47.[15] At the root of the conflict between the two women were their differing views of how to train and assign women pilots, but Jackie raised the level of animosity. Yet, on at least one occasion, Jackie ignored her rivalry with Love—probably to prove that she was not only a great pilot, but also equally good as a beautician. Nancy Love told Jackie's friend Margaret Kerr Boylan about an evening when Jackie and she shared a dressing room before an Air Force dinner. Love, who was recovering from chicken pox, complained about the remaining pockmarks on her face. "That's no problem," Jackie remarked. Producing a bag of cosmetics, she applied a perfect cover for Love's blemishes.[16]

The newly named director of the Women's Flying Training Detachment immediately began a search for recruits from the list that she had compiled for Olds.[17] While she was still in Washington, D.C., she telephoned Jean Howard, who had arranged the Ninety-Nines 1941 meeting when Jackie was elected president. She asked Howard to contact pilots in the area for a meeting at her Mayflower Hotel suite.[18] Many of the women attending did not know what the purpose of the meeting was. One, Jane Straughn, observed that "after quite a few cocktails," their hostess regaled them with stories of the American women in the ATA, then turned to Straughn and asked, "How would you like to fly for your country?" "Of course I would," Straughn answered. "Jackie never asked me how many hours I had or what rating. At the time I had barely 200 hours in a Piper Cub," Straughn recalled.[19]

While Howard was in the kitchen helping Jackie with drinks, she asked her, "What about insurance?" "Don't bring it up," Jackie replied. "I'm working on it." Nor did Jackie bring up the fact that, in addition to no life insurance, there would be no health insurance, no transportation to the place of instruction, and no burial expenses if they were killed in an accident.[20]

Jackie interviewed more than 50 women, some in her River House apartment, others in her New York office, choosing 28 with a minimum of 200 pilot hours and 20 more to enter a class after they increased their flight time.[21] She also had to find a training site, instructors, and an executive director to look after daily operations as an on-site supervisor. For the training site, she reluctantly accepted the offer of facilities leased by the Army Air Force from a former civilian pilot training contractor at Howard Hughes Field, eleven miles from Houston, Texas. Although Arnold urged her to remain in Washington where she had a desk in the office of Colonel Luke S. Smith, director of Individual Training, she moved to Fort Worth, Texas, headquarters of the Flying Training Command headed by Lieutenant General Barton K. Yount.[22] From there, she called Mrs. Leoti "Dedie" Deaton, a Red Cross swimming instructor in Wichita Falls, whose cousin worked in Jackie's cosmetic firm. Deaton later said that she was ambushed by Jackie. "That Jackie Cochran could sell a hot brick in hell! I've never seen such a saleswoman in my life."[23]

"Go down there," Jackie told Deaton, "and take care of the girls. Place them. Get them a place to eat. See that they go to [a] beauty parlor once a week. See that they stay out at the airport and have study every night from 7:30 to 9:30."[24]

Deaton arrived in Houston on November 8, 1942, a week before the first trainees were to report. She was aghast at the facilities left by the civilian training contractor. There were three hangars, some small wooden buildings, and one sheet metal building. The students were to use the municipal airport for takeoffs and landings. There was no housing, and restaurants were too far to reach during lunch hour.[25] "There were four rooms joined by a hall with a commode in it," Deaton said. "That and one at the airport were the only two toilets."[26]

To welcome the first trainees arriving at Houston, Jackie gave a cocktail party at the Rice Hotel on November 15.[27] When Jean Howard went to Jackie's room before the party, Jackie looked at her shoes, called room service, and sent them down to be polished. The appearance of "her girls" seemed to be as important to Jackie as their performances, but their grooming at a beauty parlor once a week and far more demanding problems were left to the new executive officer Deaton when Jackie left for New York the day after the party in her powerful Beechcraft L47 with the logo "Wings to Beauty" painted on its side.[28] The "dollar-a-year" volunteer for the war effort was not abandoning her business. On November 17, she left New York on a sales trip to Dayton and Cincinnati where, in the latter, she attended a dinner of the Air Power League, sitting on the dais with some of the country's most famous fliers.[29]

Back in Houston, Deaton faced twenty-eight bewildered women who were living in rooms in private homes, brought to the field in army trucks for lessons in a mix of battered civilian planes, and managed by two AAF officers who disapproved of the entire program. "Here were these kids jammed in these old trailer things, cattle trucks that didn't work," Deaton said. "No breakfast. No coffee. No nothing. They take their drill, do the physical training, fly and go to ground school in the same sweaty overalls. No place to shower. Two potties. And then they stay in the mess hall [converted from an old theater] for two hours every night."[30] Eventually, Deaton arranged for a block of rooms at the Oleander Court Motel to be leased to the AAF. For transportation, she rented a bus, a red-and-white one decorated with edelweiss and boasting a sign on the back, "Tyrolean Orchestra."[31]

Meanwhile, Jackie, who believed in approaching the military from the top down, was at Yount's headquarters in Fort Worth, where she soon gained the general's support for the new WFTD. Yount not only requested better aircraft for the Houston program, but also agreed with Jackie's plans for a course designed to qualify the trainees for jobs other than ferrying. Graduates, he said, could be assigned as glider and instrument instructors, trainer operators, and gunnery tow target pilots.[32]

Yount also chose to ignore Jackie's flouting of the pecking order among officers' wives, including his own. When Mildred Yount assigned the newcomer to do volunteer work at the base hospital, Jackie told her, "Well, you can just unassign me. I'm up at five and I'm working 14 hours a day and I'm not going to be ordered to do anything else."[33] During a visit by Arnold to Fort Worth, Mrs. Yount did not invite Jackie to a dinner that she gave for him. After dinner, Arnold asked to see Jackie. Yount's aide called, but Jackie said that she was in bed and not getting up for anyone. On another occasion, Mrs. Yount asked Jackie to send one of her two maids to help care for the Younts' infant grandson. Jackie brought a maid but bathed the child, helped the maid clean the house, and cooked the dinner; before leaving, she told Mrs. Yount that she shouldn't take advantage of the junior officers' wives. "You know," she said years later, "the old girl and I became great friends."[34]

The support of Arnold and Yount did not deter Jackie's opponents in Washington—C. R. Smith and Generals George and Tunner—from trying to gain control of the new WFTD. They wanted to put the women fliers into the Women's Army Auxiliary Corps—the WAAC—under the command of Colonel Olveta Culp Hobby. Jackie was determined to avoid militarization. Knowing that Arnold's goal for the future was to make the Air Force a separate service, she convinced him that the WFTD program was too experimental to risk associating it with the independent service that he wanted. With women pilots as civilians, she could compile and analyze for him the records of the group.[35] Only if the training program succeeded would it be acceptable as part of a new, separate Air Force.[36]

While Arnold backed Jackie, Smith, Tunner, and George enlisted the aid of Colonel Luke Smith to give them information on Jackie's every move by sending his secretary, Lillian Conner, to Jackie's Washington office to be her assistant. Jackie did not want an assistant, certainly not Conner. While Jackie was in Fort Worth, she learned that Conner had signed on her behalf a proposal advocating admission of the trainees into the WAAC.[37] Jackie demanded that Smith get rid of Conner. After he refused, she hired a private detective to follow him, then presented him with evidence of his affair with Conner, including a bill for a fur coat given to Conner. "I'll show this to your wife," she told Smith, "or you lay off."[38]

Luke Smith backed off but not for long. Promoted to Brigadier General, he would try again in January when he sent Conner, who had a private pilot's license, to audit the course at Houston. Dedie Deaton told Conner that she could not audit the course; she would have to enroll. "General Luke Smith hated Jackie with a passion," Deaton recalled. "He was trying to get Lillian [Conner] Jackie's job."[39]

Determined to keep Smith informed, Conner enrolled as a trainee. When Smith came to Houston, he told Deaton that he was taking Conner out to lunch. Deaton said the new trainee would be attending ground school at noon, followed by a flying lesson. Not until all the trainees were given a three-day pass could Conner see the general. She signed out for Fort Worth, returning a few days later with a case of measles. Deaton put her in an isolation room with no telephone, cutting off communication with Smith. A week later, Deaton saw a newspaper report that Brigadier General Smith was in the Randolph AAF Base hospital, down with measles.[40]

Luke Smith was no longer a threat to Jackie's program, but her other three opponents in Washington, backed by Arnold's chief of staff, General George Stratemeyer, renewed their efforts to militarize the women pilots.[41] Early in December, Arnold called Jackie and told her to come to Washington immediately. She flew all night through cold and freezing rain, checked in at the Mayflower and then went to the Pentagon at 6:30 in the morning. Arnold arrived fifteen minutes later. "How would you like your girls to become part of the WAACs?" he asked. "How would you like to have the Air Force back in the Signal Corps?" she replied. "Well," he countered, "suppose you were ordered to do it?" Jackie answered that the trainees were civilians and so was she, but when he asked her to see Colonel Hobby she agreed. He called the colonel for an appointment on the following day; Jackie suggested 2 P.M. because she was having lunch with Eleanor Roosevelt.[42]

Olveta Culp Hobby was a wealthy, politically powerful Texan, a friend of the Roosevelts. Jackie, who had met her in England when Hobby inspected the WAACs stationed there, not only disliked the woman, she thought the WAACs were a sorry lot—untidy, ill-disciplined, and badly behaved. But she kept the appointment that Arnold had made, escorted by Colonel R. H. Carmichael, whom Arnold had probably asked to report on the meeting of the two women. Snow was falling in Washington when they arrived at three minutes before two. Jackie was wearing a designer suit from Paris and a mink coat. She gave her name to the receptionist who told her to take a seat, but failed to take her coat. "I got a chip on my shoulder the minute I walked in," she admitted. After waiting for twenty minutes, she strode to the desk and asked for a piece of paper, writing on it, "Dear Mrs. Hobby, if you want to see me you can find me in Fort Worth, Texas. It is now 2:30 and I have to fly back tonight."[43] The receptionist glanced at the note and said, "Oh, she called that she was going to be a little delayed but I didn't realize that you were Jackie Cochran."[44]

"I have no time to wait," Jackie snapped, preparing to leave just as Hobby arrived, and was met by three of her assistants. "One person took her hat, one person took her gloves, one person took her coat," Jackie recalled. Five minutes later, Jackie and Colonel Carmichael were in Hobby's office, where they were invited to be seated, but again no one offered to take her coat.[45]

Hobby opened the conversation by telling Jackie that she had bought her young son some wallpaper "with airplanes for his room because he loved planes so much and I don't know one end of an airplane from the other." Jackie remained silent until Hobby said, "Now when we take over your outfit, naturally I expect you to come in and be their immediate superior." Jackie exploded. "Look, Mrs. Hobby, you've bitched up your own outfit. You are not going to bitch up mine. And if you think I'd work for a woman who doesn't know one end of an airplane from another we are a different breed of cat. Now do you have anything else to say to me? If you don't I have to go back to Texas tonight."[46]

In a later account of the meeting, Jackie added that Hobby said, "Well,

General Arnold is not opposed to this." Jackie replied that Arnold had not discussed it with her, and if he did approve it she would oppose him, Secretary Lovett, Hobby, and even the president. "You are not going to get these girls in your outfit," she warned.[47]

When she told Arnold about the meeting, she said, "I thought he would die laughing."[48]

Neither Jackie nor Arnold would have the last laugh. She had successfully thwarted the efforts of her opponents to militarize "her girls"—a move that would be her undoing before the war ended.

Sixteen

Cochran's Convent

By January 1943, thirteen months after Pearl Harbor, Jacqueline Cochran's control over her WFTD trainees at Houston was no longer threatened by a merger with Olveta Hobby's WAAC. But Cochran faced another major problem. The Houston facility was totally inadequate for her expanding operation with its goal of 750 graduates in 1943 and 1,000 in 1944.[1] The woman who could "sell a hot brick in hell" persuaded Air Force authorities to lease a second base on February 3 at Sweetwater, Texas, where classes for Canadian cadets were being phased out. While classes in Houston continued, the new trainees at Sweetwater, designated the 319th WFTD, were to share the field with the Canadians until early April.[2] Bigger and better than Houston, Avenger Field was no vacation spot. It was in a land of mesquite trees and buffalo grass, where northerly winds blew up clouds of red dust from April to September.[3]

Jackie left the move to Deaton and her staff, who were to bring half the classes at Houston to the new base while preparing a new class each month. The overworked Deaton already faced daunting problems at Houston. In a cold, wet winter, the trainees had no flight suits. Three of them were hospitalized with pneumonia. Tired, chilled, and often hungry, they turned on Deaton, claiming that she was "too bossy." Complaining that she was doing nothing about improving transportation to the field, about replacing worn-out planes, and about the vulgar language used by some of the male instructors, they demanded a meeting with Jackie. Jackie agreed to fly down for a meeting with her charges and to speak to Deaton. When she did, she overlaid the students' complaints with some of her own. She scolded Deaton for spending too much time on details instead of delegating authority to her staff. Shocked that Deaton allowed the students to call her "Dedie," Jackie insisted that "girl problems" be discussed only by appointment and in the office. Deaton disagreed, countering that, "if they've got something they want to tell me on the spur of the moment I'm going to stop and listen to it every time."[4] Deaton prevailed because Jackie needed her.

As a salesperson, Jackie could charm a prospective buyer. As a manager, she was a demanding perfectionist, one many of the staff and students feared. On one of her early inspection trips to Houston, as her overpowered Beechcraft approached the field, a student on duty in the tower heard her call in, "This is Jackie Cochran. Clear the field." While airborne students hastily peeled off out of the Beechcraft's flight path, the trainee in the tower sent word to Deaton's office. "Hold it careful! Goldilocks is on her way!" The "Goldilocks alert" became a code word for Cochran's arrival.[5]

When trainee Margaret Kerr Boylan first saw the logo "Wings to Beauty" on the side of the Beechcraft, she murmured to a friend, "That's a weird name for an airplane." Jackie heard her. "What's wrong with the name?" she asked. Kerr mumbled, "I don't know. It just seems kind of strange to me." "Well," Jackie snapped, "it's the slogan for my cosmetic company. I like it a lot," adding, "Why don't you meet me later today in my office?"[6]

When Boylan went to the office, there was no further discussion of the logo. Instead, Jackie asked her about the training program. Although Boylan thought that Jackie's "big brown eyes could bore holes in you," she refused to be intimidated. She told Jackie that there were "a lot of bugs in the program" and that a number of capable candidates had washed out because they were taught by incompetent civilian pilots and then tested by Army Air Force officers. The next day, after Jackie had made certain that Boylan was not one of the failing students, she asked her back to describe any other deficiencies that she had observed in the training program.[7]

Boylan was one of the students who neither feared nor disliked Jackie. Another was Jean Howard, who had already helped Jackie hold two meetings in Washington, the first for the Ninety-Nines when Jackie was elected president, and the second to recruit women for the training program. After Howard washed out, Jackie asked her to become an assistant establishment officer at Sweetwater. Howard taught trainees swimming and calisthenics and handled public relations on radio. Jackie liked her, trusting her enough to confide in her one day that although she wanted children, she had to abandon this desire after having two miscarriages. The young woman respected Jackie, but said that Jackie lacked a real rapport with the women in her command. "Her missing link was a sense of humor."[8]

Jackie was not only a perfectionist, but she was also a prude about "her girls," just as she had been with the American recruits that she brought to the

ATA in England. She was determined that they be perceived as well-groomed, well-mannered, and above all virtuous. "Young girls that are out on the loose, away from home, they go hog wild over their freedom," she said, "and I have lived a hard life working in a cotton mill, and I know what went on in life by the time I was eight years old and it's not pretty, a lot of it."[9]

As soon as Jackie was told that during the first week at Avenger Field 100 male pilots had made unwarranted "forced landings," she barred the use of the field to them except for genuine emergencies. To thwart approaches from the ground, she directed that passes be required from all male callers at the entrance gate. "That's when they began calling it 'Cochran's Convent,'" she proudly recalled years later.[10]

The self-appointed abbess laid down numerous rules to protect her charges. No unmarried officer or married officer whose wife was not living with him were to be assigned to the base. Graduates of the first four classes who were assigned ferrying duty were not to hitch a ride to their home base by plane following a delivery as male pilots did, but were to return by train or bus. Jackie declared nightclubs off-limits, and trainees attending officers' clubs were to wear skirts, not slacks. On at least one occasion, Jackie personally demonstrated how to fold a skirt for travel. "If I ever see one of you walking across the field dangling a parachute from your rump, it's going to be so sore you won't be able to sit on it," she warned.[11]

The control that she sought was often challenged. At Sweetwater, Deaton learned that prostitutes who flocked to the Blue Bonnet Hotel were telling their customers that they were trainees from Avenger Field. Deaton was forced to forbid the trainees leaving the base at night. "They were furious because they didn't understand and they needed to get off the base."[12] Balking at the confinement, the more enterprising students went to town during the day to buy moonshine from a gray-haired woman at a gift shop, then hid it in their lockers or in toilet tanks at the base.

On a night when Jackie landed at Avenger, she found Deaton in tears. One of the trainees who was drunk had struck another. Jackie was horrified, claiming, "I had never had a drink in my life and I could smell it," her temperance claim a blatant falsehood.[13] After she ordered the woman to attend a hearing before a board, Jackie returned to Washington, where she was summoned to the office of Assistant Secretary of War for Air Robert Lovett. Lovett asked her to spare the young woman, who, he said, was upset over the

16.1. Pictured in 1944 at Avenger Field, Texas, where candidates for the Women's Air Force Service Pilots (WASP) trained: *(right to left)* Maj. Robert K. Urban, Jacqueline Cochran, Col. Henry Ford, and Leoti Deaton. (National Air and Space Museum, Smithsonian Institution, SI 2005–30503.)

recent death of her father, a former law partner of Supreme Court Justice Felix Frankfurter. Frankfurter, Lovett said, was interested in her welfare. When he suggested that Jackie call on the Justice, she refused, telling Lovett that she would resign if he prevailed.[14] She could and did cultivate the friendship of the powerful, but not when they opposed her beliefs.

Working overtime to secure equipment and planes for the two WFTD bases, she made frequent trips in her Beechcraft or an Air Force AT-11, a twin-engine, advanced trainer for pilot and bombardier. During the month of January in 1943, she made flights to Fort Worth, Nashville, Washington, New York, Roanoke, Little Rock, San Antonio, and Houston in search of supplies and support for her trainees.[15] However, her fervent commitment to defense of the nation did not blind her to an opportunity for legitimate business interests. That February, she sold the Beechcraft to the Army for $18,160, then had it signed over to her by the AAF for service use. Three years earlier, she had offered the plane to a potential buyer for $12,500.[16] Later, she said that she gave the plane to the AAF for a dollar. "I then could have it on military bases, and I had a sort of gentleman's understanding that if they put it in surplus I was going to buy it back."[17]

She seemed to rest only when forced to by illness. In April of 1943, after her immediate superior, Brigadier General Kenneth McNaughton, ordered her to take a rest, she went home to Indio. After suffering an attack of severe abdominal pain, she was taken in an ambulance to a Los Angeles hospital. Although confined to a hospital bed, she continued to worry about closing out the base at Houston and eluding the Ferrying Division's opposition to her plans for WFTD assignments other than ferrying.[18]

Some reassurance was offered to her by McNaughton, who wrote to her that her Fort Worth office was being efficiently managed by Mrs. Dorothy Hawks, that forty-eight students from Houston were being moved to Sweetwater, and that the remaining trainees would be moved within six weeks from Houston to Sweetwater, where 122 more women would enter the program. But McNaughton's good news was followed by his warning that authorities in Washington were again considering putting her program into the WAAC. The WAAC would become part of the Army on July 1, to be known as the Women's Army Corps or WAC. Olveta Culp Hobby was once again a threat to Jackie's authority over the Women's Flying Training Program.[19]

Discharged from the hospital with a warning that any further attacks would necessitate surgery, Jackie hurried to Texas to attend the graduation ceremonies to be held at nearby Ellington Air Force Base for the first class of the Houston WFTD, known as 43–W-1. The graduates were brought to the base by car and bus, followed by cattle trucks carrying classes 43–W-2 and 43–W-3. As civilians, they had no uniforms, but wore white shirts, Army tan slacks, and overseas caps as they mounted the platform where Jackie stood with the base commander, Colonel Walter Reed, who presented each woman with wings. The wings had been purchased at the Post Exchange, altered to bear the designation "319th," and paid for by Floyd Odlum. To each of the twenty-three graduates, Jackie gave a silver disk inscribed: "43–1 April 24, 1943."[20]

A month later on May 28, Jackie returned for the graduation of the last class to complete their training at Houston. The forty-five graduates of Class 43–W-2 flew AT-6s and AT-17s, single- and twin-engine training planes, from Houston to Sweetwater for the ceremony. Jackie and the guest speaker,

Colonel J. H. Hills, executive officer of the Flying Training Command, alternated in presenting wings to the graduates. One of them, twenty-three-year-old Iris Cummings Critchell, had already heard rumors about Jackie as a calculating, highly motivated and driven woman. As she moved forward in the line, she thought, "Oh, no. I'll have to go to Jackie." Later, she recalled, "When I looked into those cold, steely eyes my concerns over what I had heard were verified."[21]

Another graduate, Carole Fillmore, who had met and been charmed by Amelia Earhart, remembered first meeting Jackie at Houston when she waited for Jackie to jump down from the cockpit of her Beechcraft. Cochran nodded at her and said, "Here, honey, you can carry that," handing her a mink coat.[22]

After receiving her wings, Fillmore went to the Blue Bonnet Hotel, where the exuberant graduates were already celebrating in all too hearty a fashion. At the hotel, Fillmore had her second meeting with Jackie, this one in Jackie's room, where one of the celebrants had passed out on Cochran's bed. Jackie shouted at Fillmore, "I've devoted my life to you girls these past few months and now you all are ripping this place apart! How can you do this to me?" Fillmore replied, "It isn't my fault. I just got here. They yelled my name out the window." She sat down on the end of the bed. "I've been driving all day. I'm hot and I'm tired. I haven't had a damned drink. And I could use one." Cochran turned and pulled open a drawer, took out a bottle, then went to the bathroom for a glass and poured Fillmore a tall drink.[23]

In spite of her demands for perfection from everyone in her charge, be they in her cosmetics business, in the WFTD program, or in the armed forces, Jackie perceived their problems and frequently offered advice and financial aid. In Houston, readying for a flight to Washington, a sergeant assigned to her plane asked her if she would take along an enlisted man who was trying to hitch a ride. Jasper Moore never forgot that ride. There were only four persons aboard, Jackie as pilot, her copilot, the sergeant, and Moore. "Soon the sergeant came around with chicken sandwiches and milk and I was really grateful. It had been a very long time since the last meal."[24]

If Jackie overreacted to the sophomoric antics of the graduates that day in Houston, their behavior was not the cause of her anxiety. Three weeks earlier, she had learned that all of the WFTD graduates of Class 43–W-2 would be sent to Love's WAFs in the Ferrying Command. She had already written to

16.2. United States Air Force portrait of Jacqueline Cochran, director of the Women's Air Force Service Pilots. (National Air and Space Museum, Smithsonian Institution, SI 2005–29843.)

Arnold that she wanted control over their assignments. She had designed the whole training experiment to see if women pilots were suitable candidates for multiple assignments in the Air Force. Her concept was threatened by the lack of coordination in assigning, promoting, and disciplining them. She was going to Washington to tell him that he needed a woman to do the job and that she wanted to be that woman.[25]

On June 28, 1944, Arnold gave her that job. The former Director of Women's Flying Training on the staff of the AAF Training Command at Fort Worth became director of all women pilots flying for the AAF and assistant to the Chief of the AAF staff in Washington. Jackie was to decide on who and how many women were to be trained and to set the standards for admission and graduation. She was also to determine where and in what capacities they were to be used and to allocate them to the using agencies. She was also asked to draw up plans for possible militarization.[26]

It had taken Jackie two years of unceasing effort to reach this goal, starting with the recruitment of the twenty-five American women for the British ATA. On her return from England, she had overcome the threats to her plans from Nancy Love and her WAFs, from Colonel C. R. Smith, and Generals George and Tunner. She had the support of Hap Arnold and Barton Yount, but as late as June 25, three days before her new appointment, there had been a second meeting of her opponents with Olveta Culp Hobby. Although Hobby told Jackie that she had hardly given any thought to the women pilots joining her command, Hobby had again discussed it with C. R. Smith and his assistants. Jackie stood her ground, insisting that women aviators needed a leader who understood them and their work.[27]

In mid-July, *Newsweek* magazine published a story on Jackie's promotion, along with her picture next to one of Nancy Love. The caption read, "Miss Cochran and Mrs. Love. Which one bosses the women flyers?"[28] The official answer appeared in a memo from the AAF Command on August 5. All women flying for the AAF, including those in training and those in the Ferrying Command, were to be known as the Women's Air Force Service Pilots—the WASP—under the command of Jacqueline Cochran.[29] She had what she wanted. Under her leadership, the WASP could verify whether women pilots could be used in wartime for all air assignments except those involving combat. Their failure, as civilians, would not reflect on the Air Force. Their success might warrant militarization—but only in the Army Air Force.

Seventeen

The Rise and Fall of Jackie's Empire

With her appointment in the summer of 1943, Jacqueline Cochran stretched the limits of her new command, attempting to assign specific Sweetwater graduates to an ever-expanding list of jobs. Already backed by Arnold and Yount, she turned to the newly appointed AAF chief of staff, Major General Barney K. Giles, to gain his approval for the experimental use of women pilots in anti-aircraft target towing. With his permission, she requested twenty-five women of her choice graduating at Avenger Field on July 3, and originally intended for the Ferrying Division, to be assigned to the Third Air Force base at Camp Davis, North Carolina, for target towing. She also requested Major Robert Urban, the officer in charge of Avenger Field, to choose another twenty-five students in the next class for Camp Davis. She also wrote to Mrs. Deaton asking for the height, weight, and general deportment of the women. "I am anxious that I get as many of the qualities desired as possible as they will be setting the pace for many hundreds more to be used in this capacity if this works out."[1] On July 18, the first group of twenty-five—all sworn to secrecy for an unknown mission—reported to Jackie at her Mayflower suite in Washington. There, she told them that they were to go to Camp Davis to tow targets on the end of a 1,500-foot cable while anti-aircraft gunners below used live ammunition to fire at the target.[2]

Camp Davis was a dismal place where rows of wooden buildings and army tents circled a huge swamp, and olive drab planes sent back from combat lined the narrow runway. No welcome awaited them. The pilots resented them, claiming that their help was not needed. The commanding officer, Colonel Lovick L. Stephenson, assigned them to small planes and administrative duties, and their paychecks were delayed by the Air Transport Command. Jackie immediately financed a loan system to tide them over until the paychecks arrived. Then, she flew her Beechcraft to the camp to call on Colonel Stephenson. She followed up the visit by sending WASP establishment officer at Avenger, Jean Foster, to Camp Davis to see that the women were used as Jackie intended. Soon after, they were flying Douglas Dauntless A-25s and Curtiss Hell Diver A-24s.[3]

Another challenge to her target-towing program occurred just a month later, when Wasp Mabel Rawlinson died after her A-24 attack bomber was hit by anti-aircraft guns manned by Camp Davis men on the beach along Cape Fear. The following day, Jackie arrived at Davis with her field assistant, Ethel Sheehy, on what was intended to be a routine inspection. Jackie was met by dispirited and angry Wasps who had watched the plane crash at the end of the runway where it broke in two. Rawlinson's instructor in the rear cockpit escaped injury, but she was trapped in the front section, unable to open a jammed hatch that had already been reported as in need of repair. Her horrified fellow pilots could hear her screams of agony as she burned to death.[4]

That night, Jackie listened to the distraught women's grievances and fears—the planes were discards from combat and unsafe to fly, their instructors were uninterested and incompetent, and the mechanics signed off on repairs that they had not made. At a second meeting the following day after a remembrance service for Rawlinson, Jackie told the women that she could not act on their complaints until she was advised by AAF headquarters. Meanwhile, she told them that in the interests of national security, no word about Rawlinson's death was to be released.

A month later, a second Wasp, Betty Taylor Wood, died in a crash at Camp Davis. News of both deaths was not a threat to national security. It was a threat to Jackie's expanding list of assignments for "her girls."

Before Jackie left Camp Davis, an irate Colonel Stephenson complained to her that a Wasp had refused to fly a mission that he had ordered. He said that the woman told him that Cochran had advised the group to fly no planes until they heard from her. Jackie denied this, ordering all Wasps to fly unless a plane was declared unsafe on an official form.[5]

Back in Washington, Jackie saw another opportunity to expand WASP assignments after Arnold told her that AAF pilots were complaining about the B-26 bomber as a difficult and dangerous aircraft. He said that they called the twin-engine Martin Marauder the "Baltimore Prostitute" because it was made in Baltimore and had no visible means of support. Jackie said, "I can cure your men of walking off the program." "How?" he asked. "Just put some girl pilots on it." "But what if you kill some of them?" Arnold asked. "Suppose I do. There is no difference if a woman is killed or a man if the program is to go forward."[6]

"I went out and flew it," she recalled, "and came back and said there was nothing wrong with it. . . . Eventually they had 150 women flying the B-26."[7] "These girls did a fine job. They made the male pilots' faces red for a while and then the B-26 suddenly became accepted as a safe plane."[8]

AAF pilots also criticized the new B-29 bomber. They said that the big aircraft was not safe to fly on two of its four engines, a claim of the builder. Jackie again used Wasps to counter their complaints. "We sent two Wasps in a B-29 from base to base flying back and forth on two engines. The obvious conclusion was that if a woman could do it, so could a man."[9]

Within a year of her appointment, Wasps were flying the array of missions that Jackie had envisioned. When robot planes were used as targets for anti-aircraft or airborne gunners, two Wasps were employed—one in the mother ship, the second in the target plane, ready to override the controls in an emergency.[10] Wasps also did test flights on new engines. In place of using test stands, Jackie decided that "it was cheaper and faster to take an airplane and put a new engine in it and fly it. . . . They would go on missions while they were doing it," she boasted, "towing targets while they were slow-timing the engine."[11] One Wasp, Ann Baumgartner, became the first woman to fly a jet-powered aircraft, the YP-59A twin-jet pursuit plane.[12]

Others were assigned to tracking and searchlight missions, simulated strafing, smoke laying, and administrative and utility flying. They flew B-17s, B-24s, B-25s, B-26s, B-29s, C-47s, C-6s, and the DC-3. They also flew pursuit planes—P-39s, P-40s, P-47s, and P-61s—making deliveries and flying cargo of top-secret weapons and personnel.[13]

Jackie not only wanted "her girls" to fly everything that the Air Force had, but she also wanted them to be perceived as virtuous young women, clean cut, well groomed, and stylish. They needed uniforms. She had been offered one lot that had been made for and rejected by the Nurses Corps and one sample model made from excess WAC material. Neither would do. She ordered one designed by Bergdorf Goodman in New York at her expense. To model the three, she chose two women from the Army with less than perfect figures, and one professional model, Deena Clark, to wear the one that she ordered. Arnold took Jackie and her models to the office of the Army Chief of Staff, General George C. Marshall. Marshall picked the designer suit from Paris that Jackie was wearing, but settled for the Bergdorf model.[14]

Although Jackie was getting most of what she wanted from a few senior Air Force officers, she was irritating numerous others. When Major Norman Cleaveland was posted to the 4th Air Command in Los Angeles, he was told by senior officers there, "Major, you'll deserve the Congressional Medal if you get along with Jacqueline and her Wasps." Cleaveland did get along with Jackie, but she continued to make numerous enemies, both political and military, who attempted to either eliminate the Wasps or militarize them by placing them in the WACs.[15]

Within days of her appointment as director of the WASP, she asked that special reports on women pilots be sent by the using AAF agency, reports including resignations, transfers, and the reasons for either. She also wanted immediate notice by telegram of any accident involving a woman pilot.[16] Brigadier General William Tunner protested, claiming that transfers were an internal affair of the Air Transport Command. He said that there was already a procedure for reporting accidents and that the paperwork Jackie demanded for her statistical study of women pilots was unwarranted. He also accused her of interference with the Ferrying Division's functions and saw no need to explain his reasons for ordering a transfer.[17]

Tunner was also angered by her flouting of protocol when she failed to pay a courtesy call on the commander of the Ferrying Division base at New Castle, Delaware, Colonel Robert Baker. Baker reported this to C. R. Smith as a lack of respect for his command.[18] Jackie replied that on only one occasion had she failed to call on him. He was busy, as was his executive officer. After waiting an hour and a half sitting on a bench, she told Baker's secretary that she was going to the WASP barracks. On her next visit, she said that she notified the base four hours in advance of her arrival with a general officer. No one met them. She took a jeep to Baker's office, but he was out. When she told the secretary that a general was waiting on the plane, a second lieutenant was sent to wait with the general until she finished her business. It was payback time for Jackie, who never forgot a favor or an insult. On her following visit, "having in mind the treatment accorded her on two previous occasions," she said, she went directly to the WASP barracks.[19] To Baker, Tunner, Smith, and all the officers who guarded their customary prerogatives of command, Jackie was a "cowboy" bucking the military establishment.

In addition to opposition from the military, she encountered some within her own command. On one of her visits to Love's ferrying group at New Castle, she saw the name "WAF" remained on the barracks two months after the creation of the WASP.[20] Six months later, a former WAF, Barbara Erickson, by then commander of the 6th Ferrying Group WASP at Long Beach and an outstanding pilot, was to receive the Air Medal. Presentation of the medal by Arnold was part of the ceremonies celebrating the graduation of the second Sweetwater class in 1944, witnessed by five other generals and Jackie. The graduates were all wearing their new Santiago-blue uniforms, but thirty minutes before the ceremonies began, Erickson appeared in her old WAF uniform. Only after Dedie Deaton warned her that her defiance of the new uniform regulations would result in an Arnold temper tantrum did Erickson change into Santiago blue.[21]

Erickson thought that Jackie was a brash self-aggrandizer. "She was going to be the greatest woman pilot," she scoffed, "but she never flew her Beechcraft." Erickson was referring to Jackie's inspection trips when she often used Wasp Helen Dettweiller as her pilot. On a day when Love, Cochran, and Erickson lunched together, they agreed to fly three B-25s from Los Angeles to Kansas City. "She got another pilot to fly hers," Erickson said, "because she had not been checked out in one by Ferry Command."[22] As Jackie had done with the ATA, she left most of the flying to the Wasps while she acted as CEO of the organization.

Erickson was not alone in her disapproval of Cochran. There were other Wasps about whom Deaton exclaimed, "They hated Jackie to where they could have cut her throat. . . . Nancy Love did not foster that. But some of our Sweetwater girls did."[23]

Opposition to Cochran's Wasps also came from the Congress. Senator Harry Truman, head of a Congressional committee investigating government waste, told the Secretary of War that the cost of training a Wasp was alleged to be $22,000. How the committee arrived at this figure is not clear. The actual cost was $12,500—the same as for male cadets—possibly a little less.[24]

More opposition came from the House Committee on the Civil Service led by the chairman, Representative Robert E. Ramspeck. Male civilian pilots were authorized by the Civil Service to fly military aircraft. At the formation of the WASP, the War Department asked for specific permission to employ women on the same basis, but, while the commission was still debating the issue, the Air Force started the program before permission was given. In addition to questioning the Air Force's action, the commission also asked for the cost of training the women, by what authority uniforms were procured, and at what cost and whether male pilots on administrative duty could replace the women.[25]

By then Arnold and Jackie agreed that the time had come to militarize the WASP. Representative John M. Costello of California introduced a bill, stating that the women pilots be commissioned in the Army, but assigned to the Army Air Force.[26]

But while the Costello bill was still being debated and amended into HR4219, in January 1944, the Civil Aviation Authority's War Training Service (CAA-WTS) program was terminated, and the AAF college training program was scheduled to end in June, along with a large number of civilian contract schools. Thousands of student pilots and instructors would be grounded at the time when the anticipated invasion of Europe required more men in combat units of ground forces.[27] Those who could not meet Air Force requirements as pilots, bombardiers, or navigators would be subject to the draft.

Deluged by angry complaints from the grounded pilots, Congress introduced the first of a series of bills to commission as second lieutenants CAA-WTS pilots. Arnold objected. Testifying before the House Military Affairs Committee, he said that because AAF casualties had been fewer than expected, 36,000 volunteers for Air Force training would be released to infantry units, and he wanted Wasps in expanded numbers to replace male ferry pilots.[28]

Arnold usually got whatever he asked for from Congress, but Jackie was neither as popular nor as careful to gauge the public's attitude that was so important to Congressmen. Relying on support from generals in the Army command, she worked from the top down, while Congressmen, dependent on their constituents, worked from the bottom up. On June 21, the revised Costello bill came to the floor, with the chairman of the Military Affairs Committee, Andrew J. May, who favored the bill, presiding. But lobbyists for civilian aviation organizations, veterans' associations, civilian pilots, and trainees had already turned the ensuing debate on the Costello bill into one on the disposition of CAA-WTS instructors and trainees.[29] One congressman had claimed that male fliers with more than 2,000 hours in the air would soon be cleaning windshields for "glamorous women fliers who have only thirty-five hours of flying time."[30] Both Jackie and Arnold were subjected to personal attacks by Congressman Edward T. Izak, winner of the Congressional Medal of Honor in World War I and head of the Naval Affairs Committee.[31] The vote was a close one, the bill defeated by only twenty votes.[32]

Five days later, Arnold announced the termination of further recruitment and training of additional Wasps, but said that training of those already in school would be completed.[33]

Jackie refused to give up. On August 4, she announced the continuation of a special training course for Wasps, started back in April, at the School of Applied Tactics in Orlando, Florida, a course that emphasized Army discipline, military courtesy, customs of the service, and responsibilities of an officer. All Wasps were to complete the course, she said.[34]

On the day following her announcement, columnist Drew Pearson warned that Congress was "up in arms" over Arnold's continued use of the WASP, while more than 5,000 experienced men pilots remained on the ground. "Fact is," he wrote, "the government has spent more than $21,000,000 training women fliers, primarily at the behest of vivacious Jacquelin[e] Cochran, wife of Magnate Floyd Odlum. Miss Cochran seems to have quite a drag with the Brass Hats and has even persuaded the Air Force's smiling commander to make several trips to Capitol Hill to lobby for the continuation of her pets, the Wasps."[35]

Pearson's report, published on August 6, jumped the gun on an official War Department notice to be released on August 8. In a report to Arnold, Jackie played her last card, suggesting that they try again for militarization through a Senate bill still in committee. If it passed the Senate, it might influence the House. And if the bill did not pass this time she said, the only alternative was "inactivation of the WASP program." Even then, she suggested that an effort be made to obtain military status, "if only for a day," so that the women could receive benefits, including military funerals and death benefits for their survivors.[36] Called an ultimatum by much of the press, Jackie's recommendation was headlined by the *Washington Post*: "Miss Cochran Would Commission Wasps or Junk."[37]

With regret, Arnold opted for junking. With AAF casualties in Europe far lower than anticipated, a supply of pilots that Wasps had replaced was increasingly available. On September 6, Arnold closed the classes for Wasps at the School of Applied Tactics in Orlando, a month after Jackie had declared them open until every Wasp had attended.[38]

Jackie knew that the end of the WASP was near, but as late as September, she was doggedly looking for opportunities for "her girls" to extend their experience in ever more sophisticated aircraft. If the woman who could sell hot bricks in hell could not gain her object with charm, she resorted to wearying persuasion. On September 18, she telephoned General Kenneth McNaughton to ask him that more flight time in four-engine planes be given to her Wasps. When she reminded him that he had said that women could fly any plane, he admitted it, but that at the moment he needed to have as many men as possible fly four-engine aircraft. "I see," she said. "But if they check the girls out and use them as copilots . . . is that all right?" He said it would be if there were no men to do it. When she asked if women could fly when there was a shortage of personnel, he said that he couldn't imagine that happening, but if the women were already flying four-engine planes, he didn't want to stop them.

Pouncing on this opening, Jackie said, "Suppose so many men wash out the instructors have time to check out women. Why not?" "That would be different," the general admitted. "The only thing left to do would be to check out women." While continuing to insist on men being checked out first, McNaughton agreed that if girls were already checked out, they in turn should check out men, but not other girls. Jackie closed in for the kill. "But, on the other hand, if there is some time available and there is no man available, the girls can have it?" "Yes," the general replied.[39]

Two days after her plea to McNaughton, Jackie found another opportunity to publicize the Wasps (and herself) when the ten-thousandth P-47 rolled off the assembly line at Republic Aviation in Long Island. Cochran, who had flown the plane's prototype, the P-35, to win the 1938 Bendix, broke the bottle over the plane's cowling, naming it Ten Grand. Members of the WASP P-47 squadron who were among the honored guests could boast that all domestic deliveries of P-47s were done by Wasps.[40] Forty-eight hours later, Wasp Teresa James took off in the Ten Grand from the Republic Field to Newark, New Jersey.[41]

The Wasps had done a great job, but the end was near. On October 3, Arnold directed that the WASP program be deactivated on December 20. He sent every Wasp a letter, telling each, "I want you to know that I appreciate your war service and that the AAF will miss you. I also know that you will join us in being thankful that our combat losses have proved to be much lower than anticipated, even though it means the inactivation of the WASP. Happy landings always, Hap Arnold." Jackie added that on discharge, each Wasp would be given a card as a rated pilot of military aircraft, showing horsepower rating. That and completion of a written examination of air commerce rules would give each a CAA commercial license.[42]

Was it Jackie's fault that the WASP wasn't militarized? Dedie Deaton said it was "because there was no provision for an Air Force separate from the Army and she [Cochran] would have been under Olveta Culp Hobby." But Deaton admitted that "The men pilots were fearful that the girls were going to take their jobs . . . ," adding, "The biggest commotion was caused from mainly civilian instructors who had not been in the service because of their jobs."[43] Margaret Kerr Boylan added that many believed that Jackie and Arnold lost the political battle because of the media campaign staged by unemployed male pilots. Maybe, too, Jackie was "tired of the whole thing."[44]

Jackie was more than tired. She was ill with the abdominal adhesions that had hospitalized her the previous spring. On October 16, she entered Presbyterian Hospital in New York for four days, where she was told that more surgery would be necessary.[45] Putting off the impending operation, she gave an interview to the *New York Times*, predicting the future of women in aviation as instructors and pilots of feed lines (but not for main airlines) and in aerial photography, fire watching, and crop dusting. Echoing her late friend Amelia Earhart, she said that their most important role will be in encouraging women to travel by air.[46] While expounding on the future of women pilots as a group, she never lost sight of each as an individual, for good or for ill. She received a letter from the brother of WASP trainee Mary V. Shaw, who was injured in a crash and stated that she could walk but limped and was embarrassed by the ogling and whispering of strangers. Could she wear a uniform to stop this? A few days later, Shaw received a box with a new Santiago-blue uniform.[47]

Continuing to put off surgery, Jackie attended the graduation ceremonies for the last two classes at Sweetwater. At the last, on December 7, she shared the dais with Arnold and four other generals. Four days later, she was back in New York for the operation. Recuperation was slow and was worrying Floyd. Fretting over criticism of her role in ending the WASP program, she asked Floyd to dictate a news release to Arnold's aide, Lieutenant Colonel E. A. McCabe, explaining that the failure to militarize was not the reason for demobilization, but rather the completion of their mission. She said that she did not make the original recommendation to end the program. That was made by Arnold, but followed through because of "pertinent facts and the timeliness of the action."[48] The release was too long, too repetitive, and too late for vindication.

In a summary of her final report to Arnold on the WASP, Jackie declared the experiment a success. Of 25,000 women who applied for training, 1,830 were accepted, 1,074 graduated, and 900 of them, along with the 16 original WAFs, were still on duty at the time of deactivation. They flew an estimated 60 million miles. Thirty-eight of them died in the line of duty—one to about 16,000 hours of flying. The accident and fatality rates were comparable to those for male pilots in similar work.[49]

At the close of her summary, Jackie asked that if at any time in the future, the War Department favored legislation to grant veterans' rights to civilian organizations serving with the armed forces, all Wasps should be included, and the next of kin of those who died in the line of duty should receive compensation as if the Wasp had been on military status with insurance privileges and benefits.[50]

When Arnold first announced the deactivation of the WASP, Jackie sent him a letter of thanks because, she wrote, "Whenever in your office I am so filled with awe that I cannot express myself well." After commending Generals Barney Giles, Barton Yount, and Robert Harper for their assistance, she closed with "When my work is done and my detailed report handed in I will turn the key in the door with a feeling of sincere regret that I am no longer a part of the Army Air Force."[51] For the first time since the twenty-two-year-old Jacqueline Cochran arrived in New York City in 1928, she faced failure. The Wasps were no more, and many thought that she was the cause of their demise.

Eighteen

War Correspondent

That winter of 1944, a depressed Jackie joined Floyd at the Indio ranch that had become his favorite home. But on December 20, the very day that the Wasps were officially disbanded, an announcement by Hap Arnold lifted her spirits. While on an inspection tour of the west coast, Arnold learned that Betty Gillies, squadron leader of the WASP ferry pilots at New Castle, and her forty-two charges had offered to ferry military planes as civilian volunteers for $1 a year. He immediately telegraphed Barney Giles at headquarters. "You will notify all concerned that there will be no—repeat—no women pilots in any capacity in the air force after December 20 except Jacqueline Cochran."[1] On January 19, Arnold appointed her a special assistant to the Chief of Staff on a per diem basis until June 30, 1945.[2] Her assignment, to complete a detailed final report on the WASP.

With a Pentagon office "around the corner" from Arnold's, Jackie ruled her domain with an iron hand. She sent so many prospective employees back to the civil service office that the woman providing staff called her "the most difficult woman we've ever had to deal with." Jackie replied that the women she rejected "wore petticoats that showed and makeup like that of a third line chorus girl." "All they do," she said, "is sit around and primp and chew gum and go out to the ladies' room."[3] Office rules were strict. At the close of the day, half-written letters were to be completed, desks cleared, and typewriters covered. Mid-morning coffee was to be brought for all the staff by one person listed on the blackboard. When a black woman told Jackie that a white fellow worker would not fetch her her coffee because she was black, Jackie barked, "They bring it to you or I'll fire them!"[4]

Six weeks after Jackie's appointment, President Roosevelt named her as one of fourteen recipients of the Distinguished Service Medal, the first woman civilian to receive it during the war.[5] When she heard that Roosevelt wanted to make the presentation, she told a member of his staff that she wanted Arnold to do it. If he could not, she said, "Let them mail it to me."[6] Arnold presented the medal in a ceremony that moved Jackie to tears.[7]

The citation read: "Under her leadership the WASP performed with the utmost loyalty and efficiency multiple flying services. . . . Further, her achievements in this respect and the conclusions she has carefully and wisely drawn from this undertaking represent a contribution which is of permanent and far-reaching significance to the future of aviation."[8] This was the acknowledgment that she wanted. The WASP had successfully provided "multiple flying services"—not just ferrying—in a program that could be repeated in the future if needed.

That summer of 1945, when the allies were already victorious in Europe and the Pacific war was winding down, the end of Jackie's six-month AAF appointment neared. Incapable of inactivity, she applied to the Civil Aeronautics Administration for permission to fly a Lockheed Lodestar to England and

18.1. Air Force General H. H. "Hap" Arnold presenting Jackie with the Distinguished Service Medal in August 1945, the only woman among fourteen civilians to receive it. (Courtesy Dwight D. Eisenhower Library. Photographer unknown.)

France on or about August 1 to expand her business in both countries.[9] But Floyd knew that what she really wanted was to see the post-war world, to savor the victory of American forces in Asia and Europe. To do this, she needed an authorization like that given to journalists, one that Floyd obtained for her by bidding five million dollars to buy a failing magazine, *Liberty*. Jackie was immediately hired as a war correspondent, signing a contract on August 8, two days after the atom bomb was dropped on Hiroshima.[10]

When she told Arnold that she was going to Asia as a war correspondent, she added, "There are about 175 phonies out there so I might just as well be one more phony. But I will write an article or two."[11] The woman who quit school after third grade did not lack self confidence. Arnold not only approved, he told her that she could be his consultant with priority-one traveling orders. The two most important men in her life at that moment—Floyd and Arnold—had given her just what she wanted. "I was an assistant to Arnold and I had my war correspondent accreditation."[12]

The new correspondent immediately collected letters of introduction from Arnold, the Secretary of War, the Secretary of the Navy, and numerous generals and admirals. But the letter that she prized the most was from Floyd:

> Dearest Jackie,
>
> Wherever you go on this great adventure of yours to the Pacific you carry with you my all-enduring and complete love, and whenever you get tired and lonesome turn to this note for confirmation if my wholehearted and all consuming affection for you will cheer you up. I wish I could be with you on this wonderful trip. This being impossible, my next strongest desire is to have you go. . . . You are my other half and your activity makes my enforced inactivity bearable.[13]

Floyd's "inactivity" was increasing. Working as a maid that summer, fourteen-year-old Jan Larson never saw Floyd walk. He had a nurse to attend him and spent several hours of each day in a therapeutic bath or in the heated pool where he conducted business by telephone or with visitors who donned bathing suits to join him in the pool. He was never without company for dinner. Jan saw film stars Joan Blondell, Rosalind Russell, and Alan Ladd and, in addition to corporate executives, there were admirals and generals, including Hap Arnold. The dinners were prepared by a chef and Jan's mother, Margaret Larson, the sous chef.[14]

Jackie arrived in Honolulu on August 11 and began keeping notes on the trip. She dined with high-ranking officers, but was billeted in a house for women. The house "smelled of disinfectant and cheap perfume," she recalled, and one of the occupants was a "sloppy, over-bleached blonde who looked like just the worst possible tart you could find on 42nd Street on a Saturday night."[15]

Twenty hours later, she was on Guam, where her old friend Lieutenant General Barney Giles, by then commander of the Army Air Force in the Pacific, met her plane at two o'clock in the morning. She stayed at his house and went fishing only a few hours after arrival with General Carl "Tooey" Spaatz. She cooked dinner that night at Jimmy Doolittle's quarters and played poker with four generals—Curtis LeMay, Kenneth McNaughton, Nathan Twining, and Thomas Power.[16]

Host Barney Giles arranged for her to fly a C-54E to Tinian, another of the Marianas Islands.[17] There, she gathered material for *Liberty* on baseball as a major postwar pastime for airmen stationed on Tinian. Filed in August, it was published on October 27 with a picture captioned, "The Tigers' Birdie Tebbetts, the Card's Enos Slaughter, Miss Cochran and the Yankees' Joe Gordon." The story was credited to Jackie and Corporal Robert D. John, who probably wrote most of it as she insisted that his name appear with hers.[18] Writing was not easy without a secretary. In script like that of an eight-year-old, Jackie wrote to Floyd, "I'm having quite a time for I can't get anyone to type anything for me and I find that trying to keep notes is not as easy as it sounds."[19]

On Guam, she was introduced to Francis, Cardinal Spellman after he celebrated Mass in a Quonset hut. She reported to Floyd that he was "a wonderful person," and "I hope we can have him for dinner when I return."[20] To Catholic Jackie, the cardinal was the equivalent, if not the superior, of a four-star general.

When she arrived in Manila on August 19, Jackie received the disturbing news from Floyd that his sedimentation rate—by which the extent of his illness was measured—had risen and his knees, elbows, and wrists were swollen. But he hastened to tell her that he was no worse than when she left and was acting as her "attorney in fact" to buy a six-story building at 10 West 56th Street for her office in an expansion move for Jacqueline Cochran Cosmetics.[21]

A few days later when he cabled her that he was better, she answered:

> Floyd darling,
> Thank God I just received your cable. I didn't think I could stand to go on one more day without hearing from you and now I feel as tho [*sic*] I can't stand to stay out here another day. . . . If you had not of [*sic*] arranged for me to come here I would go home at once. But I feel you had some reason for wanting me to come out here so if you want me to come home all you have to do is call me to do so. Darling, I love you very much. I want us to be happy. I feel I have failed you these past two years.

She closed the letter with "I pray to God you are better and will be well soon."[22]

Floyd replied that the only reason he wanted her to make the trip was to give her "one of life's outstanding experiences." He urged her to continue her travels while he looked after her interests at home. Her Lockheed Lodestar was almost ready after being converted from Army use, and Floyd was working on moving her cosmetic plant from Rochelle, New Jersey, to Newark into a building that the Curtiss-Wright Aviation Company had used but wanted to lease. To be certain that Jackie would meet Madame Chiang Kai-shek when she arrived in China, Floyd entertained T. V. Soong, Madame Chiang's brother, along with Harry Hopkins, Roosevelt's confidante, at lunch. Floyd was forming the Chinese-American Trading Corporation with the Soongs as partners.[23]

In another of her letters to Floyd, Jackie praised the personal cleanliness of Manila's residents, who washed and did their laundry in water carried in pails and with soap made of the bark of a tree. She thought them kind, gentle, intelligent, and deserving of American aid. "If we provide education and proper food they will rebuild their cities and do the rest," she wrote.[24]

Jackie was invited by General E. H. Leavey to witness the surrender of Japanese General Tomoyuki Yamashita, who had retreated with his forces to the mountains of northern Luzon. Leavey, who was in charge of the ceremony, said that she could go as his personal friend, but was not to write about it until he gave his permission. When he did not invite the only other woman correspondent, Shelley Mydans, Jackie protested, offering to give her place to Mydans. Shelley and her husband, Carl Mydans, both with *Life* magazine, had been prisoners of the Japanese in Manila. After their release, they were flown to Guam, where Jackie first met them, then to Manila with her. Whether by her salesmanship skills or by intimidation—she *was* Arnold's consultant—Leavey changed his mind and invited both women.[25]

The surrender was to take place at Baguio in northern Luzon, the summer capital of the Philippines. Jackie, Shelley, and two WAC officers were flown in a C-47 to an airstrip on the Lingayen Gulf about seventy-five miles from Baguio. As they taxied down the runway, she was horrified to discover that the pilot had left a lock on one of the ailerons. Hurrying to the cabin, she told the crew, one of whom climbed out to remove it. The risks that she took to break records were not undertaken with errant checkouts. On returning to Manila, she chose to make the long trip in a jeep.[26]

Witnessing the surrender at Baguio on September 3, she wrote to Floyd, "Yamashita looked like a big pig that has been fattened up and suddenly taken off his feed, losing weight. He was the most bestial looking person I've ever seen. His head was shaved as clean as an onion and his hands at the top looked like hammers and tapered down to claws."[27]

In contrast to her contempt for Yamashita was her admiration for two generals who had been his prisoners—General Jonathan Wainwright and General A. E. Percival. Wainwright had surrendered the Philippines and Percival the British colony of Singapore. The two men had been flown to Japan to witness the surrender aboard the USS *Missouri* on September 2, then returned to Baguio the following day for Yamashita's surrender.[28]

After speaking briefly to the correspondents, Wainwright, who had met Jackie at Wright Field in 1937, walked over to her and said that it was nice to see her there. Taking her notebook, he signed it, then bent down to kiss her on the cheek, causing her to burst into tears. Back in Manila a week later, she was given an affidavit by Lowell M. Limpus of the *New York Daily News*, testifying to Wainwright's kiss. Limpus wrote that Wainwright was "either charmed by a first glimpse of a charming and attractive American girl or else was hypnotized by the undoubted efficiency of the cosmetics worn by said Jacqueline Cochran, which cosmetics were presumably manufactured by said Jacqueline Cochran."[29] Jackie kept that affidavit in her personal papers for the remainder of her life.

Her long and detailed report on the surrender was rejected by *Liberty*. Editor Edward Maher wrote to Floyd, who had become her de facto literary agent, that her detailed and precise observations were unfortunately just like the newsreels of the event that readers had already seen. Maher had rewritten the next article that she sent, on the release of American prisoners of war, and published it as "From Hell to Heaven." After Floyd began to send him excerpts from Jackie's letters, Maher told him that these could be run as two-column items, possibly entitled, "Leaves from a Correspondent's Notebook."[30] Eventually, three brief pieces appeared, but Jackie's career as a correspondent was definitely waning. On her return to the United States, she received a check from *Liberty* for $1,200, payment for five articles.

After the surrender of Yamashita, although she retained her guise of reporter, her goal was to see postwar Asia while staying in more comfortable lodgings than her room at the war-damaged Manila Hotel, with its army cot, single chair, and bathroom where she showered with buckets of water over a hole in the floor.[31] To Floyd, she wrote that she was trying "to promote a nice plane ride to Tokyo as I am not too keen on the means of transportation provided for correspondents." Her old friend Barney Giles gave her that ride, first to Guam, then to Yokohama.[32]

During a three-day wait in Guam, she began to establish private supply lines for further travel. On September 16, she cabled Floyd, asking him to have Arnold's aide, Colonel Emmett McCabe, send to either Kyoto or China the uniform that she had left at home. She also wanted her personal maid, Ellen Haugen, to buy an off-duty WAC dress and have it fitted to her (Haugen was the same size as Jackie) and to buy a large quantity of nail polish and cologne.[33] Floyd cabled back the next day that the clothes were sent to McCabe, who would forward them to Tokyo.[34]

In addition to her first order, she told Floyd in a handwritten note that Giles's aide, Colonel Harry Chesley, was returning to Washington with a list of more things that she needed. Chesley would see that the items were put on a plane going to Tokyo.[35] With all the payback instincts of a master sergeant in the regular Army, Jackie suggested that Floyd treat Colonel and Mrs. Chesley to a room at the Plaza for a couple of nights.[36] Floyd booked the room, invited the Chesleys to dinner, and gave them tickets to two Broadway shows.[37]

Her next request she sent directly to McCabe. She wanted liquor—a lot of it. He sent her five cases, three of scotch and two of bourbon—all with Chesley aboard an AAF plane.[38]

On arriving in Yokohama on September 19, Jackie claimed that she was the first American woman to come to Japan after the war. The next day, she drove to Tokyo where she spent her first night in an enormous Japanese house intended for General George C. Kenney, AAF chief in the Far East, who had not arrived as yet. The following day, she moved into the Imperial Hotel, the prestigious building designed by American architect Frank Lloyd Wright, which was occupied by high-ranking officers. With her clothing and toiletries ordered, she was ready to see Japan.[39]

Accompanied by General Paul Wurtsmith, she made three attempts to see Hiroshima from the air, but each time they were forced back by stormy weather.[40] She did get to Kyoto, the city of shrines, accompanied by Major General F. L. Akenbrandt in a DC-3 with a jeep and three enlisted men aboard. (That she was the first to enter Kyoto on September 25, 1945, was verified in a certificate from Major General F. L. Ankenbrandt, dated May 31, 1949. She saved it.) Leaving the plane at the airfield with the enlisted men, Jackie and Akenbrandt drove into a city that seemed deserted. As she saw a curtain flutter in one window and tapped on the pane, a Japanese man wearing a morning suit and a silk hat appeared behind her. He told Akenbrandt and Jackie that the city's residents were waiting in their homes for the occupation forces to arrive. After a tour of the temples of Kyoto, one of which she described as the most beautiful thing she had ever seen, Jackie and the general were invited to have tea with the woman whose window Jackie had tapped. Not only an appreciator of beautiful objects, but also a collector of them, Jackie bought two lengths of silk and an obi from her hostess.[41]

To see Hirohito's palace, Jackie flew over it. "I was at the controls of the plane," she said, "and took a slow bomb run over the palace to within 20 feet of the roof and looked everything over."[42] The next day, MacArthur's headquarters issued an order banning flights within a three-square-mile area of the palace, and MacArthur's billeting officer called, telling her that she must give up her room at the Imperial because only high-ranking officers stayed there. One of her admiral friends with a combination office and living quarters in the hotel said that he would close off a room for her. Mumbling a slur about the reputation of the Navy, MacArthur's man said that she could keep her room.[43]

When she was invited by General George C. Kenney to a traditional Japanese banquet at his house, she was seated next to Kenney, with a Japanese woman in a traditional kimono kneeling between them to serve them. Jackie told Kenney that she was not eating the food, nor should he for fear for dysentery. If he was hungry, she said, there was probably a tin of corned beef in his quarters that they could share. She was certain that the waitress spoke English and was there to spy on them. After the dinner, she brought the waitress along to Kenney's house, where they ate the corned beef and plied the woman with saki until she admitted that she understood English.[44]

In another of her scrawled notes to Floyd, Jackie wrote, "I am so sure it is wrong for us to have occupied this country. We should have disarmed them and gone on about our business . . . ," adding, "Although everything here is quite [*sic*] and the people are polite I think when they are over the shock and they get even more hungry there is going to be trouble unless we feed them. I don't think we should."[45]

Having seen all that she could in Japan, Jackie was eager to move on to China, but orders were difficult to get because most officers returning home wanted to go by way of China. She got hers from Lieutenant General George E. Stratemeyer in Shanghai after she told him that she wanted to visit Floyd's cousin, General Victor Odlum, the Canadian ambassador to China. She also secured travel orders for the Mydans.[46] En route, they stopped in Okinawa, where Jackie and Shelley slept on cots in an Army tent—the kind of accommodation that Jackie had been determined to avoid after Manila. Two women, who were Army dieticians, entered the tent at midnight, occupying the cots opposite Jackie, cots that she had already noted as "messy and dirty." She said that the women were "frowzy, dirty, cheap and common," and she was horrified when the "frowziest of the two" told her that she used to date Floyd's son Stanley when he was at Dartmouth. That ended further conversation, but Jackie sent a report on both women to the Secretary of War when she returned home.[47]

She arrived in Shanghai on "Double Ten," the holiday celebrating the founding of the Republic of China on October 10, 1911. That night, the Mydans, who had previously worked in China, were invited by the owner of a restaurant to bring their friends to dinner. Jackie and the officers from the plane from Okinawa went along, driven through the streets so jammed that the trip took three hours. On leaving the car, they linked arms to fight their way to the restaurant. Jackie was so impressed by the cleanliness of the place and the elegant manners of the owner that she abandoned her plan to eat only Army food cooked at her hotel and learned to use chopsticks, eating the plainer of the dishes—but not grub worms or fish eyes. On leaving the restaurant, they found that their car had been completely demolished by the exuberant crowd.[48]

Within a day or two Jackie ended her brief career as a reporter, turning over any information that she had to *Liberty*'s regular man covering China. Before she left for Chungking, Carl Mydans asked her, on behalf of the American war correspondents, if she would get General Stratemeyer to rescind his order changing the status of war correspondents with considerable loss of privileges. Stratemeyer replaced his order, giving civilian correspondents access to Army transport, billeting, the Post Exchange, officers' clubs, and APO mail.[49]

Determined to see as much of China as possible, Jackie made two trips from Shanghai to Chungking and one to Peiping. At Chungking, she was first the guest of Victor Odlum at the Canadian embassy and then of Mei-ling Soong, Madame Chiang Kai-shek, a woman as ambitious and strong-willed as Jackie. Jackie commented, "As interesting as I found Madame Chiang I have concluded she was a dominate [*sic*] person in the family."[50] In other words, Jackie did not like her.

Victor Odlum arranged a meeting for her with Mao Tze-tung, who was in Chungking. She thought him intelligent, idealistic, and honest. "I certainly don't mean to sound sympathetic towards anything that is communistic but the man was just so powerful and so forceful and so sincere."[51]

A compulsive collector of worldly goods, she left Chungking with enough expensive Chinese silk to curtain the guest room at River House.[52] When in Peiping, she acquired a samurai sword from a Japanese general who said that he would have to give it up anyway at his formal surrender to the allies—a thought that Jackie might have originated.[53]

Near the end of October, the former war correspondent turned civilian-military tourist faced a difficult decision. She could keep going east through India, the Middle East, and Europe, completing a circuit of the world, or she could return home more rapidly via the Pacific. So far, her tour had been a great success. An admiral in Manila wrote to Paul Hammond, "I did what I could for her as have all the rest of the Navy in this area. She is very attractive, entertaining and interesting."[54] An Air Force general wrote to a friend of Floyd's, "I saw Jackie Cochran at Curt LeMay's. I think she is really a gorgeous girl. She was handling herself beautifully. Spaatz, Nimitz and LeMay all gave her interviews."[55]

But on October 2, Floyd's nurse reported to Jackie that ever since Jackie's departure, Floyd had been confined to their New York apartment. In a hospital bed for all of the first month, he was currently using a wheelchair to keep his business appointments and to have friends in for dinner almost every night.[56] However, the nurse's letter did not arrive before a cable from Floyd telling Jackie that if transportation were available, she should make her trip a round-the-world one and see India and Egypt. He would go to the ranch by December 1.[57] Reassured by his message, she cabled back that she hoped to arrange transport via Europe in the first week of November.[58]

On November 1, all war correspondents were to become civilians, who required clearances from embassies, but Jackie was cleared for France and Germany by European Theater of Operations Commander Dwight D. Eisenhower. She left Chungking on October 29 with eight pieces of baggage for a whirlwind tour, with two-day stays in Calcutta, New Delhi, Agra, and Karachi. Arriving in Cairo on November 7, she was met by Barney Giles, recently posted there. After he gave her a plane to use in a flight to Palestine, he took her to Iraq, then to Iran to visit Shah Mohammad Riza Pahlavi. En route there, a woman relative of the Shah's failed to adjust her oxygen mask. Jackie saw her "swell up like a balloon, let out a few weak squeals and pass out." Unregistered nurse Cochran leapt to the rescue, adjusting the woman's mask and loosening her clothing, possibly saving her life.[59] When Jackie left Cairo, Giles gave her a ride on a B-25 to Rome, where she had an audience with Pope Pius XII lasting twenty-eight minutes. She timed it.[60]

From Rome, Jackie went to Germany, where she wanted to witness the trials of accused Nazis at Nuremberg and to interview the German pilot Hanna Reitsch, a woman whom Jackie admired in spite of her allegiance to Hitler. "I think highly of Hanna Reitsch," Jackie wrote years later. "She not only flew the first buzz bomb [rocket-powered plane] but she flew to Berlin some German generals to see Hitler during the last days of his life."[61]

For permission to attend the Nuremberg trials, Jackie called her friend Supreme Court Justice Robert Jackson, who was in charge of them. He arranged for her attendance and took her to Buchenwald. Before she left Berlin, she saw the Reich Chancellery and the bunkers where Hitler had hidden. After her friends were refused permission to enter the underground retreat, she went back alone, and, bribing the Russian guards with cigarettes, she acquired a doorknob from the Chancellery and a medal that Hitler had intended to give a woman for bearing sixteen children.[62] But she failed to get her interview with Hanna Reitsch, who was being interrogated by both the British and American authorities. They would not let Reitsch speak to the press until December 3, and Jackie could not wait.[63]

Worried about Floyd, she went to London, where she planned to leave for home on December 3. When her plane was delayed for two days, she saw some furniture that she wanted and sought Floyd's permission to buy it.[64] On her arrival in New York, Jackie was met by two of Floyd's friends, who told her that he was very ill and unable to meet her.[65] Away from home for almost five months, Jackie hurried to Floyd, planning to spend far more time than just the Christmas holidays at the ranch.

Nineteen

The Colonel and the Air Force

Jackie returned from her postwar tour even more convinced that the AAF that Arnold had so brilliantly developed needed both independence from the Army command and more money from Congress. The time was ripe. President Truman had proposed a unification of the armed forces under a Department of Defense, with three separate departments for the Army, Navy and Air Force. She told Arnold that they should "hit it right now while the iron is hot," insisting, "This time you are going to have to take it to the public." But, she added, "It has to be done by a civilian and you or any man in uniform can't touch it."[1] She proposed to him that she be the one to take it to the public, using information from the Pentagon provided by a clever young Air Force officer, Jake Smart, later a four-star general. Smart could send her the facts and figures. She would use them in her speeches and newspaper interviews.

"I didn't go to the Pentagon for eight months," she recalled. "I would send word back through Smart as to what my progress was and I kept feeding the newspapers."[2]

In April, she spoke on the *Time Radio Hour*, telling her listeners, "Women must get behind the movement to unify our armed forces. . . . Our first line of defense against the modern weapons of an atomic age clearly lies in the skies."[3] She said that women could help by becoming informed on unification and by getting friends and neighbors interested, organizing community meetings, and writing to their congressmen.[4] Two months later, she wrote to a friend, "I have crossed the continent eight times since December and I have a very sick husband and have been trying to get my affairs in working order."[5]

Each time that she crossed the country, she stopped in cities along the way to give speeches and interviews, sometimes following her appeals for a separate Air Force with bids for free publicity on her cosmetics company. She also contacted many of the influential people whom she and Floyd knew personally, inviting them to the ranch or to dinner in New York. On June 19, she entertained thirty-one guests, including six generals and two admirals, at a dinner in a private room at Madison Square Garden. Her invitation included seats at the Joe Louis–Billy Conn boxing match for the heavyweight championship of the world.[6]

Arnold, always her principal mentor in matters concerning the Air Force, was not among the guests at dinner. He was in Washington, D.C., where he would retire eleven days later as a four-star general, but earlier, in March, he and his wife, Bea, spent three weeks at the ranch while awaiting completion of their retirement home, Ranch El Feliz, near Sonoma, California. During their stay, Arnold told Jackie, "I've got every single thing I want except a jeep and I've run out of money." Jackie and Floyd presented him with one wrapped in cellophane and parked on his front lawn.[7]

To remain an effective spokesperson for air power, Jackie needed to do some more fast flying, keeping her name before the public. That summer, she entered the 1946 Bendix Race, determined to beat Paul Mantz, whom she disliked intensely for his patronizing remarks about her and her beloved friend Amelia. Mantz had purchased a government-surplus North American P-51—the Mustang—and converted the wings into fuel tanks. Jackie also bought a Mustang, but she was too late for a wing modification like Mantz's, so she added Lockheed wing-drop tanks to her entry.[8]

She took off on August 30 from Los Angeles, buckled down in a seat atop an additional gasoline tank. Under her helmet, her face was covered by an oxygen mask. Feet on the pedals and one hand on the stick, she used the other hand to tune the radio, handle the throttle, and turn the pages of a map book tied to her knee. In place of the relief tube provided for male pilots, she opted for dehydration before the race, followed by "fighting nature" during it.[9]

After crossing the Colorado River, she saw that her radio was not functioning, forcing her to fly by compass. When she tried to release the wing tanks, they stuck at first and, when they did drop, they hit the trailing edge of the wings, damage that slowed her down. Heading into a storm, she tried to climb over it, but the engine began stopping and starting erratically. Forty-five minutes later when she thought she must be over Cleveland, she headed down. Breaking into the clear at 9,000 feet, she was surrounded by a field of other competitors, but she came in second, six minutes after Mantz.[10]

As she climbed out of the cockpit, she heard someone say, "Oh, you're all bloody!" Either during the episode of the drop tanks or the errant engine, she had hit her head against the canopy top, an injury that she had no time to notice. To Floyd, who was there to greet her, she muttered, "I'm getting too old for this." She didn't mean it, not after learning that she had set another woman's record at her average speed of 420.828 miles an hour. She donated the $6,500 second prize to the Army Air Force Aid Society.[11]

Back in the news, she resumed within a week her campaign for Truman's proposed Department of Defense. In January of 1947, her efforts were acknowledged by an invitation to dinner at the White House. Three months later, the magazine *American* noted her "stumping the country for a combined air force in between business appointments in various parts of the country where she takes care of her other enterprises."[12] That summer, her efforts were rewarded when Truman signed the National Security Act of 1947 on July 26, creating the Department of Defense with a Department of the Air Force to be headed by former Senator W. Stuart Symington. A friend to both Jackie and Floyd, Symington once observed that Jackie was the most competitive person that he had ever met. "She had to win but that's what made her great," he said. That need to compete was fulfilled a few days before Christmas in 1947, when she set two new international women's speed records, the first on December 10 and the second a week later. On December 10, she flew the 100-kilometer course at 412 miles an hour, and on December 17, the three-kilometer course at 412.002 miles an hour.[13]

For her business, Jackie flew a Lockheed Lodestar. The plane was also used by Floyd after he gained control of the Consolidated Vultee Corporation of Fort Worth, Texas, in 1946. Maintenance of the aircraft was left to Samuel Held and F. J. Bodde, with Held as pilot when Jackie was not flying it. On March 12, Held crashed in it with the wheels up after the hydraulic landing gear jammed.[14] Jackie was furious, accusing him of failing to repair the system after he had been warned about it. In sharing the big Lodestar with Consolidated, she wrote to Held, she had set up the system to defray the cost of operation and maintenance and to "give you and Mr. Bodde [both of whom were paid by Consolidated] a little better break than you could ever hope to receive from me."[15] Held learned that Jackie was a perfectionist about her airplanes, yet counted every penny spent on them.

The Lockheed was meant for business—hers and Floyd's—but the P-51 Mustang was for enhancing her reputation as a pilot. On May 22, 1948, at 447.470 miles an hour, she broke the previous world record of 440 miles an

19.1. In Washington, D.C., in 1947, Jackie adjusts her sandal for a photo op while still in the cockpit of one of her favorite planes, the North American P-51 Mustang. (National Air and Space Museum, Smithsonian Institution, SI 86–533.)

hour for a 2,000-kilometer course. In the piston-driven P-51, she had outmatched a Lockheed P-80 jet fighter flown by Air Force Lieutenant J. J. Hancock.[16] It wasn't easy. At 27,000 feet in the nonpressurized Mustang when the oxygen equipment failed, she began to feel pain between her shoulder blades and her fingernails turned blue. She remembered what Lovelace and Boothby had told her about oxygen starvation and began to hold her breath while she changed the emergency oxygen system from "on demand" to "constant flow." When it faltered, she reverted to holding her breath until the errant system flowed.[17] Forty-eight hours later, she bested her own 1,000-kilometer record when she flew 431.094 miles an hour.[18]

She didn't hold her breath, however, whenever she had a chance to praise the Air Force, and a day later, she flew the repaired Lodestar to Dallas to attend a meeting of five Dallas organizations—one of them the Air Force Association—to honor the new Secretary of the Air Force, Stuart Symington.

During a reception for Symington that night, his friend, Congressman Lyndon Baines Johnson, who was running for the Senate, was in a Dallas hospital desperately ill with kidney stones. Polls taken a week after Johnson announced his candidacy on May 12 showed that his opponent, Governor Coke R. Stevenson, was ahead with 49 percent to Johnson's 31 percent.[19] Surgery would put Johnson out of the race. At the reception, Symington asked Jackie to take the ailing candidate to the Mayo Clinic in Rochester, Minnesota. Jackie liked Johnson, whom she had first met back in 1939 when he was an executive aide to a Texas congressman and she was on the Collier Committee trying to raise funds for Lovelace and Boothby.[20] She said that she would take him in the Lodestar.[21]

The next morning, she telephoned Johnson's aide, Warren Woodward, at the hospital. "She came on the line in a very forceful, direct way," Woodward recalled. "She said, 'This is Jacqueline Cochran. I'm here in Dallas with my Lockheed Electra and I happen to know that one of the great urologists of the world is visiting here from England at Mayo's. . . . You just tell Lyndon that I'm going to take him in my Electra.'" The plane was her Lodestar not Electra, but both were built by Lockheed.[22]

Woodward reported to Johnson, "She says she's going to be here with an ambulance at one o'clock and we take off at one thirty and we'll be at Mayo's at six o'clock." Johnson moaned, "No, I'm not gonna do that. They'll say the Texas doctors are not good enough for me." But at the insistence of both Lady Bird and Jackie, Johnson agreed.[23]

In Jackie's account of the incident, Johnson was brought to the airfield along with Lady Bird, Woodward, her personal maid Ellen Haugen, and a flight engineer. Johnson was placed on a cot near the cockpit. After taking off at dawn, and two hours into the flight, Jackie heard him scream in pain. She put the plane on automatic pilot—the engineer was not a pilot—and went back to care for her patient. She gave Johnson an injection to ease his pain, stripped him of his sweat-soaked clothing, and wrapped him in blankets, leaving Haugen to watch him while she returned to the cockpit. "It was a rough flight," she said, "but we got him to Rochester and late the next afternoon I learned he was sitting up in bed, taking nourishment and on the way to recovery."[24] Johnson returned to the campaign, winning a seat in the Senate by less than 100 votes. Recollections of the incident differ. Symington maintained that Johnson told him that he wanted to go to the Mayo Clinic before Symington asked Jackie to take him.[25] Beverly Hanson Sfingi said that she and

19.2. Jackie and President Lyndon Johnson at the White House in 1964. Her friendship with LBJ had begun in 1946 when the then-congressman became desperately ill during his first bid for the Senate. Evading the press, she flew him to the Mayo Clinic, where he recovered. (Lyndon Baines Johnson Library. Photo by Yoichi Okamoto.)

Helen Dettweiler, a former Wasp, were also on board. Sfingi and Dettweiler, professional golfers, had been guests of Jackie's at the ranch and accompanied her to Dallas, where they stayed in a hotel suite with Jackie. [26]

Back in the news that fall, Jackie entered the 1948 Bendix, determined to wrest first place from Paul Mantz, but he won again for the third consecutive year. She came in third, described by one reporter as "a disappointed flier who doesn't lose easily. By her calculations she was an easy winner but the official timers figured it was four minutes longer."[27]

She was lucky to have finished the race. Three days later, the wing of the Mustang that she used in the race fell off while Sam Held was taking it west for her. He was killed when the plane crashed on a farm near Sayre, Oklahoma.[28] The following year, Jackie bought another Mustang, the "Beguine," for $27,000. She loaned it to pilot Bill Odum, who was killed in it during a pylon race at the National Air Races in Cleveland.[29] Mike and Ben Howard both dismissed the assumption of pilot error, telling Jackie that the plane had "some strange characteristics."[30] Superstitious Jackie said that he crashed because he failed to repaint the tail with her lucky number "13" as she had asked.[31]

If some in the aviation community viewed Jackie as a poor loser and an overly ambitious egotist, Symington and most of the general officers in the new United States Air Force did not. In September of 1948, she was commissioned a Lieutenant Colonel in the U.S. Air Force Reserve, as was her wartime rival, Nancy Love—the only two women officers in the Reserve.[32] The freshman senator from Texas, Lyndon Johnson, was one of the group of staunch supporters. On the last day of the year, he wrote to Jackie, "Finally I take my seat in the Senate. Thank you for your friendship."[33] A month later, Johnson warned Jackie of the coming battle over appropriations for the military: "We are going to go through much the same fight this session as we did last."[34] Both the Air Force and Navy wanted more bombers—the Air Force land-based, the Navy, carrier-based—and when the congressional wrangling peaked in July of 1949, Floyd Odlum was under fire.

As chairman of the board of Consolidated Vultee Aviation Corporation, Floyd had negotiated a contract to build 100 B-26 bombers for the Air Force at a cost of $6,200,000 each. Supporters of the Navy accused him and a former board member, Louis Johnson, the Secretary of Defense, of arranging the deal in exchange for raising funds for Truman's election campaign. Opponents claimed that thousands of dollars were listed as coming from Odlum's Pine Street office in New York and that Symington had been a too-frequent houseguest of Odlum's at the ranch.[35] Washington columnist Tris Coffin wrote, "One reason big-time financier Floyd Odlum is up to his ears in the noisy hard-fought Air Force versus Navy fight is that his wife, Jacqueline Cochran, the famous flier, is Mrs. Odlum. She is an ardent air power advocate and good friend of the unofficial spokesman for that school, tough old Gen. Tooey Spaatz."[36]

Floyd had been a prominent backer of Truman. Invited to the inauguration, Jackie wrote to friends, "Floyd was practically the only business man in America who backed Mr. Truman both financially and publicly. We were among the white-haired children at the White House, invited to all the festivities in Washington including the inner sanctums to witness the swearing in ceremony."[37]

The investigation failed to produce evidence of misconduct by Odlum, Johnson, or Symington, and Jackie was to remain an ardent supporter of the Air Force for the remainder of her life.

Twenty

The Purposeful Traveler

Addicted to travel, Jackie Cochran did not take trips, she made tours. While the case against Floyd's Consolidated Vultee agreement was still brewing, she was designing an itinerary that included eight countries, with dates, conveyances, and wardrobe. To her friend Hoyt Vandenberg, chief of staff of the Air Force, she wrote that she would be in Paris from April 23 to May 14, 1949, when she intended to go to Germany for a week, followed by two or three days in Austria, Trieste (Italy), Israel, Greece, and Turkey. She had also obtained permits to enter the military occupation zones of Europe from the Americans, the British, and the Russians.[1] On the way home, she hoped to visit Belgium, Sweden, and England before sailing on either the *Queen Mary* or the *Queen Elizabeth*.[2]

Jackie traveled in what she termed comfort and others might describe as luxury—and never alone. For this trip, she invited former Wasp Mary Nelson, manager of the Palm Springs Airport, to accompany her. To Georges de Sonchen, Floyd's representative in Paris, she was sending ahead on the *Queen Elizabeth* Nelson's trunk, her trunk, a packing trunk, a suitcase, and a wooden crate, along with a list of the contents of her wardrobe. Another trunk would be sent later on the *Queen Mary*, but she would be there to receive it. The list included coffee, cosmetics, medical supplies, stockings, foodstuffs to be used as gifts, and five cartons of cigarettes.[3]

In place of her personal maid, Ellen Haugen, de Sonchen hired a maid in Paris. He must have known her preference in hotel accommodations, too, because he received no letters of complaint. Jackie was a master of demand and complaint. In Dallas the year before, she had embarrassed her golfing partners Beverly Hanson and Helen Dettweiler when she signed in at a hotel, had all the luggage brought to the suite, found that she didn't like it, and moved to another hotel across the street.[4] "We ended up with a living room you could have hit pitching wedges in," Hanson said.[5]

Jackie seldom traveled with a single purpose in mind. In Paris, she planned to attend the International Air Show and to receive the Legion of Honor, awarded to her by the French government. For her business, she wanted to visit designer Nina Ricci, whose perfume she had agreed to distribute in the United States, and to buy clothes. In Germany, she meant to board an Air Force plane bringing supplies from Frankfurt to the beleaguered city of Berlin. In the other countries on her list, she looked to meet as many famous persons as possible, including the King and Queen of Greece and Chaim Weizmann, the first president of Israel.[6]

She was ill before she left, but refused to change her plans. On April 23, she left New York on an Air France plane. Instead of resting during the eight-hour flight, she accepted the pilot's invitation to sit in the cockpit, and at one point took the controls. The sleepless night was followed by four days and nights of luncheons and dinners, culminating on April 28 in a reception for 300 guests at the Aero Club of France, where she was presented with the cross of the Legion of Honor. In letters to friends, she reported that the parties, including the one at the Aero Club, were wonderful, but she was too sick to enjoy them: "They are a blur."[7]

Stubbornly refusing to surrender to pain, she left Paris for Weisbaden, the guest of Air Force General John Cannon. He arranged a flight to Berlin, where another general, William Hall, put her on a Berlin airlift plane. She was eager to see how the ground control approach worked in bad weather and sat on a jump seat between the two pilots. After the pilot recognized her, he let her call in all the positions on the radio. She was delighted. Imperious, even aggressive in so many situations, with experienced Air Force and commercial airlines pilots she was an appreciative and respectful student.[8]

Returning to Weisbaden, she joined Cannon's wife LaVon for a trip to Vienna, but three days later the sickness that she had been fighting finally felled her. She spent ten days in a Vienna hospital with a severe back pain and a high temperature until Cannon arranged a flight to Paris for her. Her friend Howard Hughes, by then president of TWA, ordered his Paris office to put a berth for her aboard a flight to New York.[9] Hospitalized at the Lovelace Clinic in Albuquerque, she had a large abscess in the abdominal wall that adhered to the peritoneum removed during extensive surgery.[10]

To Jackie, a major operation meant postponement, not an end to her European tour. During three months of recuperation, she answered letters from friends, thanking them for their messages of concern and describing her operation in graphic detail. Just as she never forgot an insult, neither did she forget a kindness. For de Sonchen, she had already ordered fifty boxes of streptomycin to be sent to him for a relative in Spain, who was without medication for tuberculosis.[11] She wrote to Air Force Assistant Chief of Staff Lieutenant General I. H. Edwards on behalf of Lieutenant James Callahan, who ran the army hotel in Vienna where she had awaited her flight home. Callahan wanted a transfer to the Air Force, but his request through channels had not been answered. Ignoring protocol, she told Edwards, "If you can properly give this request your personal blessing, I'm sure it will be granted."[12] For Jinx Falkenberg and Tex Rankin she secured two seats on an allegedly sold-out Air France flight, and for her friend former Secretary of War Robert Patterson, she asked President Truman to appoint him to the Supreme Court as a replacement for the late Justice Frank Murphy.[13]

Jackie did not write to Harry M. Durning, the Collector of Customs at New York, who was incensed by her ceaseless efforts to evade paying duty on the designer clothes and other goods that she purchased in France. Instead, Floyd wrote to him, explaining that Jackie had left her maid to fetch the trunks that were arriving by ship and that the maid was ignorant of the rules and thought that she should give a tip. "We have cautioned all our people so that nothing like this will ever happen again," Floyd said.[14] The explanation was accepted.

By late September, after she attended the National Air Races, she was ready to return to France, this time with Floyd. Again she requested de Sonchen to make arrangements, including a two-bedroom, two-bath suite with one sitting room. They were to be met at Cherbourg, with a maid to help them through customs and return to Paris with the luggage by train, while they traveled by car. Because Floyd was not feeling well, and on his first vacation in years, de Sonchen was instructed not to tell even personal friends of his arrival. "I don't want him burdened with social and business appointments which are unnecessary," Jackie wrote.[15]

Floyd left for home after three weeks, but Jackie stayed on until December 5, returning on the *Ile de France*. Her secretary in New York, Florence Walsh, wrote to Durning at Customs House asking for permission for four persons to board on Jackie's arrival—Walsh, Floyd's nurse, Jackie's maid, and a butler. Walsh also enclosed a list of clothing that Jackie had previously purchased from Paris designers and on which she had already paid duty, including two suits, five blouses, five dresses, and four nightgowns with bed jackets.[16]

The following summer, Jackie rearranged her previous itinerary that was canceled by illness. Armed with visas for Sweden, Norway, Denmark, Finland, Russia, Spain, Germany, and England, she arrived in Stockholm in early June to attend the forty-third conference of the Federation Aeronautique International. The purpose of the FAI, a federation of national aeronautical organizations, was to create performance standards for airlines and airfields and to establish rules for the verification of record-setting flights. Already named one of five "members of honor"—the only woman—and the Harmon Trophy's outstanding woman aviator of the decade, Jackie told friends that she was escorted up the stairs to the dinner table by Prince Bernard, right behind the king and queen, and her place at the table was higher than that of any other member except the FAI president.[17]

On this trip, her traveling companion was LaVon Cannon. They sampled Norway, Denmark, and Finland, reaching Russia in mid-June, where they were guests of the American ambassador. On a sightseeing tour in the ambassador's car about eighty miles south of Moscow, Jackie heard the sound of aircraft. Pretending to be ill, she asked the chauffeur to stop and she left the car. Overhead, she saw nine delta-winged planes—"monsters," she said.[18] When she reported the sighting to Air Force intelligence officers, they didn't believe her. Irate, she wrote a magazine article about the planes, but withdrew it, receiving thanks from the director "for the sake of the Moscow embassy's personnel."[19]

From Moscow, she joined Floyd for a trip to Spain, where he had negotiated the sale of a number of Stinson aircraft to the Spanish Air Force. In a typical Odlum move for Consolidated Vultee, he had closed its Michigan factory because of low sales of the small airplanes and union demands, disposing of the excess airplanes in Spain for a profit. Both Jackie and Floyd were enchanted by Spain, Floyd by a dinner given in a house presented to Columbus by Ferdinand and Isabella, and Jackie by an audience with Generalissimo Franco. She thought that the Moorish guards at the palace gate were "even more impressive in a simple but more exotic way than the palace guards at Buckingham Palace." As for Franco, "The title 'dictator' should really be forgotten in connection with Franco," she wrote, claiming that he was not like Mussolini or Hitler, but came to power when the only choice was either Franco or communism. "Like Latin American governments, a tighter central control seems more suited to the Latin temperament," she reasoned.[20]

Floyd left Spain for New York while Jackie went on to Greece and Turkey.

Impressed by royalty, but not intimidated, Jackie advised Queen Fredrica of Greece that she should wet her finger in sherry from a glass she had spilled and rub it behind her ear for good luck. The queen did so. In Turkey at an air show given by the Turkish Air Force, a pilot crashed into the spectators, killing the wife of the air minister. When a doctor in the crowd tried to give an hysterical woman an injection, Jackie offered to help until she saw that it was morphine. Backing off, she told LaVon, "He shouldn't give this woman morphine when she's in a state of shock." Later she added, "She was still breathing, but I think he finished her off."[21]

She returned to the United States in October, but not for long. Air Force chief Hoyt Vandenberg invited her to accompany him on a flight from Washington to New York. When he asked her what she thought of the WAF (Women in the Air Force) program, she told him, "They're a pretty messy looking bunch of females, but I don't know anything about your program." He immediately asked her to accompany him on an inspection tour of American bases in ten countries, to leave in two days. She said that she would go with him, but only if his wife, Gladys, accompanied them. "I don't want to be on the plane with all those men."[22] She would regret the request before the trip was over. "Mrs. Vandenberg nearly drove me crazy. She wanted me to go shopping with her," Jackie said. Jackie told her, "I came on this trip to work. I didn't come to entertain you."[23]

Having said repeatedly that a woman's place was at home with children lest she lose her femininity, Jackie didn't want to be one of them.[24] When she had dinner with General Lauris Norstad, commander of the allied forces in Europe, at the house provided for him by the French government, his fourteen-year-old daughter Kristin said, "My father talked to her like she was a man. He never talked to any other woman like that."[25] The teenager saw Jackie as "a big woman with bright yellow hair and lots of makeup. Her clothes were elegant and her jewelry plentiful—big and gold." Kristin's mother, Isabelle Norstad, a beautiful and gracious woman, described Jackie as "an amazing woman" who wore stylish but not too feminine clothing because she was "very muscular," adding, "she loved jewelry. It was very beautiful, very dramatic."[26]

Vandenberg had placed Jackie on active duty as a lieutenant colonel to serve as special consultant on all women in the Air Force—their procurement, orientation, training, and utilization. He was especially interested in her advice on uniforms and equipment.[27]

On arrival in Weisbaden, she went straight to the WAF headquarters. "I found girls who had been on duty in Europe for six years . . . and I found the darnedest looking mess you've ever seen. They couldn't tell me what work they were doing," she said. She asked for a report before her departure the next day, but never received one.[28]

As she traveled with Vandenberg's team from country to country, Jackie racked up complaints about the WAFs everywhere. They were immoral, sloppy, and inefficient. Never in doubt about her own ability to analyze and solve problems, she assumed an additional task, acting as the medic that Vandenberg had failed to bring along. When his assistant, General William F. McKee, became very ill with a fever of 104 degrees at Alexandria, Egypt, she gave him antibiotics and other drugs from the supply that she always carried with her overseas. She treated others as well, reminding them that she was trained as a nurse even though she hadn't taken the State Board examinations.[29]

On her return to the United States in November, she continued her inspections, visiting base after base, where she frightened and angered both enlisted and commissioned WAFs. In December, she sent Vandenberg a scathing, ten-page report. She described the WAFs at Lackland Air Force base as "the most tattered, bedraggled persons I have ever seen in the services."[30] As an example, she chose one WAF who was four feet, nine inches tall, weighed 134 pounds, and was cross-eyed. The Lackland training center had failed to eliminate recruits who "appeared to be emotionally or hormonally maladjusted."[31]

One of the most capable and well-known officers in the Air Force, Major General Jeanne M. Holm, commented later that if any other woman had made such a report, it would have been lost in the files, but, Holm wrote, "Cochran was the kind of person who could sweep into George Air Force base at the controls of her own C-47 with a perfect three-point landing, toss her fur coat to the nearest colonel, talk over old times with the commanding general, meet a few military women and be off again—all in the space of an hour."[32]

Jackie wanted the WAFs to be not only trim and attractive, she wanted them to be well-educated, an elite corps within the Air Force. Her vision recalled an earlier one for "her girls"—the Wasps—the women to whom she had denied a place in the military with all its benefits, rather than see them as part of the WAC. Since then, she had backed their acceptance as Air Force

Reserve officers, although she continued to disapprove of their having flying status. In a letter to former Wasp Margaret Ann Hamilton, she wrote, "I am so grateful that I finally got the WASP accepted in the United States Air Force Reserve. Already 100 have received their commissions."[33]

Vandenberg acted on Jackie's recommendation by appointing Millicent McIntosh, the president of Barnard College, to head a committee of administrators from twenty women's colleges who met with him at Jackie's New York apartment in early January of 1951. He told them that he did not want WAFs doing menial jobs. WACs could work alongside men, but WAFs would be better employed as technicians or in administrative work.[34]

Their commander, Colonel Geraldine May, did not agree. When she first saw Jackie's memo, she exclaimed, "What do you want us to produce? Beauty queens?" May insisted that WAFs be an integral part of the Air Force, trained to do the same work as men, with the exception of flying.[35]

By June, news of the WAF controversy peaked in the media. Radio commentator Paul Harvey reported, "There's a cat fight in our sidesaddle Air Force, and it's a corker. Tomorrow Colonel Geraldine May will quit before they fire her, and the new commander will take over, Mary Jo Shelly, former commander of the WAVES. Some say this'll make Jackie Cochran the real behind-the-scenes boss of our Women's Air Force." Harvey's report was repeated by Drew Pearson.[36]

May resigned, replaced by Mary Jo Shelly, the former head of the Navy's WAVES and one of the four women whom Jackie had pre-selected.[37] The media storm continued. A typical headline stated, "Glamour Vs. Grease Battle Splits WAFs."[38] WAF officers were reported to be fearing that Cochran's goal would result in the WAF becoming a corps of "beautiful women doing ladylike jobs."[39]

Jackie was in Madrid when the press caught up with her. She had her answers to their queries ready—answers cabled by Floyd on the advice of Harry Bruno. Bruno recommended that the suggestions of the Air Force public relations office be followed. Jackie took the advice. She told newsmen that she hadn't heard of May's resignation. "I've been on a motor trip through North Africa and southern Spain. I haven't read a paper for 12 days." When told of the appointment of Shelly, she said that she knew Shelly and regarded her as "very capable but that is all. I have no comment."[40]

The change in command was followed by accusations that Jackie was paid, as a civilian consultant, $400 for eight days of advice on how to manage women enlistees, recommendations that Air Force officials admitted had not as yet been adopted.[41] The story ran in newspapers from coast to coast. Pentagon officials were pressed to explain why a wealthy cosmetics manufacturer would be paid that much. Jackie was identified as a "famed woman pilot, wife of Floyd Odlum chairman of the board of Consolidated Vultee Corporation," and the charge that he had contributed to the Truman campaign in exchange for the B-36 bomber contract was raised again.

Jackie might have persisted in her attempts to reshape the WAF if her old friend Hap Arnold had been around for advice, but Arnold was dead. She was in Berkeley in January when she found a note in her hotel box. "I hope you are going to have time to come and see us," Arnold wrote. "I'm not feeling very well so I'm not going to come to the meeting." He died the next morning.[42]

Five months passed after Mary Jo Shelly took command of the WAF before Jackie received a letter of thanks for "a splendid job" as advisor on the WAFs. The letter was not from Vandenberg but written on his behalf by his deputy. In answer, Jackie said that she wondered why she was told by the Air Force public relations office to say nothing to the press after the media sided with Colonel May, causing "damaging effects to her personally."[43] The damaging effects to the WAF were probably far greater than any to Jackie. Having thoroughly disrupted the organization, she turned her attention to a new interest—politics.

Twenty-one

Ike

In the pre-election year of 1951, Jacqueline Cochran was asked to be a candidate in the Democratic primaries for the twenty-ninth Congressional District of California. Registered as an Independent, she refused.[1] About the same time, Representative Henry Cabot Lodge, Jr., of Massachusetts traveled to Paris to ask Dwight D. Eisenhower if he would become a Republican candidate in the presidential primaries. Eisenhower, former leader of the Allied forces in Europe and president of Columbia University before becoming commander of NATO, told Lodge that he would think about it.[2] While Eisenhower thought about it, Jackie was advised by Floyd that the Democrats no longer represented her, or his, views. The federal government, he said, was engaged in "wasteful national spending accompanied by destructive taxes and a heavy overburden of bureaucracy.[3]

Jackie agreed with Floyd, but she wanted to enter the political arena. As early as October 1945, while she was in Shanghai, she wrote to Emmett McCabe that if he thought she had a chance in the 1946 elections for Congress, "I might run for my district. . . . It would be wiser to wait until 48 but I wish it was possible in 46."[4] When, early in 1951, she had yet to run for office, John Hay "Jock" Whitney offered her the opportunity to test the political waters as a volunteer. Chairman of the Finance Committee of the Republican Party, Whitney asked her to work with a group that sought the nomination of Eisenhower as the Republican candidate for president. A rally for Eisenhower, who was in Paris and still not certain that he wanted the nomination, was the scheme of Tex McCrary, columnist and radio and television personality, and his wife, Jinx Falkenberg. Jackie later claimed co-chairmanship of the event, taking credit for renting Madison Square Garden for February 8 at 11 P.M. following a boxing program.[5] However, Jackie's recollection differs from those of Virginia Waring. Waring, whose husband, Fred, led the popular orchestra the Pennsylvanians, said, "Fred, Tex McCrary, and George Murphy [film star] organized and arranged the rally. Jackie helped."[6]

Falkenberg was famous in her own right as a fashion model, movie actress, and, with McCrary, originator of the radio talk-show format. To prepare for the rally, she asked Jackie to accompany her to Texas, where they recruited three trainloads of Eisenhower backers and a "cowboy band" from Hardin-Simmons College. Two more bands were booked later, one from Brooklyn and another from New Hampshire. Banners and placards were provided bearing slogans such as "We Like Ike," "Ike's Our Boy," "Draft Ike to Run," and "Taxpayers for Ike." Other banners testified to the support of Eisenhower by businesswomen, veterans, and commuters. Jackie claimed authorship of two slogans—"Holler with the Dollar" and "We Want Ike."[7]

The show was held in the boxing ring, with a roster of stars of stage, screen, radio, and television, some of whom were left waiting awkwardly for missed cues. Ethel Merman sang. So did Mary Martin long distance from London, offering "I'm in Love with a Wonderful Guy," with lyrics suitably altered. She was accompanied by composer Richard Rodgers on piano in the boxing ring. Also appearing were Henry Fonda, Lauren Bacall, Humphrey Bogart, and Steve Allen. Clark Gable introduced Irving Berlin, who sang the theme song that he had written for the campaign, "I Like Ike."[8]

Jackie said later that her plan to use the lingering fight fans to assure a good crowd resulted in the event "getting out of hand for everyone who was working on it, including me. . . . We couldn't get rid of the people already in the garden. We couldn't get the people we had brought here inside the garden. Oh, it was a real mess."[9] A reporter from the *St. Louis Post-Dispatch* agreed with Jackie that it was a mess but denied her claim of throngs trying to get in. He wrote that the 18,000-seat auditorium was not filled to capacity, there was no storming of the gates, and relatively few fight fans stayed for the well-advertised appearance of the stars.[10] Theater critics panned it. Tex McCrary explained to the theater publication *Variety* that he took over the job only after Arthur Godfrey, Milton Berle, George Jessel, Eddie Cantor, Jack Benny, and Ed Sullivan had all backed out.[11]

New York Post columnist Leonard Lyons wrote: "This was the worst produced show ever held at the Garden. . . ." and, on learning that Jackie was to fly to Paris with moving pictures of it to show Eisenhower, said, "She would be wise to dump the film into the Atlantic. For a man of Eisenhower's stature and sensitivity it probably would be most discouraging."[12]

Lyons was wrong. After Eisenhower saw the film, Jackie said, "His whole outlook had changed. I saw tears. It was apparent he had made a decision."[13]

21.1. Jackie with Jinx Falkenberg on the *Tex and Jinx Show*. Falkenberg and her husband, Tex McCrary, were pioneer stars of radio and TV talk shows. A cover-girl model in World War II, she worked with Jackie raising money for the Republican Party during the Eisenhower campaign. (Ann Wood-Kelly Collection, the Woman's Collection, Texas Woman's University, Denton, Texas.)

For the next three months, Jackie was among the Eisenhower backers raising funds and recruiting supporters in the face of predictions that Taft would be supported by most of the party's leaders. The *Kiplinger Letter*, a popular political publication, claimed that the Eisenhower campaign was failing to gain momentum, he was "a candidate in name only," and was needed at home. His backers were poorly organized, bungling their collection of funds, Kiplinger said, while the Taft machine was smooth and well oiled.[14]

Raising funds for Eisenhower did not prevent Jackie from preparing for her next tour of Europe, starting in early May, with the annual FAI conference in Madrid. With her customary attention to detail and her penchant for what she called comfortable travel, she wrote to a French friend asking about availability of parts for the Lodestar that she planned to fly to Europe.[15] She asked an English friend, J. E. Bacon, to process her application for a Customs Carnet.[16] A trunk was to be sent to Paris aboard the *Queen Elizabeth*, sailing on May 6. A three-page list of its contents, compiled by her secretary, Florence Walsh, included eight bottles of scotch; two of bourbon; three pounds of coffee and a coffee pot; twenty-three jars, boxes, and tubes of makeup; and twelve cartons of cigarettes. The liquor was to be packed with boxes of Kleenex, along with a bedboard, canasta cards, golf balls, shirts, and shoes.[17]

Jackie flew the Lodestar to Paris with a copilot, a flight engineer, Walsh, and maid Ellen Haugen, refueling at Presque Island, Greenland, Ireland, and Paris, where she spent a week before going on to Madrid. After the FAI meeting, she returned to Paris to meet Floyd, who arrived by ship with his nurse, Elizabeth Jenkins. Floyd and Jackie joined forces in a combination of business calls and sightseeing, using the Lodestar and bringing along Haugen, Walsh, and Jenkins, as well as a few friends. For eight weeks, the Eisenhower nomination campaign had to get along without Jackie while she toured Grenada, Nice, Rome, Catania, Zurich, and Amsterdam.[18]

Although she missed the later days of the campaign, she intended to take part in the convention in Chicago on July 7. While she was still in Madrid, she wrote to Paul Hoffman, head of the Ford Foundation and an Eisenhower backer, asking him how she might play a role in Chicago.[19] She also wrote to John Hertz, who instructed his Chicago man, Benjamin Weintraub of the Chicago Motor Coach Company, to secure a sergeant's badge for her, which would admit her to any part of the convention hall.[20]

After Eisenhower was nominated on the first ballot, Jackie asked Sherman Adams, governor of New Hampshire, to get her a seat on the podium for Ike's acceptance speech. She got it and a kiss on the cheek from Mamie Eisenhower as the couple left the podium.[21] Eisenhower wrote a letter of thanks to both Jackie and Floyd for their "heart-warming messages" during the convention. It was signed, "Ike."[22] Soon after, Floyd sent a letter to General Lucius Clay marked "Very Personal and Confidential." He told Clay that watching Ike on television the night before he had noticed that Ike had no makeup, "looking drawn and rather pasty." Floyd said that when he had been on television, the studio people put makeup on "his face and bald pate." He was writing this suggestion to Clay, he said, rather than the people handling the campaign—people who had "frozen out the amateurs, hurting the Republican party." It is likely that Floyd meant his favorite amateur—Jackie.[23]

Jackie was again involved in a botched rally for Eisenhower—this time in Los Angeles on October 10. He was to arrive in the afternoon, talk to newsmen at the airport, be driven along a confetti-strewn route lined with cheering crowds, and speak that night at the Pan Pacific Auditorium. Jackie was responsible for pre-arrival publicity, including print, radio, and TV. She was to meet the plane with the media, plan the motorcade route to the hotel, and later, to the Pan Pacific to see that the auditorium was filled with supporters.[24]

But before the rally, Jackie was ousted from the committee in, she claimed, "an untidy incident," probably a clash of wills between her and two other committee members. Whether she or they were at fault, the difficulties in seating encountered at Madison Square Garden were repeated. Two or three thousand blue ribbons designating distinguished guests were mailed. Recipients assumed that they would get a seat if they arrived before 6:45 for the eight o'clock appearance of Eisenhower. But as early as 6:15, the seats were filled and the doors locked, leaving thousands outside, including 500 angry blue-ribbon holders.[25] The *Los Angeles Times* said that 20,000 people were turned away.[26]

In answering a letter from Floyd's friend and hers, Los Angeles lawyer Mendel Silberberg, Jackie said that the California experience was good for her, that she had done some good work, and that the buses that she had chartered to bring supporters to the auditorium saved the day, assuring an overflow crowd. Undeterred by her critics, she was working on a $100-a-plate dinner at the Waldorf Astoria hotel, a fund-raiser for Ike and Nixon, and also on another rally at Madison Square Garden on October 30.[27]

Not all of her efforts were fruitless. Prompted by Jackie, Roy Disney suggested that a group of employees supporting Ike at Disney studios volunteer to design and produce a one-minute spot and a twenty-second spot for television. Jackie arranged a showing for Jock Whitney and Roy Disney at her apartment.[28] Following their approval, 225 prints of the one-minute spot and 210 of the twenty-second spot were shipped to TV stations, which later reported that they were played more than any other Eisenhower television material.[29] Jackie saw to it that individual letters of thanks were sent to each of the fifty-three Disney employees who worked on the project.[30]

As the election neared—with Eisenhower leading Democrat Adlai Stevenson in the polls—Jackie was a special guest at a dinner given by Francis, Cardinal Spellman for the Alfred E. Smith Memorial Fund. She sat at a table on the dais four feet away from Ike. She wore a new evening gown and an Indian rajah's diamond pendant given to her by Floyd, who purchased it from Cartier's. On her wrist was a miniature diamond airplane adorning a bracelet, and on her ring finger a huge, square-cut diamond.[31]

For election night, Jackie and Floyd were at the ranch, where they had a television set installed, only to discover that it didn't work. But they turned on the radio in time to hear Adlai Stevenson concede to Eisenhower. The happy pair went out onto the lawn, shouting and cheering under the desert stars.[32]

Floyd thought that the new administration would approve of the speech that he was preparing to give to the Wings Club of New York in a few days. He was asking that compensation be given to aircraft companies for inflation, with its increasing costs for labor and materials. He also wanted factory workers to work more efficiently, a cut in the number of government bureaucrats, increased research and development of military aircraft, and the purchase by commercial airlines of domestic rather than foreign aircraft.[33]

Jackie was as conservative as Floyd, but she was also eager to be perceived as a friend of the most powerful man in the world—the president of the United States. She had already received telegrams of thanks from him and a letter signed "Ike." She had approached Ike as a political ally. She approached Mamie Eisenhower as the wife of a future president.

Three days before the Chicago convention, she offered to send operators from her beauty salon—"one of the finest in Chicago"—to Mamie's hotel.[34] Two weeks later, Jackie wrote to her again, inviting her and the general to visit the ranch, listing its amenities and suggesting that they make it their first stop after the election. Jackie told Mamie that the ranch was open from October to May and offered a golf course, heated pool, tennis courts, a skeet-shooting range, and riding horses. Of the five guesthouses with private gardens, she hoped that the Eisenhowers would occupy one that had two bedrooms, a living room, and a large garden about a city block from the main house. Promising to invite no other guests until she heard from Mamie, Jackie said that they could enjoy complete privacy, with facilities for any personal staff they might want to bring.[35] The invitation was not accepted then, but laid the ground for continued acquaintanceship if not close friendship with Ike. For the moment, it was enough to be an invited guest, along with Floyd, at the inauguration.

At 46, the former Bessie Pittman had been a guest at two presidential inaugurations.

Twenty-two

The Fastest Woman in the World

In the spring of 1951, while Jackie was in Europe, another Jackie—Jacqueline Auriol—set a new international women's record of 510 miles an hour on a 100-kilometer closed course. In December 1952, she boosted that speed to 534 miles an hour, almost seventy miles an hour faster than Jackie's four-year-old record.[1] In the twenty months that Auriol concentrated on speed, Cochran had spent her time traveling, trying to reshape the WAF, expanding her cosmetics business, and campaigning for Eisenhower. The time had come to do what she loved best, flying—flying for speed, for records, and for international recognition.

Jackie was being challenged by her equal in courage and determination. Eleven years Cochran's junior, Auriol was the daughter-in-law of the French president, Vincent Auriol. The beautiful and wealthy Parisian socialite had resumed flying after a 1949 crash that left her with facial injuries requiring twenty-two plastic surgery operations.[2] As skilled a pilot as Cochran, Auriol had set her records in French, jet-powered military aircraft, the Vampire and the Mistral, while Jackie's last was in a World War II propeller-driven P-51. To challenge the Frenchwoman, she needed a jet plane.

Floyd immediately offered help. Two weeks after Auriol set her first record while Jackie was still in Europe, he wrote to her, sending a list of suggestions for getting the use of a jet-powered aircraft. First, he said, she should ask Vandenberg for an Air Force jet. She could say that, as a lieutenant colonel on active duty and with temporary flying status, she could test the capability of a woman as a jet pilot if needed in wartime. If Vandenberg refused this offer, then, Floyd wrote, perhaps he could get the loan of a jet "from Canada Air [*sic*] or some such name." Otherwise, he said, she might get the Lovelace Foundation to propose research that compared men and women as jet pilots—"you, naturally, to be the woman pilot."[3] Vandenberg had to refuse her request. All American jet planes were owned by the military, and much as he may have admired Jackie, he could not give her flight status when WAF officers were denied it, a restriction that Jackie had once approved.

As it appeared impossible for Jackie to get the use of an American plane, Floyd turned to the Canadians. The U.S. Air Force used the F-86 Sabre, but it was manufactured under license from the North American Corporation in Canada by Canadair, Ltd. Canadair was controlled by General Dynamics. Floyd would buy the use of an F-86 for Jackie. As chairman of the board of both Atlas and Convair (Consolidated Vultee), Odlum negotiated a deal with the chairman of the board of General Dynamics, John Jay Hopkins. Odlum sold 17 percent of Atlas's holdings in Convair to General Dynamics and resigned as chairman of Convair's board, to be replaced by Hopkins. There was no written agreement in the deal regarding Jackie, but before the end of 1952, she became a newly appointed member of the flight test advisory board of Canadair, an eligible test pilot for a Sabre jet with a new Orenda motor.[4] The plane was to be tested by the company before being released to the American Air Force.

Canadair officials suggested that she have a 100-kilometer closed course laid out and certified by the National Aeronautics Association, but the NAA reported that winter weather in Canada would limit the plane's speed. Heat was needed to reach the speed of sound, known as Mach 1.[5] When Jackie asked to use Edwards Air Force Base near Lancaster, California, Vandenberg consented. She was, after all, a test pilot for Canadair, builder of U.S. Air Force jets. With the right plane and the best air base, all she needed was a master pilot of jets to teach her, a chase pilot flying alongside her in constant radio contact. After Vandenberg told Colonel Fred Asconi at Edwards to arrange for her flights, Asconi appointed Major Charles "Chuck" Yeager, the first man to fly faster than sound in the Bell rocket-powered X-1, to be her instructor.

With Jackie's intuitive recognition of the best pilots, she already knew and liked Yeager. They first met in 1947 in Stuart Symington's office when she invited the young Air Force officer to lunch. Recalling the very expensive restaurant, Yeager said that he was first embarrassed and then amused when Jackie sent back half the courses and then marched into the kitchen, "to give the chef hell."[6] But the former country boy from West Virginia recognized in the former poor kid from Florida's panhandle an intelligent and dedicated pilot.[7] Asconi agreed. Years later he remarked, "There are cautious pilots who never know what the plane's maximum performance is and then there are pilots like Yeager and Cochran."[8]

By the time that Jackie arrived at Edwards to fly the Canadair Sabre jet, Yeager, his wife, Glennis, and their two children had already been frequent guests at the ranch, a three-hour drive from the base. They had recovered from their initial awe at the unbridled luxury of the place, with its groves of citrus trees, green grass in the desert, the staff of servants, the golf course, stables, skeet range, and Olympic-size swimming pool. On their first visit, they stayed in the guesthouse where Eisenhower would write his autobiography a decade later.[9]

Yeager the instructor was not intimidated by the mistress of the ranch, the woman of wealth who played poker with generals and called congressmen by their first names. For her first lesson in the F-86, he told her to be at the briefing room at five o'clock for a six o'clock flight. Jackie was in the habit of remaining in bed for breakfast, often remaining there until noon while she dictated letters to her secretary and made telephone calls before taking one of her four daily showers followed by an application of makeup and donning a Paris designer suit. When she appeared that first day at 6:15, Yeager took her into an office, closed the door and told her, "If you want to fly this program you're gonna be on time. . . . Look at the man time you've already wasted for the Air Force, not to mention the guys who are busting their tails for you."[10]

From that day forward, Jackie was on time for the training program designed to make flying a dangerous experimental aircraft as safe as possible. During thirteen days between October 31 and January 9, she made fifty-six takeoffs and landings in an Air Force training plane, the Lockheed T-33. After a break for Christmas and a six-week trip to Europe, she returned to more practice in the T-33 on March 9 of the new year. By April, she was ready for an Air Force F-86 before testing the Canadian model with the new Orenda motor.[11]

For the F-86 flights, she moved into Yeager's home near Edwards, while he went to bachelor officers' quarters on the base and Glennis and the children stayed at the ranch. Before Glennis left, she cleaned the house and waxed every floor only to discover later that Jackie, who brought along her secretary and maid, had all the wax removed for fear that Floyd might slip and fall. It was not the first nor the last time that Jackie would anger Glennis Yeager.[12]

On May 12, Jackie was ready to fly the Orenda-powered Canadian Sabre jet for the first time. She knew the risk that she was taking to reach Mach 1 on the meter in front of her. (The Mach meter was named for Ernst Mach, an Austrian physicist who discovered the ratio between the speed of an object moving through air to the speed of sound in that air.) At that speed, the force of gravity, measured in Gs, caused blood pressure in the head to drop rapidly, or as she put it, "Blood is forced from the head and what is known as a red-out results with almost immediate occurrence of numerous small hemorrhages in the whites of the eyes."[13] A loss of vision follows. To prevent this, she was given a G-suit with rubber tubing binding the abdomen and legs, tubing that would expand as pressure increased, forcing blood back toward her head. She knew that in her initial dive from a high altitude, she needed to execute a special "S" maneuver, almost but not quite straight down lest the plane roll over on its back or break apart, the engine pushing it while gravity pulled it.[14]

She radioed Yeager, who was flying alongside her, "This cockpit is burning me alive." He saw through her canopy that someone had turned on the defroster meant for high altitude. He explained how to shut it down, but the heat had raised the smell of sweat and kerosene in the cockpit and on her parachute—odors that she hated. From that flight on, she fought odors by spraying every cockpit she used with perfume. "Every airplane she flew smelled like a French whorehouse," the laconic Yeager observed.[15] On another flight when she roared over a poultry farm, the loud noise frightened 2,000 chickens. Panicked, the birds rushed to a fence where hundreds smothered in the crush. Jackie had to pay for them.[16]

After two trial flights of the Canadair jet on May 17, she made two more, ascending to 30,000 feet on the first before putting it into a gentle dive, reaching Mach .97 on the meter. On her second flight that day, she climbed slowly all the way to the Mexican border to reach a higher altitude. Turning back toward Edwards, she flew over the ranch so that Floyd could see the plane's contrail of ice crystals formed by exhaust gas striking the surrounding cold air. When Yeager radioed to her asking what she was seeing, she told him that she could see the shock waves rolling off the canopy.[17]

On May 18, one week after her forty-seventh birthday, she was ready to reach Mach 1. Climbing to 45,000 feet in "a dark blue sky" where she could see "the stars at noon," she put the Sabre jet into an "S" dive, radioing her speed on the Mach meter to Yeager—Mach .96 . . . .97 . . . .98. On this flight

22.1. Jackie climbing out of a North American F-86 Sabre jet, the plane in which she became the first woman to break the sound barrier in the summer of 1953. (National Air and Space Museum, Smithsonian Institution, SI 2005–29842.)

as on a previous one when she reached Mach .99, the air became turbulent, first one wing then the other dipped, and once more she saw the shock waves roll off the canopy. Pulling out of the dive at 18,000 feet as she passed Mach 1, the turbulence stopped. She was ahead of sound, flying in an eerie silence. The sound she had left behind hit the ground, two sonic booms in quick succession, strong enough to shatter window panes.[18] Although the Mach meter had recorded her speed, when she learned that the men in the tower had not heard the sonic boom, she took off again an hour later, exceeding Mach 1 twice in the same day.[19]

The first woman to fly faster than sound was not finished for the day. She was determined to set a world speed record for the 100-kilometer closed course that she had paid to have laid out over Rogers Dry Lake bed. The photographic equipment was there at the start and finish of the twelve-pylon course of approximately sixty-three miles, and she had enough fuel to complete the course twice with two minutes left over. Yeager flew chase as she roared around the pylons at 300 feet, the plane at a thirty-degree bank.

22.2. In 1953, while flying a Sabre jet F-86, Jackie became the first woman to break Mach 1, the sound barrier. Congratulating her is Chuck Yaeger *(left)*, her mentor and the first man to reach Mach 1. (Courtesy Dwight D. Eisenhower Library. Photographer unknown.)

Pushing the aircraft to its limit, she felt it begin to roll over on its back and had to pull the throttle to keep the plane from breaking up. But on the first run, she exceeded Asconi's record of 635 miles an hour when she averaged 652.33 miles an hour and broke the sound barrier on the straightaway part of the course. She had also bested Auriol's record by more than 100 miles an hour.[20] As she climbed out of the cockpit, Asconi was there to congratulate her, along with Yeager. Nothing could have pleased her more than the approval of these two great jet pilots.

Jackie was eager to set more records. On May 23, with extra fuel tanks installed on the wings of the Sabre jet, she set another record over a 500-kilometer course (310.5 miles), averaging 590.273 miles an hour. But she had proved that she was a great pilot at a price. After seeing that Yeager and a few of the other experienced jet pilots sometimes flew without their G- suits, she had discarded hers on several of her early flights at Edwards. In spite of her public stance on the need for women to act like women, her carefully applied makeup, bleached blonde hair, and designer clothing, Jackie wanted to be one of the boys—if the boys were pilots. In tests given at Mayo Clinic before her jet flights, she had endured four Gs without blacking out. But she learned at Edwards that a forty-seven-year-old woman with abdominal adhesions from earlier surgery needed a G-suit. In such severe pain that she could not continue the F-86 flights, she entered the hospital in Albuquerque, where her friend Dr. Lovelace prescribed rest in a hospital bed with the foot elevated and three hours of pure oxygen each night.[21]

Six days later, she returned to the base to resume flying.[22] With only four days remaining before the plane had to be returned to Canada on June 2, she attempted to better the record of 698.5 miles an hour for three kilometers set by USAF Captain J. Slade Nash.[23] On her first attempt, the electrical and photographic timers failed. Stopwatches showed 690 miles an hour.[24] On the following day, she tried two passes, but the plane wings dipped, threatening a rollover. Giving up, she had the plane refueled and flew the fifteen-kilometer course, reaching 690 and 680 miles an hour on two runs. On the third try to better the record that she had already set, the plane again started to roll over. After gaining control, she decided to return to the base. Yeager, who was flying chase, saw fuel pouring from the plane's left wing and radioed, "You're a big girl now . . . but you look all wet on the bottom."[25] Smelling fuel, Jackie knew what he meant. Ignited fuel could blow the plane apart. He suggested she bail out, but she refused. She did not intend to lose the Sabre jet. He told her to land on the dry lake bed and she did. Raising the canopy she stood and looked down. It was too far to jump without risking a broken leg. She saw two men in a truck nearby, but when they eyed the fuel leaking from the hot plane they left. Moments later, Yeager landed and ran over to break her fall as she jumped from the cockpit.[26] Two days later, the F-86 was shipped back to Canada.

Before Jackie left the Edwards base, she was the guest of honor at a dinner celebrating her record-breaking flights. Seated at a V-shaped table, Jackie's smile faded when she saw another of Yeager's admirers at the other end, Florence "Pancho" Barnes, a woman whom she despised. Pancho Barnes was the proprietor of the Happy Bottom Riders Club, described by Glennis Yeager as "a desert whorehouse," its customers pilots from the base. Pancho was a pilot, licensed three years earlier than Jackie and a Hollywood stunt flier whose parties were notorious for their mingling of film stars, pilots, liquor, and narcotics. Glennis thought both Jackie and Pancho wished they were men and were bored by women. She observed that Jackie was large-boned with big, strong hands, "But she also had big, beautiful brown eyes and blonde, curly hair. Pancho was a mess."[27]

The dinner marked the end of months of hard work by Jackie, of seemingly endless training flights capped by pushing the Sabre jet to its limits. She had done all that she set out to do, from securing the jet in the first place to test-flying it at a military base with qualified observers. She was the first woman to break the sound barrier and now held all but one of the principal world speed records for straightaway and closed-course flight.[28]

Jackie paid a high price for those records. She was hospitalized again with severe abdominal pain—pain caused by an intestinal obstruction that Dr. Lovelace said would require surgery. Knowing how upset Floyd would be if he learned of the operation, she flew her Lockheed to Albuquerque, was admitted to the hospital, then telephoned Floyd's secretary. She said to tell him that she was going into the mountains to see an old Indian patient of Lovelace's and could not be reached until the next day.

Lovelace operated immediately, assisted by a young doctor, Charles McAdams, who described the procedure as a Noble's plication in which the bowel was "reamed out" and "fixed so that it was one segment instead of a lot of little ones."[29] With a gastric tube into her stomach and unable to eat or drink for five days, Jackie was visited daily by McAdams. "After three days," he said, "she wanted that tube out and she just grabbed ahold of it and jerked it out and called her maid and sent her out for a bottle of whiskey. . . . She called me a few names," he added. "She was a real card. She wanted what she wanted, immediately if not sooner."[30]

Released from the hospital, Jackie faced both praise and criticism for her F-86 flights. Some of the praise was self-generated. In an *American Weekly* story, "I Flew Faster than Sound"—by Jacqueline Cochran as told to Curtis Mitchell—she described herself, very ineptly, as "a sort of Daniel Boone of the air, going into higher speeds and higher altitudes."[31]

Although receiving praise in another article, "The Fastest Woman in the World," in Canada's *McLean's Magazine*, Jackie protested to publicist Harry Bruno that the author claimed that she had attempted to beat Nash's three-kilometer record and had failed. Jackie said that the writer had not even interviewed her, and she denied that she tried to break Nash's record, although it was public knowledge that she had.[32]

Although most of the articles lauded her breaking the sound barrier, her use of Air Force facilities was criticized. *Aviation Week* published a letter from a former fighter pilot who asked how the USAF could justify the money spent on her for T-33 trainers, Sabres, maintenance, fuel, and manpower. Why, he asked, did the Air Force not use one of its own jet pilots? A Pentagon spokesman answered that the "USAF is embarrassed" and "permission came from 'high up.'" She did indeed, he said, disrupt day-to-day flight testing at Edwards.[33]

Both Yeager and Lieutenant Colonel Frank Everest, chief of flight test operations at Edwards, came to her defense. Yeager said, "She had six hours' flying time and only 13 takeoffs and landings [in the F-86] before setting three world records and diving three times past the sonic barrier." Everest wrote to *Newsweek* that he could not see why USAF headquarters should be embarrassed by Cochran's flights that were "semi-official" and of real value. He denied that day-to-day flight testing was disrupted and said that the bill for her F-86 flights was footed by Canadair and Cochran. He said that anything that she owed for the T-33 training was outweighed by her offering, at her own expense, her ranch as a rest camp for pilots during the war and for her service as commander of the WASP.[34]

As always, Jackie Cochran had mixed reviews.

Twenty-three

The Stars at Noon

In the late summer of 1953, not even a major operation could quell Jackie's determination to remain in the public eye. She had already signed a contract to write her autobiography with Atlantic Monthly Press, a division of Little Brown and Company, with Dudley Cloud as her editor. Floyd, who had agreed to help, would actually write most of it from her oral reminiscences, leaving Jackie to pursue pre-publication publicity. Less than three months after breaking the sound barrier, she was still regarded as newsworthy and she intended to remain so, to promote the as-yet-to-be written book.

Finding fault with an article in the magazine *Air Force* that cited her as holding women's records, she wrote to the editor, "My records are men's records," carefully listing all of them. "I am opposed to women's records," she said. "A record is a record, whether made by man or woman and there would not be two."[1]

"Practically, without exception," she claimed, "my records are men's records. For piston engine planes I hold the open class records for 100 kilometers, 500 kilometers, 1,000 kilometers and 2,000 kilometers. For jet engines, I hold the 15 kilometers as well as the 100 kilometer and 500 kilometer records. That takes in all of them except the 3 kilometer in each case. I recently passed up the three kilometer record for jet planes because I could not beat Captain Nash's record in the plane I had and did not want just a woman's record."[2]

Her claims suffered a major blow when, on August 29, three days after Jackie mailed her letter to *Air Force*, Jacqueline Auriol became the second woman to break the sound barrier. Already the winner of the 1952 Harmon Trophy, the Frenchwoman did it in a French Mystere II jet fighter. Her friends said that she would challenge all of Cochran's records as well as attempting the three-kilometer course that proved too much for Jackie. For future record attempts, Auriol had been promised the use of the new Mystere IV by designer Marcel Dassault as soon as the French Air Ministry gave him permission.

After a *New York Herald-Tribune* editorial named Jackie and Auriol as rivals with Auriol in the lead, Jackie wrote a long letter to Helen Rogers Reid, chairman of the paper's board. She told Reid that Auriol pursued women's records and that she did not. Furthermore, Auriol had a better plane than the F-86, while she was "a rider without a horse, unable to use Air Force jets for records." The French government let Auriol fly the prototype of its fastest plane, an aircraft developed with the aid of NATO.[3] Jackie left further defense of her records to Floyd while she spent three weeks visiting department stores on a tour that served a triple purpose. While appearing at cosmetics counters, she could both increase orders for her products, give interviews to reporters eager to write features about her as a businesswoman-aviator, and continue to publicize the upcoming book.

While she traveled, Floyd asked Harry Bruno to come to her defense after E. V. Durling, a columnist for King Features Syndicate, wrote that, of the two women aviators, "At the moment Jacqueline Auriol is on top."[4] Bruno said that Auriol held no speed records at the moment. Although two of Cochran's had just been broken by USAF pilots, she retained the one of 500 kilometers and the woman's record for the 100- and 15-kilometer courses. On September 1, 1953, Captain Harold Collins reached 707.889 miles an hour over 15 kilometers, and the next day, Brigadier General J. Stanley Holtner flew at 690.118 miles an hour on the 100-kilometer course.[5] If Jackie objected to women's records, Floyd and Bruno did not.

A week later, Floyd sent a three-page, single-spaced letter to Bruno complaining about the *New York Times* headline—"Frenchwoman Sets a Flying Mark, Breaks Sound Barrier at 687 M.P.H.; Daughter-in-Law of President Auriol Exceeds Speed Set by Jacqueline Cochran."[6] Headlines like that one were misleading, Floyd wrote. "Madame Auriol—as nice a person as she is—set no new mark and did not better any speed of our own Jacqueline Cochran." Furthermore, he said, Auriol's speed in a dive through the sound barrier could not be compared with Jackie's on a high-altitude-level closed course.[7]

Floyd even suggested to Bruno that he see if the newspapers might agree to telephone their headlines to Bruno for his verification before publication. The publicist rejected Floyd's attempt to control the *Times* headlines, but he did what he could, writing a letter that appeared three days later at the top of the "Letters to the Times" on the editorial page.[8] "The sonic barrier," he wrote, "is an area around the speed of sound defined by Mach 1." But, he explained, Mach 1 varies with the temperature of the air from about 680 miles an hour in cold air to 790 miles an hour or even more in very warm air. There was no "mark" or "record" in Auriol's reaching Mach 1.[9]

While Floyd was defending her records and working on her manuscript, Jackie was traveling again, this time to Asia, with Japan as her first stop. At her departure, Floyd, who was ill, sent her a yellow rose with the message, "The rose carries, as always, my great love for you and my hopes that all your expectations will be more than realized. I'll be traveling with you in my mind." He might well have added, "And working on your book."[10] She was still in Japan when he reported to her that he was "making progress with rest and writing," meaning that he was feeling better and working on the manuscript.[11] Four days later, he wrote again, saying that "the book was so preoccupying me that I was getting no rest, so I mailed it back to the office today for retyping."[12]

After a month's stay in Japan, Jackie completed the remainder of the trip in her customary fashion with one-, two-, or three-day stops in Formosa (Taiwan), Hong Kong, Thailand, Bali, Australia, and the Fiji Islands.[13] In Melbourne, Nancy Bird, a well-known bush pilot, was appointed her aide-de-camp. "She was given the V.I.P. treatment she expected," Bird said. "However, on this trip nothing seemed to please her and her behavior was, at times, extremely ungracious."[14] Worries over the autobiography, Floyd's health, and her own may have contributed to her behavior, but she was acquiring a reputation as an arrogant, impatient, and demanding woman.

If Jackie worked on the manuscript at all, she did it on the road. After Christmas at the ranch, she left again on a six-week trip to London, Paris, and Madrid, returning just in time to be with Floyd, who was scheduled for surgery—a triple operation for gall bladder stones, a double hernia, and chronic appendicitis. While Jackie was visiting him at the hospital, Eisenhower's aide, Paul Hoffman, telephoned her to say that Ike was on a golfing vacation and would like to call on her and Floyd at the ranch. Floyd, accompanied by Lovelace, went home early, eight days after the operation, to meet the president, who stayed for an hour. After Eisenhower left, Lovelace took Floyd to his bedroom, where he removed the stitches. Neither Floyd nor Jackie was about to miss meeting the president of the United States in their own home[15]—it was material for the book.

23.1. Jackie and Floyd were hosts to President Dwight D. Eisenhower at their ranch in Indio. Later, Eisenhower wrote his memoirs there. (Courtesy Dwight D. Eisenhower Library. Photographer unknown.)

Not long after, Jackie was also ill. She summoned a young doctor, Earl A. Thompson, newly arrived in Indio, for a house call. The maid who answered the door told him that Jackie was in the library. As soon as he entered the room, Jackie looked up at him and said, "I'm Jacqueline Cochran and I want a shot of penicillin." He came to attention, clicked his heels, and asked, "How much and where do you want it?" She stared at him for a minute, then sighed, "Let's start over." He went out, closed the door, and knocked. "Come in," she said, then, "I'm Jacqueline Cochran and I don't feel very well." Thompson became her family doctor when she was at the ranch.[16]

While she was still at the ranch, Jackie received a letter from Dudley Cloud. "Your material is first rate," he wrote. "The presentation is not." He said that after her initial success was revealed by chapter 6, she listed one success after another in a boring plateau. "What was driving you on, where were you going, and what did you get from each fragment of your experience?" he asked, offering to insert her answers in strategically placed paragraphs throughout the manuscript. Otherwise, he warned, "The last half of the book is dull." She would lose the reader if she lapsed into listing her triumphs and the great people that she had met. "It sounds like boasting and people are annoyed by boasting."[17]

Either she took the manuscript with her or left it for Floyd to work on because during the following month she was a guest speaker in five cities—Miami, St. Petersburg, Cleveland, Dayton, and Dallas.[18]

Whatever Jackie lacked in literary skills, few authors could have had better publicity than she received before the book was even on the market. On May 21, Jackie and Floyd were on Edward R. Murrow's CBS television program *Person to Person*. Morrow was attracting audiences in the millions interviewing celebrities in their homes. Viewers saw a devoted couple against the background of their River House apartment, its entrance hall shelves filled with trophies and models of the planes that she had flown.[19]

Six weeks after the Murrow show, Jackie was named a Harmon Trophy winner for 1953, along with Chuck Yeager. She won it for being the first woman to break the sound barrier on May 18, 1953, and Yeager won it for piloting the rocket-powered Bell X-1A more than 1,600 miles an hour on December 16, 1953. A *New York Times* picture of them was captioned, "King and Queen of the Air."[20]

Although the book was scheduled for distribution in October, the publisher released excerpts to *Life* magazine in August, headed, "I Reached the Stars the Hard Way—A Great Flier Poignantly Recalls Her First Bleak Earthbound Years."[21] In Jackie's description of those early years, she claimed that she was an orphan, that her foster mother was cruel, and that the family was indifferent to her basic needs. She made no mention of her given name, her marriage to Robert Cochran, and the death of her son. When the magazine requested a childhood photograph of her, her secretary, Florence Walsh, sent one taken with her sisters Mamie and Myrtle, along with the instructions, "As I explained to you on the phone, Miss Cochran does not want the other two girls in any picture you may use in *Life*—only herself."[22]

The article was followed by yet another honor for Jackie when she was awarded the FAI's De La Vaux medal for her contributions to aviation since 1934. She went to the annual meeting in Istanbul to receive it, traveling by way of Paris, London, Athens, and Beirut before accompanying Floyd to Argentina in late September.[23] They brought the galley proofs of the book with them, although when they worked on them is a mystery. Floyd was trying to arrange a business deal with President Juan Perón involving crude oil production, a uranium mining concession, and building atomic power plants. They were the guests of Perón, and Jackie, who had already decided that Franco was a benevolent dictator needed by the Spanish people, thought that Perón was "the acme of courtesy" with "a great warmth of personality."[24]

The book reached the stores that October. Its title, *The Stars at Noon*, was taken from a paragraph in which Jackie revealed more about herself than much of the text. She wrote, "Earth bound souls know only the underside of the atmosphere in which they live. . . . But go up higher above the dust and water vapor and the sky turns dark and up high enough one can see the stars at noon. I have."[25]

Reviews were good, some of them as enthusiastic as one by the *Kirkus Reviews*: "The success story of an era sparkles with the vigor and decisiveness of a great woman and pilot."[26] In spite of Cloud's reservations about the manuscript, the critic for the *Saturday Review of Literature* found that the material following her childhood account was well organized and smoothly presented. "Throughout, of course, Miss Cochran dominates the book," the reviewer wrote, "but she does it with little interpretation or egotism."[27]

Jackie set off on a unique book tour—one in which she not only promoted her book but also Jacqueline Cochran Cosmetics, often doing both at the cosmetics counter of department stores. Flying her Lodestar in ten days in October, she visited ten department stores in the Northeast and Midwest, giving press and radio interviews along the way. After a week's rest at the ranch, she resumed her marketing on the West Coast before moving on to stores in St. Louis and Indianapolis, with a stop at Kansas City for a Camp Fire Girls convention. She was then a member of their board.[28]

Floyd also viewed the book as a marketing tool for Jackie's business. He ordered 300 copies to be sent along to stores. To Jackie's office staff, he sent a detailed version of an insert to be placed in each book—a mix of quotes from the text with praise for her products—and price lists for them. Another 200 books were ordered to be given guests at the ranch.[29]

During the following eight years, 24,000 copies of *The Stars at Noon* were sold. A French-language edition was published in 1955 with a gracious introduction written by Jacqueline Auriol. But Cloud had rated the text correctly. It sounded boastful and the last half was dull.

Twenty-four

Life According to Jackie

Early in 1955, Jackie decided to have a living room fit a rug. The living room was in the main house at Indio, the rug in storage for more than a decade. Originally displayed in the Romanian exhibit at the World's Fair in 1939, the forty-by-fifty-foot carpet was the work of 600 women. When Jackie told her friend Romanian diplomat Radu Irimescu that she wanted to buy it at the close of the fair, he refused, saying that it was to be returned to a Romanian museum. But when the war began in Europe, the rug was put up for auction, and Jackie bought it.[1]

For the revised living room, she hired architect Wil Hanson, a frequent visitor to the ranch after his marriage to Max Constant's widow, Mary, in 1951. Floyd was the trustee of Mary's estate. He approved of the bridegroom, but introducing Hanson, who was not like most of his guests a financier, politician, aviator, scientist, general, actor, or movie producer, was a challenge. He settled on "Mary's artist husband."[2]

Hanson had not seen the rug that was still in its wrapping when the impatient Jackie flew him to Santa Fe to order furniture made by native American craftsmen. She told him that she had a collection of Kachina dolls and Indian rugs and blankets, a theme that she wanted throughout the house. Wondering how all these would look with a Romanian rug, Hanson telephoned the contractor Bud Libbot, who had promised to unpack and inspect the rug after they left. Libbot said that there was no damage to it, but that it was odd looking—"full of square chickens." The "square chickens" proved ideal for Jackie's Indian theme.[3]

Jackie aimed to make the remodeled ranch with its Romanian rug adorned by "square chickens" into a showplace for her expensive tastes. In addition to her Kachina dolls, throw rugs, and wall hangings made by native Americans, she had a dozen silver boxes set with turquoise and semiprecious stones insured for almost $5,000. Among the artifacts that she bought in her travels were three Japanese bronze elephants, a Victorian organ, English Regency book ends, a Sheffield inkstand, a silver dish and two icons from Russia, a pair of elephant tusks from Africa, two eighteenth-century German chairs, and a drawing by Mexican muralist José Clement Orozco. Paintings for the walls included three by Eisenhower, one of them a portrait of Floyd. Altogether, the fine arts collection was insured for more than $100,000 at a time when a new, three-bedroom house in the suburbs of New York City cost $15,000.

The new living room was fifty-by-sixty feet, with massive leather furniture grouped around a fireplace. Three dining tables, each seating ten persons, were at the far end next to the dining room where food was served buffet style. Drinks before dinner were mixed at a bar in the hall at the other end of the room. While Jackie's center of interest was the new carpet, Floyd's was the huge fireplace. At his bidding, Hanson faced it with samples of uranium ore illuminated by tubular black lights hidden under the mantel, a spectacle that drew gasps of awe from guests when the room was darkened. "It was really hokey," Hanson recalled, "and it embarrassed me no end, but it gave Floyd a lot of pleasure which is what counted."[4]

Floyd had been a sailing enthusiast and an avid horseman, but by then he was so crippled by arthritis that he spent much of the day in a wheelchair or in the swimming pool that was heated to 103 degrees. His elbows resting on rubber floats at the edge of the pool, he moved his legs back and forth in the heated water while carrying on his business. Nearby, his secretary, Cecelia Edwards, sat at an umbrella-shaded table on the patio, taking dictation and placing long-distance calls for him through the ranch's telephone switchboard. Visitors who came to the ranch on business had either to squat at the poolside or change into swimming trunks and get into the pool. In addition to Mrs. Edwards, Miss Jenkins, a registered nurse, was in daily attendance, preparing hot packs for Floyd's swollen joints, supervising therapy and medication, and reporting to the doctors who treated him.[5]

Jackie and Floyd had separate bedroom suites. Hers was furnished with a French Provincial bed and lounge chair and had a mirrored dressing room and black-tiled bathroom with a sunken tub and separate shower, its door of etched glass. The walk-in closet was filled with expensive clothing and rows of shoes on shelves. It also held an ironing board for Ellen's use in preparing her employer's wardrobe. Like Mamie Eisenhower, Jackie spent most mornings in bed, dictating letters to her secretary, Margaret Currin, and making numerous long-distance telephone calls.[6]

Although both Jackie and Floyd would deny that they were extravagant, and on occasion both would ask for a strict accounting of charges levied by tradespeople and employees, they lived like the millionaire that Floyd was. When a friend of Jackie's died in an airplane accident and left an estate of twenty million dollars, she remarked, "I knew he had a million or two but I didn't think he was really wealthy."[7]

On one occasion, Wil Hanson drove Floyd to the little airport in nearby Thermal to meet Charlie Steene, one of the two men who had sold Floyd the Hidden Splendor uranium mine. While they waited for Steene to taxi down the runway in his Lodestar, the architect asked Floyd if everyone around him had a Lodestar. "Well," Floyd replied, "we have one. And Charlie has one." He paused for a moment, then added, "And Charlie's mother has one because she won't fly with him."[8]

The residents of Indio liked and admired Floyd, but they either were wary of Jackie or disliked her. Although she employed a chef, she often shopped for food at the Mayfair Market, where the cold room was opened for her to select her vegetables. Dr. Thompson heard that she was so particular that she picked green beans one at a time, adding that he had never known another woman who drove to the market, chose the food, and then had it delivered. At a general store run by a Mr. and Mrs. Gummer, when Mrs. Gummer saw Jackie approaching, she was heard to say, "Oh, God, there's that bitch."[9] She was no more lovable to the control tower personnel at the Santa Fe airport when an Air Force plane crossed her approach to the runway. Passengers in the back could hear her yelling a vulgar protest over the roar of the Lodestar's engine.[10]

Jackie still played golf with Helen Dettweiler, who had laid out the nine-hole course at the ranch, and Beverly Hanson, married by then to Edward Sfingi. Invited to be godmother to their two sons at their baptism in the Episcopal church, Jackie first asked for approval from the local Catholic priest. Having received it, she arrived at the church dressed in her finest Paris suit. The service was a long one. When the rector asked her what she thought of it, she said, "I was afraid my suit would go out of style before it was finished."[11]

Although the rich and the famous were guests at the ranch, there was an inner circle composed of Mike and Benny Howard, Mike and Louise Rosen, Georges and Rosita de Sonchen from Madrid, Chuck and Glennis Yeager, Randy and Mary Lovelace, Harry and Nadia Bruno, and Mabel Willebrandt.

24.1. Beverly Hanson Sfingi *(left)* professional golfer, with Rosalind Russell and Jackie on the course at the Odlum–Cochran ranch in Indio. Golf and gambling at Las Vegas were Jackie's favorite recreations. (Courtesy Patricia Laflin via Beverly Sfingi.)

Vi Strauss, who was still managing the household, was a confidante of Jackie's. Another was Father Charles Depière, a Catholic priest from Spokane and an aviator who flew to his scattered parishioners in a sparsely populated area of Washington State.[12]

Jackie's favorite card game was gin rummy, her favorite partner was Dr. Edward Teller, labeled by the press "the father of the H-bomb." Teller was a colorful fellow, a Hungarian immigrant who had had one foot amputated. He went swimming without his prosthesis, hopping along the diving board on one foot in an amazing display of balance. While suffering from an allergy, he appeared at the breakfast table with tufts of cotton protruding from his nostrils, presumably to arrest the flow of mucus. He played gin with Jackie in a little room off the hall where drinks were served. Their voices rose as they played, his a rumble of heavily accented English, hers an octave higher. She repeatedly protested that he broke the rules. He countered that she made up the rules as they played. Witnesses agreed with him.[13]

A second equally colorful guest was aerodynamicist Dr. Theodore von Karmen. A Hungarian immigrant like Teller, Karmen was already recognized as one of the world's great aeronautical theorists when he fled Hitler's Germany to teach at the California Institute of Technology in Pasadena, where he remained for almost three decades before retiring. He was a short, stout man with frowzy white hair who gave the impression of a fictional mad scientist when he peered through the thick lenses of his rimless eyeglasses. Actually, a gentle, witty man, he was a frequent guest at the ranch. On a day when Floyd asked him how he had spent the morning, he answered, "From 7 to 8:30 I was developing a theory, and from 8:30 until a quarter to nine I proved myself wrong."[14]

Jackie loved visiting the ranch, but seldom stayed more than a few days. Once Hanson had begun to work on the house, she spent the remainder of the spring either in her New York office or traveling for her business before leaving for Europe in June. In May, she received two honorary degrees, a doctorate of law from Elmira College and a doctorate of human letters from Russell Sage. Her first stop was in London to witness the opening of parliament. Enchanted by the ceremony and pageantry, she wrote to the American official who had arranged for her seat, "The queen looked like a fairy queen and I could only have had a better seat by being a Lady, or a Lord, or a Peer."[15] At her next stop in Paris, she attended the fiftieth annual conference of the FAI. She was interviewed by *New York Herald-Tribune* columnist Art Buchwald. She told him that the FAI had abolished women's records, a change in which she no doubt had a hand.[16]

She left Paris for a forty-day African safari "to see the Watusi and the pygmies," an adventure undertaken with her customary attention to creature comforts, including fifteen pieces of luggage and the company of Ellen Haugen.[17] After a week in Cairo and a few days in Addis Ababa, she arrived in Nairobi for an extended safari. In Uganda, a seven-year-old boy came to her camp seeking treatment for a large carbuncle on the back of his neck, which was accompanied by a high fever. After estimating his weight, she gave him half of the adult dosage of codeine with emparin and 400,000 units of penicillin from her well-stocked medicine kit. To open the abscess, she asked the safari guide to use the knives he carried for animal skinning. After he did this, she drained the abscess, applied penicillin powder, and gave the boy a hard candy. Pointing to the sun, she indicated that he should return the next day when she would reopen the abscess and apply more penicillin powder. On the third day, his fever was gone and the wound was healed. His confident, if unlicensed, nurse described the incident in detail years later.[18]

Jackie cut short her safari to meet Floyd in Naples after he had attended a nuclear energy conference in Switzerland. A major player in this new field of uranium production, Floyd had added to the Hidden Splendor Mining Company in Colorado more claims to mines in Utah, Australia, and Argentina.[19] He was going home to close a deal with Howard Hughes, who had already sold the physical properties of RKO Pictures but not the corporate structure that would provide Odlum with $18 million in cash and $30 million in capital losses to offset future taxes. Hughes had agreed in principle to the merger of RKO with four other companies into Atlas. The final settlement was completed by the reclusive Hughes in his limousine, the two men in the back and the chauffeur in front, during a long drive from Indio to Yuma, Phoenix and Kingman before returning to the ranch. Floyd had made Atlas the world's largest owner of uranium ore.[20]

Jackie planned to remain in Europe until mid-October to see to her own business in Paris and in Madrid, where she held the contract for the release of Walt Disney films in Spain. Instead, she was hospitalized for three weeks in Madrid with lobar pneumonia. From her hospital bed, she used a dictaphone to answer her mail. Two of her letters were to her sisters, Myrtle Alford and Mamie Hydle. To Myrtle, she sent fifty dollars for a dental bill.[21] To Mamie, who was complaining of troubled vision, she recommended an ophthalmologist, offering to pay any bills.[22]

Jackie had been sending a monthly allowance to both women for years, but continued to deny that they, or Joe Pittman, were her siblings. Not even after receiving a letter from an admirer in Fort Worth, who wrote, "You were something of a legend when I left DeFuniak Springs. There was a Mrs. Pittman who cared for us when my parents were ill and a Joe Pittman, a neighbor, who I thought were your relatives. Anyway, they were great boosters of yours."[23] Jackie replied, "I knew the Pittmans in DeFuniak Springs—they were probably the same family you refer to in your letter."[24]

In a letter to her friend Randy Lovelace, she asked him to evaluate Mamie both for the need for eye surgery and in a general medical checkup. "I will pay for her medical bills," she said, adding, "Because her mother brought me up, I have looked after this family for years. . . . It was her mother to whom I referred in my book as a 'no good, slovenly woman,' which she was." However, she wrote, if Mamie did come to see him, he was not to let her know that he was Jackie's close friend. "She might be embarrassed if she thought you knew my opinion of her mother etc. [*sic*]."[25]

However, none of her concerns—the Pittmans, the ranch, her aviation career, her business, or Floyd's health deterred her in her pursuit of a new goal, a seat in Congress. In its November column on celebrities, *Time* magazine stated, "Aviatrix Jacqueline Cochran who arrived as a guest of Spain's Air Ministry in September boarded a plane for Paris and tossed a flying helmet that landed in a ring way over in California's 29th Congressional District."[26]

She had been waiting for the right time for ten years. That time had arrived.

Twenty-five

The Candidate

In the fall of 1955, Jackie came home from Madrid already a declared candidate for California's Twenty-Ninth Congressional District. More than a decade had passed since she first entered the political arena as a lobbyist for the militarization of the WASP in 1944, an effort that failed. Believing that Representative Edward Izak's blistering attacks on her and Arnold were responsible for the defeat of the WASP bill, she took aim at Izak. She asked Lieutenant Colonel Emmett McCabe, who had been a congressional aide, to find a candidate who could defeat Izak in the next election. McCabe found one who won the seat, and Jackie wired Izak, "The people of South Dakota are to be congratulated on your return to private life."[1] Jackie had long been fascinated by congressional power. A year later during her post-war tour of Asia, she wrote to Floyd, "If I run for Congress this trip will have great value. I hope to run and that I can win."[2] She even asked McCabe to check on her chances.[3] But Republican John Phillips, who represented the twenty-ninth district, was too popular to take on.

Jackie's chance did not come until the summer of 1955 after Phillips told her that he intended to retire. While she was still on her African safari, she wrote for help from Mrs. Frank Bennett, a Republican activist in Palm Springs.[4] Melba Bennett immediately offered her assistance in raising campaign funds and advised Jackie to enlist a good manager. She also warned her, "Your straight-forward and business-like attitude is perfect but I wonder if you might blow your top if they get nasty which they certainly do. If you can laugh at them instead, it's a cinch."[5]

With Bennett's approval, Jackie chose Harry C. Harper, former campaign manager for Phillips, to direct her bid in the Republican primary election. Although Harry Harper was to be her official campaign manager, Floyd became her political mentor. On the day that she arrived in New York, he sent her a memo asking her to bring to the ranch the letters that Ike had written on running for office and to check the campaign records of other women who had been elected to Congress. He also reminded her to reread a paper she had written on the problems of the district and to save favorable press comments for a composite campaign flier.[6]

Within weeks of her arrival in Indio, she was flying from town to town in her Lockheed Lodestar with her picture painted on the fuselage, covering a district that included 11,000 square miles. "Between now and next March when I shall file my nomination papers for the congressional endorsements from my district at the June primaries I intend to have met and appeared before 10,000 persons in the two counties of the district I hope to represent in Congress," she told the press.[7]

Near the end of January, she wrote to Stuart Symington that she was averaging two or three speeches a day and had talked to "some 4,000 people."[8] Assuming that local voters would be impressed by her nationwide fame, she also accepted speaking engagements outside the twenty-ninth district, like the one in Tulsa, where she was honored by the National Women's Aeronautical Association as "Woman of the Year." A Tulsa newspaper reported that she arrived in her Lodestar loaded with baggage, women, and a copilot, whom she had taxi down the runway so that she could change clothing and comb her "silvery-blonde hair."[9]

Harper arranged for her to meet local voters, but Floyd told her what she should say to them. He gave her lists of questions that she might be asked with the answers that she should give; one of the lists was set in large print so that she could refer to it from the speaker's dais without her glasses. Her platform included protection of existing water rights and the development of new sources for farmers, but she was against fixed price supports. She was for the protection of small business and for organized labor "within limits needed for the stability and economy of the country." She wanted a strong military and foreign air bases, and she was against Communism, One World Federalism, and all "isms" except Americanism.[10]

While Jackie was meeting and greeting voters, Floyd looked for material that might discredit her chief opponent, Democrat Dalip Singh Saund. The fifty-seven-year-old Indian-born Sikh who had become a citizen in 1949 was a successful businessman and popular district judge. Floyd asked Eisenhower's former appointments secretary, Thomas Stephens, a lawyer, whether Saund might be ineligible for office, but Stephens answered that Saund's naturalization oath in 1949 had made him eligible.

Floyd then asked one of his Atlas executives, J. E. Proffitt, to read and review a book, *My Mother India*, which Saund had written in 1930. Proffitt reported that Saund was a Hindu of the Sikh sect that rejected the caste system. The Sikhs believed that all humans were equal, regardless of color, rank, or gender; that women deserve respect; and that no one should harm any living being. Proffitt predicted that Saund would wage a high-level campaign and suggested that Jackie limit hers to three themes: "1) A vote for me is a vote for Ike; 2) Keep America free from foreign ideologies; and 3) Saund believes in lowering immigration barriers, flooding America with cheap Asiatic labor. I don't."[11]

On the eve of March 7, when Jackie was to collect her nomination petition papers from the Riverside County Courthouse, she invited members of the press to dinner at the Riverside Inn and offered them overnight lodging so that they could come with her the next day. Her guests included two from *Life*, two from the *Los Angeles Examiner*, two from CBS television, one from the *San Diego Union*, and three from local papers. The next morning, they accompanied her, first to the courthouse where she picked up the petition forms, then on plane rides to five towns where she collected signatures before returning them to Riverside. Between 9 A.M. and 3:30 P.M., she had done what would take other candidates a week or more.[12] That day, she received nationwide media coverage.

Democrat Saund was not the only threat to Jackie's candidacy. To get her name on the election ballot, she faced considerable opposition from a Republican, Fred Eldridge. A Corona rancher, Eldridge had resigned as the president of the Riverside County Farm Bureau to run on the Republican ticket. When he heard that Jackie had offered to fly Secretary of Agriculture Lloyd Benson in her own plane from San Francisco to El Centro where the secretary was to give a speech, Eldridge wired Benson that the flight would be exploited as his endorsement of Cochran. That endorsement, he said, would disturb other Republican candidates because the farmers were "less repeat less than happy about the Cochran candidacy."[13]

Like Saund, Eldridge had written a book, his about the war in Burma. He wrote that Chinese soldiers were thieves, but so were American servicemen in occupied Germany, who "stripped the Germans of everything they owned—silver, jewelry, cars and radios." Jackie had excerpts from the book with page numbers printed and sent to the local Veterans of Foreign Wars.[14]

Eldridge also belonged to the United World Federalists, a group formed to promote public interest in the United Nations and to eventually develop the U.N. into a world federation. Jackie labeled the organization as subversive and questioned Eldridge's patriotism.[15]

To beat Eldridge in the primaries, Jackie called on outside help from her friend Earl Squire Behrens of the *San Francisco Chronicle*. He told her that Eldridge's backers thought that Jackie would "blow up" when asked difficult questions. They also saw weakness in her reliance on wealthy friends while she neglected low-income voters. Behrens advised her to spend more time in Eldridge's power base of Riverside and to follow up her meetings by immediately signing up supporters.[16]

Behrens's advice was followed by a warning from one of her own campaign workers who did sample interviews with a cross section of voters. A rancher and member of the Republican Central Committee said that Jackie's campaign was "amateurish," with too many coffee hours and teas instead of tours of businesses in small towns. Another criticized her riding around in large cars and an oversized airplane. "Where are the Fords?" he asked. An Indio man said that she was not interested in local people until she wanted to run for Congress and added, "The old man [Floyd] can be vicious. If he gets it in for anyone he'll use his money to break them."[17]

In April, the *Calexico Chronicle* published an editorial headed, "Glamour Is Not Enough." Using *The Stars at Noon*, the editorial said, "From the pages of her own story, the picture is drawn of an immensely ambitious, ruthless individual using an engaging personality as a key for unlocking doors otherwise closed to her or anybody else, using powerful friends to break the rules, using any weapon available to get what her unstable, immature but powerful ego wants."[18]

The editorial left Jackie bewildered, hurt, and angry. Her book had been so well received. Why was it being used against her? What was so wrong about all that she had achieved? She was tired, she told Behrens. "They have me seesawing between Riverside and Indio. I feel like a rubber ball."[19]

Her campaign treasurer, Melba Bennett, wrote to Jackie that she had received reports from Riverside that Jackie was on the defensive, almost belligerent. Bennett told her that she was overtired and looked and acted cross. "That is why you MUST rest." In addition, Bennett said that she had been told that Jackie had remarked at a Young Republican meeting that retiring Congressman Phillips was "not getting around the country."[20] Jimmy Allen, another campaign worker, sent word that Jackie must avoid even by implication any criticism of Phillips.[21]

When Phillips failed to lend his support to Jackie, Floyd considered buying it. He wrote to his friend, Washington, D.C., lawyer George Allen, that he understood the retiring congressman wanted to continue living in Washington, but had no income except a government pension. Jackie would hire him as a consultant for a year or two, Floyd told Allen, "but he should publicly state in due time that he is going to vote for her."[22]

Support for Jackie appeared to come more from outside the Twenty-Ninth District than inside it. In May, *Life* magazine ran a two-page picture story on her, and on May 11, the *New York Herald-Tribune* marked the twentieth anniversary of her marriage to Floyd with a picture of the couple taken in 1936.[23] On May 27, a "Salute to Jackie" barbecue at the Riverside County Fairgrounds in Indio was attended by 6,000 people. The entertainment was headed by Bob Hope and Rosalind Russell, neither of them locals.[24]

Ten days later, on June 6, Jackie won the Republican primary in what the *Riverside Enterprise* described as "one of the most energetic campaigns the district has ever seen." The contest between Jackie and Eldridge was more than energetic, it was bitter and nasty. She bested Eldridge by only 4,000 votes out of 33,000 cast, while Saund swept the boards for the Democrats.

Primaries over, campaign manager Harper sent Jackie a two-page plan for the November election. Saund, he warned, was a persuasive campaigner, supported by the Democratic National Committee and the radical wing of labor. His "whipping boys" would be Jackie's wealth, her lavish campaign, and her connection to the Atlas Corporation. Jackie's big spending had to stop. She needed to check on upcoming fairs and group meetings where she could speak.[25]

Jackie ignored Harper's plan. She continued to gather endorsements from her famous friends, among them Eisenhower's brother Edgar; Generals Barney Giles and George Kenney; and Admirals Adam Kirk and John Reed Kilpatrick, national chairmen of the Citizens for Eisenhower. After her local friend, Mabel Walker Willebrandt, spoke on her behalf to every lawyer and judge in the district, Jackie refused to accept speaking engagements, saying that the end of July to the beginning of August was the only time she could rest.[26] Her "rest" was an assignment to active duty with the Air Force in France and Spain from July 11 to August 7.[27]

On her return, she called on Eisenhower at the White House, had her picture taken with him, and was given a letter of endorsement by him. She used copies of the picture and the letter as campaign fliers.[28]

Among Jackie's supporters outside the district was reporter Dick Habein of the *San Diego Union*. He sent her a long letter describing Saund's campaign strategy. Saund was registering voters and promising rides to the polls and was receiving undercover help from Fred Eldridge. Saund was accusing Jackie of wanting office to help her husband's business interests, of failing to register as a voter from 1935 until 1948, and of spending $54,000 on the primaries to Saund's $11,000. Jackie had also made it easier for him to win minority votes by remarking to an El Centro publisher—off the record, she thought—that Saund's color would make it difficult for him to win support from southern congressmen.[29]

Two days after Habein posted his letter, the *Calexico Chronicle* ran a second, devastating editorial on Jackie, "A Look at Mrs. O." Describing her as the "blonde flyer and wife of [a] multi-millionaire investment trust operator," the editorial claimed that both Saund and Eldridge were well qualified to serve the district, but that Jackie was not. To win, she had spent more than any of the California candidates for Congress. She was "an unstable political novice" who had no contact with the people of the district. And in her twenty-six years of residency, she had never served on a school board, a city council, or a central committee, nor had she participated in the Chamber of Commerce, the community chest, or other civic activities.[30]

In early October, *Time* ran another article, contrasting the campaigns of the two candidates. Jackie drove in her air-conditioned Oldsmobile or flew in her plane. She brought along several changes of clothing, insisting that a rumpled woman could not win votes. Saund drove 26,000 miles in a six-year-old Buick to speak at morning coffees, lunches, and dinners, stopping along the way to talk to field hands and construction workers. She had four professional organizers; he used his wife, son, two daughters, and "a couple of in-laws" in a registration drive that added 6,000 voters to the registry in eleven weeks. In a battle "as hot as the sun," Saund referred to Jackie as "that woman" and she called him "that Hindu." She refused to share a platform with him, saying, "I'm the popular national figure; why should I give him the publicity?" He asked how Jackie could oppose government support of farm prices, but favor them for uranium. She now openly claimed that his color would hinder deals with Southern Democratic congressional leaders.[31]

When Saund predicted victory, a *Time* article reported that local pundits said that "they never underestimate the power of Jackie Cochran."[32] But Jackie was running on nerves and was making mistakes. Melba Bennett wrote a second note to her, telling her to stop worrying about everything and everybody. "If you don't relax, for heavens [*sic*] sake, and smile and give us a pleasant word you are going to have either a bunch of jibbering idiots or a fist full of resignations." Bennett said that Jackie was acting like a spoiled prima donna. "So don't waste your time on being hurt, defending your position or feeling you aren't appreciated."[33] Jackie was doing all three.

As election day neared, Jackie feared that she was losing. With only seventeen days to go until the polls opened on November 6, columnist Drew Pearson renewed his ongoing attacks on Jackie. In his "Washington Merry-Go-Round" column, he called her a "glamor millionairess-aviatrix-cold cream manufacturer" who "flits around the cotton and date ranches of Southern California, piloting her own Lockheed Lodestar, shaking hands, and changing clothes three or four times a day in the sweaty heat of the Imperial Valley." Claiming that she spent $58,000 on her campaign—more than seventy-two other California candidates for Congress—he revived the rumors about Floyd's getting the Consolidated Vultee B-36 contract aided by Jackie and Air Force brass. Like Saund, Pearson asked how Jackie could oppose price supports for farmers while her husband accepted them for uranium. Repeating much of the material in the *Calexico Chronicle*, Pearson said that Jackie and all her millions might be defeated by Saund.[34]

Pearson was right. In the early morning hours of November 7, she learned that Saund had won. Conceding the election in a telegram to Saund she said, "I doubt that the absentee vote will change the presently known results. If you have been elected as our representative in Congress I warmly congratulate you."[35]

Jackie blamed Fred Eldridge for her defeat. When she asked for his support, he had refused it, citing her questioning of his patriotism. In a letter written ten days before the election, she denied his accusation. The only reason that she chose not to make a public statement on the matter was because he or others might think that her motive was political.[36] It was.

Eldridge's answer came the day before the election. He repeated his charge, saying that whether she or the people at her headquarters had raised the question of his patriotism, he held her responsible for it. However, he said, he hoped that they both would be able to forget about "this whole business" after the election.[37]

Jackie refused to forget it. In a bitter, two-page letter to Eldridge she said that the time to forget had been after the primaries and before the election. He had cost the Republicans a seat in Congress. Party leaders would not forget his refusal to support the Republican ticket, even after Vice President Nixon asked him personally. "I want to say in closing," she wrote, "that a personal attack against me of the smear variety was waged by a large group of your supporters in the last days of the primary." The smears, she said, were used by Saund, resulting in her defeat.[38]

Years later when she was asked about her run for Congress, she said, "Yes, and I lost by approximately 700 votes to a Hindu who was born in Panjab [*sic*] India, whom I'm positive was a communist and who got into the country under a fraudulent visa." She said that he avoided arrest until his stay was legal, after Claire Booth Luce introduced a law that made it possible for Asians to become American citizens. Furthermore, Jackie said that Saund was not the man he claimed to be on his passport. "I think it was his uncle."[39] She said that Saund held the seat in Congress for three terms, but was ill during the last year "and the taxpayer's money was keeping the Hindu in a hospital."[40]

But the Hindu had not robbed Jackie of her conviction that careful planning, influential friends, hard work, and courage brought success. She had not dared enough, planned correctly, selected the right influential friends, and worked hard enough. Politics was not the only game in town. She would find another.

Twenty-six

Speed and Space

Within weeks, the defeated candidate returned to her first love—flight. She was determined to set a supersonic speed record and, in the wake of Russia's launching of *Sputnik I* in 1957, to find a role for herself in the American race to catch up with the Russians.

The speed record came first. Her former record in the F-86 was four years old and had been broken in 1956 by Jacqueline Auriol in the French air force Mystique IV. Jackie needed an American Air Force plane, one still denied to women pilots. To get one, she used every contact that she had in Congress, the corporate world, the military, and aviation organizations like the FAI. Elected senior vice president at the 1957 FAI meeting in Majorca, she became president in 1958, in charge of arrangements for the annual meeting that year in Los Angeles. She met the delegates from forty-seven countries in Washington, dined with them there, and escorted them the next day to Fort Worth for a second banquet in their honor. While they spent the night in Texas, she flew ahead to Los Angeles, to check into a suite at the Ambassador Hotel arranged by her two secretaries, Florence Walsh from New York and Margaret Currlin from the ranch. In the suite were items ordered by Jackie, among them a white ermine stole and black purse with a special pocket for documents; her passport and driving license; ten boxes of tissues; a crate of citrus fruit; four bottles of scotch, two of bourbon, one of gin; two small pillows; an electric hot plate; an iron for Ellen, there to help her dress; stationery from the New York office and Indio; and glossy prints of Jackie for distribution to the press.[1]

The new president treated the delegates to a two-hour luncheon and a tour of Disneyland given by her friends Walt and Roy Disney. The visitors also spent a day at the ranch, where Jackie had asked Bob Hoover, a test pilot, to buzz them in an F-100 pursuit plane. In thanking Hoover, she wrote, "Some of the delegates fell into the pool with their clothes on trying to photograph every detail."[2]

The following year when the conference was held in Moscow, Jackie flew her Lodestar there with Yeager as copilot and passengers Currlin, Haugen, and a woman officer from the State Department to serve as her translator. In addition to her extensive wardrobe of designer dresses, she brought twenty-six pieces of jewelry. The jewelry included a four-carat diamond ring, a bracelet with a three-and-a-half-carat diamond and 210 smaller diamonds, and a brooch in the shape of an airplane, the propeller centered with a three-and-a-half-carat diamond. For her medical supplies, she brought dramamine, dexadrine, bandages, throat lozenges, penicillin with disposable syringes, and mystecline.[3]

With Yeager, she flew by way of Spain, where she was feted for a few nights, then to Yugoslavia and Bulgaria. From Belgrade, they were assigned a Soviet navigator who redirected them to Kiev after the Lockheed's wings iced over in a storm over the Carpathian Mountains. Jackie was at the controls, flying in zero visibility through black clouds and buffeted by strong winds. "But," Yeager noted later, "Jackie laid that airplane down right at the end of the runway on one wheel—a great piece of piloting."[4]

Jackie's disapproval of the Russians deepened during her stay in Moscow. "All the Russians did," she claimed, "was drink and make speeches. They never gave you a chance to eat."[5] At dinner, Deputy Premier Anastas Mikoyan, who was seated at her right, told her that he wanted to give a speech before they ate. "Look," she said, "I've done nothing but listen to speeches in three languages. And I've gone without my dinner every night because you never fed me." He ignored her. "Mikoyan got up and talked out of both sides of his mouth for 20 minutes and not even the Russians were polite enough to listen," she said.[6]

At the close of the meeting, the Russians refused her request to fly out of Russia over Siberia and the Aleutians to Alaska, insisting on a route through Bulgaria. In Sofia, officials would not let her cross into Turkey. Furious, she telephoned the chief of the Turkish air force, but after the Bulgarian air marshal, who was listening, heard her say, "these idiots," he said to her, "Madam, you have exactly one hour to leave this country and you will fly to Yugoslavia."[7] She did and from there returned to more receptions in Spain and on to the Paris Air Show, plagued all the way by intestinal pain.

On her return to the ranch in November, she was hospitalized while doctors debated on the need for further surgery. Recovering without it, she accepted an invitation to speak to the Riverside Zonta Club, adding to her letter, "I have just accepted the presidency of the NAA which is the sole representative of the FAI in this country. I am," she boasted, "the first woman president of this organization."[8] With the presidencies of both organizations, Jackie could be certain that the NAA and the FAI would be available to verify any new records that she might set.

To retain her Reserve commission and her contacts in the Air Force, she went on active duty on a ten-day inspection tour with Curtis LeMay, visiting air bases in Belgium, the Netherlands, and Spain. She also did a recruiting film for the WAF.[9] On returning with LeMay, she added to her foreign address book the names of eight generals, Queen Juliana of Holland, and King Baudouin of Belgium.[10]

As a lobbyist for the Air Force, she was so effective that in spite of regulations limiting women officers to the rank of lieutenant colonel, her promotion to the rank of colonel was recommended by the legislative liaison officer. He cited her close association with "certain key personnel on Capitol Hill."[11]

In spite of all her efforts, by 1960 Jackie was still waiting for the Air Force plane that she needed. She did wrangle a ride as a passenger in the rear cockpit of a Navy jet, the A3J Vigilante, becoming the first woman to fly as a passenger at twice the speed of sound, but the pilot was James Pearce, flight-test manager for North American Aviation. Although the press called it a record for Jackie, it was not her kind of record. Pearce reached a speed of Mach 2.02, 1,320 miles an hour, at 47,000 feet.[12]

She had to wait for another fourteen months to fly the plane that she wanted—Jack Northrop's T-38 "Talon." In the summer of 1961, Northrop agreed to her use of a company-owned model, the Air Force gave her permission to use Edwards AFB, and the NAA sent officials to verify records. She arrived at the base on the first day of August, met by Chuck Yeager and NAA officials. Not all the officers there were pleased to see her. To First Lieutenant Henry Steele, she seemed a very demanding, middle-aged woman, her face weathered and her hair bleached. "We were imposed upon," he said, "to set up calibration mechanisms for her to make a speed record. When she left we all breathed a sigh of relief."[13]

Jackie was there for more than two months. Fifteen days and five flights after her arrival, Yeager pronounced her ready to solo. On August 24, with Yeager as her wing man, she set a record for the 15–25-kilometer straightaway course. The next day, she held a press conference at Northrop's factory. CBS television filmed her in the cockpit of the T-38, and wire service photographers took her picture standing beside the plane, helmet under her arm, and not a hair out of place. Between September 8 and October 12, she set seven more records for speed, distance, and altitude in the T-38.[14] Cochran's records included: August 24, speed over 15–25-kilometer straightaway: 842.20 miles an hour; September 8, speed over 1,000-kilometer closed course: 639.38 miles an hour and distance in a closed course: 1,346.36 miles; September 17, speed over 500-kilometer closed course: 680.75 miles an hour; September 18, distance in a straight line: 1,492.39 miles; October 6, speed over 100-kilometer closed course: 784.28 miles an hour; October 12, sustained altitude: 55,253 feet and absolute altitude: 56,071.80 feet. She had bested Frenchwoman Jacqueline Auriol's record of 711 miles an hour by 131 miles an hour.

The woman with influential friends in high places had acquired the plane and the use of an air base. The same woman, a fearless and superb pilot, set the records.

Having restored her claim to be the best woman pilot in the world, Jackie was already seeking a role for herself in manned space flight. In 1958, the Americans had founded the National Aeronautical and Space Administration to monitor research and development of a manned vehicle in their race to overtake the Russians. Jackie was briefed on the medical aspects of space flight by her old friend Randy Lovelace, who had established the Lovelace Foundation for Medical Education and Research at his Albuquerque clinic. She took the extensive physical and psychological tests, but at fifty-five, she could not pass them. However, another woman did—twenty-eight-year-old Geraldine "Jerrie" Cobb, winner of the FAI's Gold Wings in 1959. A veteran pilot who had flown the TF102 Delta Dagger faster than sound, Cobb hoped to become the first female candidate of NASA.

Forced to look elsewhere for a slot in any program for women, Jackie had donated funds to the Lovelace Foundation for the testing of additional women pilots and began actively recruiting them. In an article for *Parade* magazine, she told her readers, "You might become the first woman astronaut who really earned that name."[15] However, she warned applicants that the medical research program for women was unofficial and that NASA would "put at least several men in space over a considerable length of time before they try it with women." To be eligible, recruits had to be under thirty-five years of age,

26.1. Jackie Cochran holds a flight test barograph after setting a new FAI record on October 12, 1961, at Edwards Air Force Base, where she maintained a sustained altitude of 55,253 feet in a Northrop Grumman T-38. (Courtesy Northrop Grumman Corporation.)

in good health, less than five feet, eleven inches in height, and hold an FAA instrument rating and medical certificate.[16]

Of the twenty women who applied for the Lovelace tests, twelve, in addition to Cobb, passed. They were Jean F. Hixon, Myrtle T. Cagle, Bernice Trimble Steadman, Irene Leverton, Geraldine Sloan, Sara Gorlick, Gene Nora Stumbough, Jan and Marion Dietrich, Mary Wallace Funk, Rhea Hurrle Allison, and Jane Hart. But on the day before the women were to leave for a third and last series of tests at Pensacola Naval Base in Florida, NASA notified them that the qualifications had been changed. Candidates had to be pilots of military jets and hold a degree in engineering.[17]

Two of the women, Jerrie Cobb and Jane Hart (Hart was the wife of Senator Phillip Hart of Michigan), protested the change of rules and demanded a hearing before the House of Representatives subcommittee on Science and Astronautics. The testimony of the two was followed by that of John Glenn, first to orbit the earth in February of 1962, five months before the hearing. Glenn said that women were not in the program because of "a factor in our social order."[18] Scott Carpenter, who followed Glenn into orbit, said that "unknowns" had to be eliminated, implying that women were the "unknowns."[19]

In her testimony before the committee chaired by Representative Victor L. Anfuso, Jane Hart said that even if women were not allowed to go into space, their exclusion did not justify cancellation of a research program already begun. While Cobb was being questioned by Representative Joseph Karth of Minnesota, any hopes that she or Hart had of receiving support from the committee were dashed when Anfuso rose to welcome Jackie. Reading from a prepared statement, she said that she did not believe that there had been any intentional or actual discrimination against women in the NASA program. Male pilots who were selected had already proven themselves. To include women, she said, would slow down and complicate an already expensive program.[20] Instead, in a proposal that sounded like a replay of her plan for the WASP, she suggested the creation of a program that included a large number of trainees—not necessarily pilots—to be tested in a single effort with sufficient control over a long period of time. This would afford reliable statistics on the suitability of women as astronauts in the future. It is likely that she envisioned herself as director.

As early as 1961, she probably knew that NASA had no intention of accepting women candidates for the foreseeable future. That summer, during a visit to Dallas, she mentioned the probable cancellation of the final tests for women at Pensacola to one of the candidates, Geraldine Sloan. After Sloan replied that Jerrie Cobb had not notified the group as yet, Jackie "let loose a string of epithets," ending with "Jerrie is not running this program. I am." Although Jackie had paid for the tests given to the women at the Lovelace Clinic, Sloan thought that she was a "self promoter and grandstander."[21]

Another woman in Cobb's group, Bernice Steadman, who admired Jackie, said that she thought the pilots at Edwards AFB had convinced Jackie that women were not wanted in the program.[22] A third woman, Irene Leverton, said later that once Jackie knew that NASA would not support a long-term program, she put an end to it with her congressional testimony.[23] Even before the hearing, Jackie had sent a letter to the editor of *Current Biography* claiming that an article written by Cobb contradicted a statement by NASA director James Webb. Webb had said that there had been no program adopted for women astronauts as yet and that no woman candidate had been selected for training. Jackie added that the Lovelace tests that cost the government nothing were pure medical research—the women who took them, all volunteers.

Webb did appoint Jerrie Cobb special consultant to NASA, but after she spent months traveling around the country as an advocate of the space program, Cobb commented, "I'm the most unconsulted consultant in any government agency."[24] A week later, she was fired, and on June 11, 1963, Webb appointed Jackie to replace her.[25]

Less than a week after Jackie's appointment, Russian Valentina Tereshkova became the first woman in space. *Life* magazine published a story headed, "Soviet Space Girl Makes U.S. Men Sound Stupid." Photographs of all thirteen American women volunteers accompanied it, under the subtitle, "The U.S. Team Is Still Warming the Bench." Claire Booth Luce added an editorial, claiming that "the U.S. could have been first to put a woman in space merely by deciding to do so."[26] Jackie countered with a quote from Gordon Cooper after his Mercury 9 flight: "All this talk about brains and dames [there had been proposals to send scientists as well as women] is bunk. . . . If there had been a scientist on my flight I don't think we would have gotten him back. As for the ladies, to date there have been no women—and I say absolutely no women—who have qualified to take part in our space program."[27]

Too old to be an astronaut and without the directorship of a program for younger women, Jackie was to settle for being a guest at space launchings at Cape Canaveral.

Twenty-seven

Mach 2

Looking for and failing to find a significant role in space exploration while destroying the hopes of thirteen other women took but a fraction of Jackie's time. At fifty-six, she was on a restless search for an undefined goal. In the fall of 1962, she spent two months motoring through Europe on her way to an FAI conference in Greece. To meet Jackie's standards of comfort, she drove a Dodge Rambler, hauling a huge trailer filled with luggage and food. She was accompanied by Vi Strauss, manager of the ranch household, and maid Berthe Schwab.

Starting in Paris, they went through Germany, over the Brenner Pass to Italy, with Strauss noting in her diary, "Set up a kitchen along the way and had a feast of mountain trout, string beans with new potatoes, cucumbers and tomatoes. Wonderful!"[1] Jackie was the cook. At an inn in Trieste where Jackie prepared breakfast in their room, Strauss wrote, "Much better than their food."[2]

In Yugoslavia, the roads were so rough that it took Jackie fourteen hours to drive from Dubrovnik to Uzice. As she approached the town about midnight, a policeman on a motorcycle sped past her, set up a roadblock using a farmer's cart, and delayed her while he examined her papers. When Jackie followed him into the town, he blocked her way again. Anti-Communist, conservative Republican Jackie protested vehemently in a telegram to the president of the Yugoslavian Aero Club, "He insisted I get out of the car and put his hand on my shoulder. . . . He made me turn around under difficult and dangerous conditions with my baggage trailer. . . . I never before suffered such indignities from the police."[3]

Back from Europe and after a short trip to Ethiopia as a guest on a Boeing 720 jet marking the start of a service from Paris to Addis Ababa, she arrived at the ranch for Christmas. She remained there for the first two months of 1963, entertaining friends, flying to Las Vegas to gamble, and playing golf. One of her partners was President Eisenhower, who had accepted Floyd's offer of the use of a ranch guesthouse for his office. The Eisenhowers were passing their winters at the El Dorado Club in nearby Palm Desert and celebrated Christmas Day at the ranch with their children and grandchildren.[4]

Too restless to stay at the ranch any longer, Jackie flew to New York in March accompanied by Ellen Haugen. In a single week, she saw an ophthalmologist, bought clothes and had them fitted at Saks, and inspected her cosmetic plant in New Jersey before flying to Washington. There, she moved into a suite at the Statler Hotel, visited department stores that carried her line of cosmetics, and was presented with an achievement award at an NAA dinner. The following day, in twelve hours, she attended a luncheon and meeting of the board of trustees of George Washington University, then flew back to New York in time to host a cocktail party with Floyd, followed by a tribute dinner for Bob Hope.[5]

In spite of drumming up business in Washington, Jackie had already decided to ease out of the cosmetics business. With Floyd's guidance, she sold 45 percent of the stock, retaining 55 percent and continuing as president and chief executive officer for one more year. The following year, she was to become chairman of the board and a consultant for five years after.[6]

Meanwhile, Jackie's restless search for a significant test of her will and her fame had ended. Five days after the sale, she wrote to Russell Adams, vice president of the NAA, "I have already begun preparation for a series of flights in an extremely interesting aircraft."[7] The plane was Lockheed's F104 Starfighter—the one that she was allowed to fly—a two-cockpit, company-owned demonstrator. There would be no wrangling with the military over her use of an Air Force plane, and Lockheed needed her. Like the B-24 Martin bomber, the Starfighter had a bad reputation among pilots, who called it another "Widow-Maker." Years later when she was asked, "How did you get to fly a military jet?" Jackie replied, "I flew it because it killed about 150 Luftwaffe pilots. When a plane had a little trouble I got to fly it."[8]

After Tony LeVier, Lockheed's chief of test pilots, put Jackie on the company payroll on March 20, she rented a house in Lancaster near the test field at Palmdale, bringing along Ellen and a driver. "Snake" Reeves, the test pilot assigned to coach Jackie, declared her ready to solo after only two flights of less than a half hour each.[9] Any grumbling from other pilots over a woman doing their job soon stopped when she began bringing picnic lunches for them, often including her Southern fried chicken. She also invited them to

27.1. Jackie Cochran steps from the Lockheed JetStar *Scarlett O'Hara* after a record-breaking flight in 1962 from New Orleans to Washington, New York, Boston, Gander, Shannon, London, Paris, and Bonn. (Courtesy Lockheed Martin Corporation and National Air and Space Museum, Smithsonian Institution, SI 80–16081.)

the ranch. Test pilot Robert Gilliland said that the pilots liked her because "She enjoyed talking aviation to the max."[10]

Their respect for her courage and skill in the cockpit soon followed. With permission to push the plane as far as she wanted, she flew it while taking directions from a controller on the ground who told her to skim pylons of smoke at 1,000 feet and to time the flights for the limited fuel capacity. Some of the flights were done with movie cameras in the cockpit to give her Mach numbers and engine temperatures. "I flew it with the red light as to excess temperature on all the time," she recalled.[11] On April 12, she flew the fifteen–twenty-five-kilometer straightaway course at 1,273.109 miles an hour. On May 1, she covered the 100-kilometer closed course in 1,203.686 miles an hour, surpassing Auriol's last record.[12]

Jackie's records brought a flurry of media attention, including two interviews on national television—one on the "Today" show and the other on Mike Wallace's "Personal Closeup." She was asked by the director of the Smithsonian's new Air and Space Museum, Philip Hopkins, to sit for a portrait that was to be placed with those of "famous persons of flight from Wilbur Wright to John Glenn."[13] Jackie was where she wanted to be—"a famous person of flight."

For her annual trip to the Paris Air Show, the Air Force assigned her to accompany a group of senators and congressmen on the presidential plane. They left from Andrews Air Force Base on June 11. Two days later while she was in the Aeronautical Salon at Bourget Airfield outside Paris, she was told that Jacqueline Auriol, flying a Mirage III, had just broken her F104 record by sixty-three miles an hour.[14] On June 13, Auriol flew the 100-kilometer closed course at 1,266 miles an hour. Cochran's May 1 record was 1,203.686 miles an hour.

Rivalry between the two women was news. *Sports Illustrated* magazine published a story headed, "Sweet Explosions in the Air." It cited their different backgrounds, the French aristocrat and the American orphan, but also their similarities. Both had "entered a man's world, facing inscrutable hostility." Jackie had written her autobiography. Auriol's biography was to be published soon. Neither woman would admit to personal rivalry. Auriol said that she made the flight to prove that the French Mirage III was a better plane than the F104 and that when she received the 1952 Harmon Trophy, it was Jackie who had presented her to President Truman. Jackie credited Auriol with helping her to receive the Legion of Honor. But the writer quoted an unnamed source who sat between them at a luncheon and claimed to be a friend of both. "They didn't claw each other over my body. They were so sweet to each other for a half an hour that I thought the place would explode."[15]

If Jackie was just being nice about Auriol's triumph, Floyd was not. In a handwritten letter to "Dearest Jackie," mailed the day after Auriol's flight, he said, "I don't know what the top speed of a 'Delta Wing' Mirage III is but unless it is well over 2 Mach there is some trick to the record just as those who seem to know planes and their speeds think there was about her former record."[16] That fall, he asked Chuck Yeager, who was accompanying some astronaut trainees to Paris, to check the FAI records on the 100-kilometer course that Auriol flew for proof that she followed the same flight path as that of Jackie.[17] Years later, Jackie wrote that she had gone to the FAI to compare Auriol's course with the one that she had flown. Hers resembled a race track, oval in shape, curved at both ends. Auriol's, she said, resembled an open parachute, beginning with the harness, following the shroud lines up and over the top of the chute and down the other side, and ending at the point that it began. Curves cut down on speed. Jackie's course had two, she claimed, Auriol's only one.[18]

Home from Paris in July, she stopped in New York for golf in Long Island and Washington, where she dined with Yeager and James Webb of NASA before leaving for the ranch. During the following twenty days, she flew her Lodestar to Las Vegas; St. Louis; New York; Boston; Springfield, Missouri; and back to Albuquerque. In August, she vacationed in Alaska for two weeks, again flying the Lodestar and returning in time to take Floyd to the Lovelace Clinic and back to the ranch. In October, she flew to Mexico City for a five-day meeting of the FAI. She dined with film star Merle Oberon and went to the races in Acapulco.[19]

It was in the Yukon that a reporter for the *Whitehorse Star* wrote, "Miss Cochran said she doesn't fly simply to go fast. She flies to win."[20] To win meant taking that record from Auriol. Early in 1964, she won the approval of the Air Force to fly the plane that she needed—Lockheed's updated single-cockpit F104G Starfighter—and to fly it at Edwards Air Force Base.

She was fifty-eight years old. During the previous eleven years, her body had been repeatedly subjected to the G forces of sonic speed. Yet she made forty flights in the plane, pushing it past the permitted 121-degree centigrade temperature until the dial rose to 151 degrees centigrade, the red warning light on most of the time. On the 100-kilometer closed course, she flew the aircraft at an eighty-degree angle at a fixed altitude down a corridor one quarter of a mile wide, its inner border sixty-three miles long. To land the aircraft, she had to keep her speed up to at least 225 miles an hour until the wheels touched down before she released the plane's parachute to slow it down on the runway. A power failure while airborne meant a fall of 11,000 feet a minute and certain death.[21]

Between May 4 and June 3, 1964, she set three new records, including one eclipsing that of Auriol. Her speeds were: May 4, 15–25-kilometer straightaway, 1,429.297 miles an hour; June 3, 100-kilometer circular closed course, 1,303.23 miles an hour; and 500-kilometer closed course, 1,135 miles an hour.[22]

The first woman to fly faster than Mach 1 had reached and passed the speed of Mach 2.

Twenty-eight

Jackie's Circus

For the remainder of the 1960s, Jackie's life resembled a traveling circus, with Jackie as the ringmaster. The performers included the Pittman family, Floyd and his relatives, the staff and guests at Indio, Air Force generals, and two American presidents. At a relentless pace, she pursued multiple objectives, seeking help from influential friends just as she had always done.

At the same time that she set a new agenda, she discontinued a number of former items, among them assistance to the two women whom she said were not her blood sisters, Myrtle Pittman Alford and Mamie Pittman Hydle. For more than thirty years, Jackie had been sending monthly checks to them. The feckless Myrtle's were mailed to her children. Her son, Thomas Alford, once reported that he hadn't seen his mother in a week. "She just comes home when the money runs out." On April 10, 1965, the sixty-two-year-old Myrtle died in a Hialeah hospital. She had been working washing dishes in a café, and Jackie's offer to pay for the funeral was refused by Myrtle's husband and children.[1]

Jackie also stopped her payments to Mamie Hydle because she said that Mamie should be receiving Social Security checks and could ask her children for further help. She reminded Mamie that she had sent the Pittmans more than $200,000 in the past. In a lengthy, bitter reply, Mamie accused Jackie of doing more for Myrtle and Joe and their children, while she had never told her own children about Jackie's monthly checks for fear that they would ask for more assistance. Jackie stopped the allowance.[2]

The only intimate relationship that Jackie needed was with Floyd. As he became increasingly handicapped by rheumatoid arthritis, he stayed for most of the year at the Indio ranch, where he was attended by a nurse, a secretary, and a chauffeur. He spent the days in the heated swimming pool or therapeutic bath, but at night, he hosted dinners for neighbors, business associates, and friends, many of whom stayed in the guest houses.

Although Jackie was not in Indio for much of the time, she exchanged daily telephone calls, wires, and letters with Floyd, who often penned answers until he could no longer hold the pen. He reveled in every record that she had made, the publicity that she had received, and the honors that she had been awarded. For his comfort, she hired and fired nurses, maids, gardeners, and cooks, sending them lists of their duties, their working hours, and Floyd's menus. In a continuing search for a good cook and while accompanying Curtis LeMay in 1966 on a tour of the Far East, Jackie took a commercial flight from Taiwan to Hong Kong. There, she rented a hotel apartment with a kitchen for two weeks to try out cooks. She hired two. After interviewing more than 100 applicants, she also hired four maids, a gardener-chauffeur, and a secretary, arranging for their visa applications through friends at the consulate and in Washington.[3]

The cleanliness fanatic was a hard taskmaster, inspecting everything, including the servants' rooms and baths. Two years later, with the Indio staff again depleted, Jackie sent a memo to a housekeeper on trial. The duties of maids were to be scheduled for each day of the week, showing days off, and they were to sign in and out.[4] When that housekeeper proved unsatisfactory, Jackie wrote to the employment agency that she needed a trained, executive housekeeper to supervise the work, keep inventories, and do the marketing. They need not send people with pets, including birds. She did not want couples or anyone who expected to be off every weekend. Under her signature, she wrote, "Stop spending my money for useless phone calls."[5]

While Jackie attempted to assure Floyd's comfort, she also tried with mixed results to be attentive to Floyd's family, although he showed little interest in its members. His two sons, Stanley and Bruce, had been raised by their mother. After the war, Stanley worked for him at the Atlas Corporation, but in 1953, Floyd wrote to Jackie, "Stanley is a mess."[6] Rumored to be a heavy drinker, Stanley had died of hepatitis in 1957.[7]

Bruce Odlum also worked for his father. Family friend Virginia Waring described him as "a renaissance man—artist and pianist, good enough at tennis to play with professional Don Budge, and always wanting to please his father but he never seemed to succeed." In 1967, when his mother, Hortense, was seriously ill in New York, he brought her to his home on the ranch where he lived with his second wife, Judith, and their daughter, Wendy. While he was having a home built for Hortense nearby, he lodged her in a nursing home, but she was so disruptive that the management sent her back to him.[8] Caring for her was a problem. Incompetent and disillusioned, she was certain that she was to be united with Floyd and had to be prevented from meeting him.[9] Hortense died in Indio on January 12, 1971.

Jackie was no help. At a Christmas party for children, one of the guests pointed to Jackie and asked Wendy, "Who's that?" "That's my grandmother," Wendy answered. Jackie heard her, turned to the child and said, "I'm not anybody's grandmother." She also asked Wendy to call Floyd "Uncle Floyd."[10] "Jackie didn't understand children," Mrs. Waring said, "and the Yeagers were reluctant to bring theirs to the ranch."[11]

She was more understanding with Floyd's aunt, Mary Barbour, who lived in Toronto, and with his sister, Marguerite Steele, and Marguerite's son, Arnold. When Marguerite needed surgery, Jackie made the arrangements for it and she offered to hire a private nurse for Aunt Mary when she was ill. During the war, young Arnold Steele, who received orders to report for duty in the Navy, drove his wife, Jean, and daughter, Patty, back to Boulder. On the way, they stopped at the ranch for the night. "The ranch was short of help," Steele said, "but Jackie cooked dinner for us and made up our beds in the guest house."[12]

Jackie's hunger to see all of the world—no matter how remote the place or expensive the trip—was never sated. From September to mid-December of 1964, she traveled first to the Farnborough Air Show in England, then to Paris, staying long enough for first fittings of some designer clothes at Nina Ricci's, before moving along to the Middle East. On a trip down the Nile to Luxor, she was accompanied by Helen LeMay, whose husband, Curtis, was by then head of the Joint Chiefs of Staff in the Department of Defense. After playing golf in Italy and dining in Rome with Francis, Cardinal Spellman, Jackie returned in time to join LeMay on an official visit to Japan.

During the next two years, more and more of her travels would involve attending air shows and the fulfillment of her annual duty as a lieutenant colonel in the Air Force Reserve.[13] After dropping out of LeMay's Far East tour in 1966 long enough to hire servants in Hong Kong, she went to Vietnam with General Hunter Harris. Although she was eager to see the Air Force in action, the best that she could do was one helicopter ride in a Huey on a combat mission forty miles out of Saigon. From there, Harris took her to Manila for a visit with Chuck and Glennis Yeager. She returned to Washington in time to accompany a congressional delegation to another Farnborough Air Show.[14]

Jackie could no longer fly jets, but she passed her tests for a helicopter license during the summer of 1967 at the age of 61. She had become a power in the Air Force—a friend of generals. This was not enough. She wanted to become a power in the White House. A former president was already writing his memoirs at the ranch after accepting an offer of "Office and quarters for self, Mamie, bachelor chauffeur and secretary, Lillian 'Rusty' Brown." In accepting Floyd's invitation, Ike wrote that after seeing Jackie with President John F. Kennedy at the dedication of Dulles Airport, he rushed over to give her a kiss on the cheek. Kennedy said to him, "Well, I gave her a decoration too."[15] Ike had presented her with the Distinguished Service Medal in 1945 and a Harmon Trophy in 1953. Kennedy gave her her fourteenth Harmon Trophy in 1962.

Three weeks after Kennedy was assassinated in November 1963, Jackie sent a telegram of support to Lyndon Baines Johnson. He answered promptly. "Dear Jackie," he wrote, "nothing has meant more to me than the messages from friends like you."[16]

A flurry of letters between Jackie and Lady Bird Johnson followed, and in July, Jackie and Floyd were invited to a Rose Garden ceremony.[17]

Arriving in Washington from Europe on December 14, 1964, when Johnson had been in office only thirteen months, Jackie telephoned the White House requesting an appointment with the president the next day. Her request was denied by his chief of staff, Jack Valenti, who must have been startled by such short notice to gain an audience with the most powerful man in the world.[18]

Jackie wanted a job—a presidential appointment. In a letter to her friend Assistant Attorney General Edwin L. Weisel, she told him that although she was a Republican, most of her friends were Democrats and she was a good friend of the president's. But the job, she said, had to be "in keeping with my capacities, experience and reputation. . . . I am well known in Europe and many parts of the Far East and believe I am qualified to serve as Ambassador in certain countries. Also I could do a good job as an Assistant Secretary of Air. No one not a career officer has as many friends in, or a broader knowledge of, the Air Force than I."[19]

Weisel sent her letter to Jack Valenti, who turned it over to John W. Macy, Jr., chairman of the Civil Service Commission.[20] Macy sent a memo stating that there would be no mission for Jackie. "Those who have worked with Miss Cochran tend to be somewhat reluctant to renew such associations," was

28.1. Jackie and President Lyndon Baines Johnson examine the menu while Floyd Odlum seats Lady Bird at a White House dinner. (Courtesy Dwight D. Eisenhower Library. Photographer unknown.)

his comment.[21] Twenty months later, Macy's assessment of Jackie was more blunt. She was, he said, "an insufferable egotist."[22]

Jackie would not give up. On August 27, Johnson's birthday, she wrote to him that few messages from well-wishers would "pack the same punch as mine because for historical reasons I feel very close to you and having seen you in some darker moments of your health I glory in the vigor that is now yours."[23]

During the next two years, Jackie had two off-the-record meetings with Johnson alone in the Oval Office, one for thirty minutes and a second for one hour.[24] But by February 1968, when she realized that she would get no appointment, she asked Johnson to arrange for her to go to Vietnam on active duty as a reserve air force officer.[25] He refused her request, but two weeks later during a trip to California, he stopped at Palm Desert for a golf game with Ike, followed by an hour's visit by both men to Jackie and Floyd at Indio.[26]

Jackie was ecstatic, boasting, "So far as I can ascertain this is the first time an incumbent president and an ex president have ever paid a joint visit to a private citizen in a private home."[27]

Johnson followed up with an invitation to a White House dinner in April. Floyd was too ill to go, but Jackie accepted. That night, Washington was under a curfew after riots followed the death of Martin Luther King, Jr. Jackie slept at the White House. Only a few weeks later, while she was in Europe, Johnson announced that he would not run for reelection. Refusing to give up on Johnson, she told him of her previous plans to campaign for him, either severing her ties to the Republican Party or working as a Johnson for President Republican.

Her support for LBJ was based as much on genuine admiration as on self-promotion. She saw in him a good old boy from Texas who had the intelligence and will to become the president. Only after she was convinced that he would not run for reelection did she belatedly offer to campaign for the Republicans. In a letter to the head of the Nixon for President campaign, she said that she had refused to work in the primaries because Johnson was "a dear friend of many years['] standing, one of the most abused human beings ever to have served the republic."[28] Her other friend and hero, Ike, died on March 28, 1969, two days before Floyd's seventy-seventh birthday. Instead of their customary celebrity-laden birthday party at the ranch, Jackie attended Eisenhower's funeral service in Washington. Nixon's presidency closed down the political action in Jackie's circus, to be replaced by Air Force duty and lobbying, travel, witnessing space launches, and recognition of her past accomplishments. But a chill wind was creeping under the tent.

Twenty-nine

Grounded

A month before Eisenhower's funeral, Jackie sold her Lodestar and with it her lucky number—N13V. She had always insisted on the transfer of that identification for each plane that she bought, but to the new owner of the Lodestar, she wrote, "Since you bought the Lodestar partly out of sentiment, the number N13V should stay with the aircraft."[1] Jackie sold the plane to dealer Blake Tucket, with the agreement that she would keep the number N13V. Blake sold it to H.M. Hutches, who wrote to Jackie, "I could tell it had been operated properly, with the best of maintenance, and it really hurt me to think that this plane with such a colorful past should be dismantled and sold for junk."[2]

The sale of the Lodestar was a gravestone marking the burial of her days as a pilot, a joy that she shared with Earhart. But her pursuit of recognition continued unabated.

In eighteen days of the previous December, she attended her last White House dinner—one for the astronauts—and went to Kill Devil Hills with Chuck Yeager as the guests of honor at an anniversary celebration of the Wrights' first flight on December 17, 1903. From there, she hurried to Cape Kennedy to witness the launching of Apollo 8. The next day, she was in New York for the wedding of Julie Nixon and David Eisenhower. On December 27, she was in Houston for the recovery of the Apollo capsule before driving to Indio the same day. Early the next morning, she awakened with a high fever and spitting blood. She was hospitalized with bronchial pneumonia. Nurse Jackie should have realized that her aging body could no longer endure the frantic pace that she set for herself, but if she did, she ignored it.

At the ranch that April, she entertained 400 members of the WASP and their guests at their annual reunion. In May, she received the Distinguished Flying Cross after reporting to Washington for active duty in the Air Force Reserve and escorted a group of congressmen to the Paris Air Show. From Paris, she went to Spain, returned to witness the launching of Apollo 11 at Cape Kennedy on July 16, and again moved along to Houston for the splashdown on

July 24. Celebrating the launch, Jackie gave a dinner for fifty guests at a Coco Beach restaurant. George Mueller, associate administrator for manned space flight, asked three of his staff to assist her. One of them, Patricia Newcomer, said that while they placed cards at the tables, Jackie told stories—hangar stories. The only time that Newcomer could ask where the cards belonged was when Jackie stopped to take a breath. "I was a nervous wreck, I, who had been told by my boss that I didn't have a nerve in my body," Newcomer said, adding, "but she was a delightful hostess and when she talked, you listened."[3]

Away from Floyd for months, she wanted his company but not in the heat of an Indio summer. Instead, she arranged a three-week motor tour of Europe and a month's stay in Spain for both of them. After a visit with the Yeagers in Germany where Chuck was the vice commander of Ramstein AFB, Glennis accompanied Floyd on a boat trip down the Rhine while Jackie took a flight back to Los Angeles to attend a dinner honoring the astronauts.

On her return, they set off on the motor tour. Jackie drove. The car was a Chrysler and towed a trailer with 200 pounds of luggage. The passengers were Floyd, a secretary, a nurse, and Jackie's maid, Ellen. In a letter to Chuck, Floyd wrote, "From the time I got off the Rhine boat, one day has been about like the others in that we have traveled anywhere from 2 to 4 or 5 hours a day by car. Jackie enjoys this and sees much in the countryside to interest her, but I was too tired for complete enjoyment." In pain from arthritis, barely able to walk with a cane and bored by the passing scene, Floyd still took a vicarious pleasure in anything that Jackie enjoyed. After staying in Spain at an elegant country club where Jackie played golf, he sailed for home with the secretary, the nurse, and nine pieces of Jackie's luggage.[4]

After seeing Floyd off, Jackie went on another of her high-intensity sightseeing circuits of the world, including, in India, Agra, Fatehpur, and Jaspur and five days on a houseboat in Srinagar; Bangkok; the temples of Angkor Wat in Cambodia; and Hong Kong. She arrived at the ranch in early December. But before she left Spain, she had written instructions for Floyd's newly hired valet. "Certainly he [Floyd] needs certain of his clothes buttoned for him and his trousers tightened around his waist which either I do or Mai-Hing or whoever happens to be handy. . . . I want him [the valet] to learn how to press Mr. Odlum's clothes and to keep them clean and to spot them, and if he doesn't know how to spot them I will get Ellen to teach him when we get home."[5]

Jackie could look after Floyd's health and his comfort, but not his money. Retired, he was no longer the newsworthy tycoon with the Midas touch. He was not broke, but he was less rich. In spite of this, he still financed Jackie's expensive tastes and extensive travels. His happiness continued to rest in her accomplishments, her awards, and her recognition by the press and public. In a Christmas letter in 1969, he wrote to her, "This year my wrist is so unstable that a handwritten letter would be undecipherable. After viewing what is going on in the world of the kooks and the hippies, I have decided to make a specialty of four-letter words. Some come to mind right now in your connection so I will throw them at you. They are:

fine
good
warm
nice
and finally, Love.

"I don't know how many Christmas letters I have written to you but they stretch well over more than thirty years and they each are attempting to tell you how much happiness you have given me in life."[6]

When Donald Henzel at Harvard University's observatory informed Floyd after Jackie's retirement that her friends Lovelace and von Karman were being considered in naming craters on the far side of the moon, Floyd suggested that Jackie's name also be considered. Floyd said that she had been credited by Lyndon Johnson for teaching him the meaning of space and that as a Collier committee member, she was instrumental in gaining the trophy for Lovelace. At that date, the only woman to be honored was Marie Curie.[7]

Two months later, Floyd left the comfort of his heated pool to attend Jackie's interview by two Department of Defense historians. His pleasure in the status given to his wife was not diminished by his listing as "Fred" Odlum.[8] He returned to Washington in June to attend Jackie's official retirement from the Air Force and the presentation of the Legion of Merit to her by the Secretary of the Air Force. Jackie returned his love. A few days before the ceremony, she wrote to their friends Supreme Court Justice Stanley F. Reed and Mrs. Reed, "I have arranged to drive underneath the Pentagon to the elevator going directly into U.S. Air Force Secretary Robert C. Seamons, Jr.'s office so that Floyd will not have to walk this very long distance from the river entrance.[9]

Soon after the reception that followed this latest award, she checked into the Mayo Clinic. The recipient of the DFC and the Legion of Merit had not flown a plane for three months. On her last flight as she approached the landing strip, the muscles in her legs cramped so severely that she had to pull up and circle the field until the pain subsided. At the clinic, she complained of muscle cramping in all her limbs, of frontal headaches, of night sweats, and of gaining weight while eating less. The clinic reported that she bore surgical scars from mammary reduction, from multiple abdominal operations, and from lumbar disc disease. After she also complained of "tightness" in her chest, she was given tests that showed that she had a scar on her heart muscle, but the report said that the duration of her chest pains was not long enough to indicate any treatment.[10]

Jackie was told that she had a mild case of diabetes that could be corrected by reducing her weight from 155 to 140 pounds and that she should stop smoking and get more rest. She went on a diet, but kept on smoking, and her concept of rest included driving a huge Winnebago mobile home through four states, accompanied by Floyd, his nurse, and Ellen.[11] Two weeks after this journey, she was in England at the Farnborough Air Show before circling the globe again with Neil Armstrong and Charles Conrad for an FAI meeting in New Dehli.[12]

On her return, exhaustion evolved into another case of bronchial pneumonia, but by May, she again accompanied a congressional delegation to the Paris Air Show of 1971. She took along ten pieces of luggage, including her golf clubs and a jewelry case with eighteen different pieces: pins, rings, earrings, bracelets, and two watches, most of them adorned with diamonds.[13] There for only a few days, she suffered chest pains so severe that she had to go home. Assuming that all she needed was rest, she refused to see a doctor until she fell unconscious and was taken to a hospital. She had had a massive heart attack, damage that would require a pacemaker, the first of three that she was to have surgically implanted in two years.

Jackie Cochran was grounded. She knew that she could never fly again. At the time, she held ratings on more than a dozen single- and multi-engined land planes including the Convair, DC4, Piper Military Cub, and Lockheed Jet Star—and a rotor helicopter.[14] She faced the loss with action—another motor trip in another motor home, this time without Floyd, for a twenty-one-city drive from Indio to Wichita, Kansas, and back. Her hands were on the controls—if not a plane at least a vehicle that called for an accomplished driver. Every night, she telephoned the ranch employees, asking them to tell Floyd where she was and where she was going. She had given the motor home's license number to the highway police so that they could locate her if Floyd became ill.[15]

That fall, Congressman George P. Miller placed a lengthy paean to Jackie in the *Congressional Record*, titled, "Twentieth Century Renaissance Woman,"[16] and on December 17, 1971, she was inducted into the Aviation Hall of Fame in Dayton, Ohio. Her friend Amelia had been enshrined, but Jackie was the first living woman to be honored.

Too frail to attend the ceremony, Floyd sent her the following message: "A man is lucky who has a wife he loves, or one he admires, or one he respects for character and accomplishments. I am thrice blessed . . . in that I have all three of these values in the same person and heart broken [*sic*] that I can't be with you in Dayton tonight, to bask in your glory."[17]

Floyd's praise and having her name ranked with Amelia's was comforting. But months later after attending a reunion of the WASP at Sweetwater, she reported to former Wasp Florence Marston, "No one will ever know how ill and exhausted I felt at the reunion. It was not only the shock of having the heart problem and surgery but the fact that I knew I would never be able to fly again and this was almost more than I could swallow."[18]

Thirty

The Last Years

Jackie had entered a no-fly zone littered with obstacles—ill health, a waning prestige, and the loss of the Indio ranch. Her stays in the hospital were more frequent and longer, her ailments involving attacks of bronchial pneumonia, intestinal troubles, and failed pacemakers. Floyd had sold the ranch. Her home for more than thirty years and the golf course that Floyd had built "to keep Jackie at home" were both part of a plan for a country-club community of 3,000 condominiums and single-family houses. The sale followed two years of negotiations that involved and alienated his son Bruce, who was the reluctant head of the project.

Early in 1973, Jackie and Floyd had bought a house nearby from William Kerstheimer, who had been foreman of the ranch. The pool for Floyd was smaller, the servants fewer in number, and the dinner parties less frequent, with guests seated at one table instead of three.

Jackie met the new and drastic limitations in her life head-on, lobbying for the Air Force and for a larger national defense budget. At every opportunity, she aired her opinions on women in the Air Force (they should not be admitted to the new Air Force Academy), the women's liberation movement, welfare, modern education, and the conduct of the younger generation—all of which she disapproved. But the first item on her agenda remained travel. Prohibited from commercial flight by the pacemaker, she was limited to the roads of the United States and, in place of her Beechcraft, she drove a motor home. In 1972, she bought a thirty-seven-foot, two-bedroom Travco and took Floyd, his nurse, and Ellen Haugen on a six-week trip to Yellowstone, across Idaho and Oregon, and down the California coast.[1] That December, she drove the Travco to Cape Kennedy to witness the launch of Apollo 17, the last manned space flight to the Moon.

Between trips in her Travco, Jackie was gathering her correspondence, records, files, and scrapbooks with the aim of placing them in a library at a university or museum. Years before, she had been approached for them by the Arthur H. Schlesinger Library at Radcliffe College, where the papers of many prominent American women were held, among them Amelia Earhart's. She dithered until 1968, when Dr. John E. Wickman, director of the Dwight D. Eisenhower Library in Abilene, Kansas, asked her for them. Although there were more than 200 boxes in Jackie's collection, she had been selective. She had removed material relating to her business, the River House apartment, her secretarial staff, her expense accounts, and her work as a director of Northeast Airlines. In addition, there was no material on her childhood and youth, nor any describing Floyd's financing of her activities. She had already been interviewed in oral history sessions at the Department of Defense and Columbia University and was soon to add to those interviews at the U.S. Air Force Academy and the Lyndon Baines Johnson Library in Austin, Texas. The material at the Eisenhower Library would complete Jackie's version of her life and career.

She may have refused the request from Radcliffe because of her often repeated aversion to the women's liberation movement. Fond of Hap Arnold's son Bruce, she offered to assist him in his effort to secure veterans' status for the Wasps, but she was delighted to hear that many of the Wasps disapproved of the women's movement. "I think it's terrible," she said.[2] To a woman who was writing a history of women's struggles to retain their surnames after marriage, she replied that although Floyd urged her to do so, "I have never belonged to or been part of any feminine movement to acquire more freedom for women. In fact I think many women have more freedom than they know how to use." Among the occupations that she thought unsuitable for women were bartender, on-the-beat police work, and foot soldier.[3]

Jackie also disapproved of women as commercial pilots. She claimed that it was too expensive to train them when they would probably marry and have children. As for their continuing to work, she said, "I have no desire to fly behind a pregnant woman."[4] Nor did she want to see women enter the Air Force Academy. Her old friends, retired generals Ira Eaker and Hunter Harris, had given their approval for women cadets, but she continued to insist it was too expensive to train them when most would resign their commission at marriage.[5] In testimony before Congress, she stated that women would be a disruptive force in all of the academies.[6]

Jackie had become a conservative of the far right. When a Chinese-American group asked for her support for the promotion of Air Force Colonel Richard Hum, whom she had befriended in Hong Kong, she wrote, "I don't believe that because one is of an ethnic group of people is justification for promotion in the U.S. Armed Service[s].[7]

Even changes in the Catholic Church upset her—Mass in English and nuns in ordinary dress instead of the habit. She backed the Church's continuing ban on birth control but feared that the people whom she thought fit to bear children would use birth control and the ones who were not fit would not use it. "In fifty years," she wrote to a friend, "we will become a mentally third class nation which we are becoming anyway. We need education and perhaps forced sterilization for certain classes of people."[8]

Jackie was against unions, welfare programs, and raising taxes. She was for drastic increases in appropriations for defense, especially for the Air Force. On a more personal level, Jackie wanted Chuck Yeager to have a Congressional Medal of Honor. "You are the first in my affections after Floyd," she once wrote to him, and to prove it, she was determined to see he received the medal.[9] She wrote on his behalf to Stuart Symington and the senator from West Virginia, Jennings Randolph. Symington told her that there were two problems: it had to be granted within three years of exceptional accomplishment and in the face of the enemy.[10] Eventually, Congress passed a special bill exempting him from these stipulations. Two years later, in 1976, Yeager got the medal. He gave full credit to Jackie for her efforts, claiming that she lobbied everyone from the president on down. But his friend Dick Frost, an X-1 designer, said, "A lot of us thought that the reason Chuck didn't get the regular medal was that Jackie had made too many enemies over the years."[11]

Soon after her initial effort to gain the medal for Yeager, Jackie took Floyd on a month's trip through Utah and Montana to the World's Fair in Seattle and down the west coast. She rented two vehicles—a Pace Arrow motor home and a bus—and took along C. C. "Chuck" Chu, who was both cook and second driver; Helen Grace; a nurse for Floyd; and Ellen Haugen, who had been with her for thirty-seven years. She may have planned the trip to distract Floyd from a serious financial setback. That spring, Bruce Odlum, head of Odlum Properties—created for the development project called Indian Palms—had filed for bankruptcy. A month after their return, a despondent Bruce Odlum committed suicide.

If their income was less, Jackie and Floyd were still living comfortably. He was by then confined to the pool, a special chair at the dinner table, or his bed. A Dalmatian, Spot, was his constant companion. The household staff included a gardener, maid, secretary, and cook. To economize, Jackie resigned her memberships in the Washington Aero Club and the Army and Navy Club. She also complained to the State Board of Nurses' Examiners that after a recent illness, two of the nurses whom she had hired charged her $3 a day for transportation.

Among the last official accolades that Jackie received was one given to her by the U.S. Air Force Academy—a permanent display of her memorabilia, including her WASP uniform and models of Lockheed's Jet Star, F104, and F104G. At the dedication ceremonies on September 10, 1975, she was presented with an Air Force cadet's sword, and the following March, academy historians came to Indio to interview her for an official oral history.[12]

The elation that she felt at being honored by the institution that she respected more than any other—the Air Force—was shattered just three months later by the death of the person whom she loved more than any other—Floyd Bostwick Odlum. She was at his bedside, holding his hand. Dr. Earl Thompson, physician to both Jackie and Floyd, said, "I think when Floyd died a little bit of her died. She never gave another party . . . just like she'd given up on life."[13]

On July 1, 1977, in one of her last public appearances, she was one of two official starters at the thirtieth annual Powder Puff Derby with Milton Coniff, creator of the comic strip "Terry and the Pirates." The temperature was 127 degrees when they rode onto the tarmac in Coniff's Rolls-Royce. Jean Howard Phelan, who went to the car to greet her, said, "She didn't know me. She was out of it."[14]

A year later, Jackie moved again to a modest California ranch house, one of twenty-four on Humming Bird Lane. During the last months of her life when the National Air and Space Museum was preparing an exhibit, "Pioneers of Flight," curator Claudia Oakes went to Indio to interview Jackie. Before Oakes left Washington, she told Louise Thaden, "I'm frightened to death." Thaden replied, "As well you should be." Blanche Noyes added, "You know the only time I thought she was human was when she was with Floyd. She was a different person."[15] But Floyd was gone. So were six other men who had been her friends and mentors—Hap Arnold, Randy Lovelace, Dwight Eisenhower, Alexander Seversky, "Tooey" Spaats, and Lyndon Johnson.

When Oakes arrived at Jackie's house, she was greeted by Chuck Yeager. With Yeager present during the interview, occasionally prompting her, Jackie repeatedly stated that a woman could be as good a pilot as a man and that women should not attempt separate records, but compete with men. As Yeager listened, she said that she had always been treated fairly by male pilots and that her F-86 flight through the sound barrier was the most important event in her professional life.[16]

In the summer of 1980, Jackie's niece, Joe's daughter, Gwen, and her husband, Bud Erickson, went to Indio to see her in the house on Humming Bird Lane where she lived with old friends Yvonne Smith and Aldine Tarter. "She was in a wheelchair and her pacemaker wasn't doing its job. She had so much fluid in her she was swollen and it seeped out of her skin," Gwen said, adding that although Jackie asked about the Pittman family, they did not discuss Jackie's childhood or youth. "It was a taboo subject."[17] Dr. Thompson, who was looking after her, said, "Her legs were cracked and bleeding but she would not go to bed." She told him that she was not going to die in bed. "She sat in that chair and just literally died," he said.[18]

Jackie died on August 9, 1980. Three days later, under a clear blue sky, she was buried in the Indio cemetery. Buried with her in the simple pine coffin were her rosary and the doll that she had won, lost, and regained years later from Willie Mae. She had initially decided to have the Air Force cadet's sabre also buried with her but changed her mind, sending it to the academy for display with her other memorabilia.

The graveside ceremony was conducted by Father Charles Depière of Spokane, Washington, pilot and longtime friend of Jackie's. He had already administered the Roman Catholic sacrament, anointing of the sick, earlier in the summer. Of her long illness he observed, "Such a slow, peaceful exit might have been fine for someone else, but she was bored."[19]

At the grave site were Floyd's grandchildren, Stanley and Wendy Odlum, Chuck Yeager, Aldine Tarter and her husband, Jack, Vi Strauss, Yvonne Smith, Maggie Miller, Mike Rosen, Ann Wood-Kelly, Tony Marimon, and Charles and Jane Shibata. Wood-Kelly said, "It hadn't been planned that way, but the number of those present happened to be 13, Jackie's favorite number."[20]

Two memorial services followed on September 19 and November 6. The first, at Patrick Air Force Base in Florida, was attended by Wasps and members of the Ninety-Nines. The second was held in the Air Force Academy chapel. Yeager and WASP president Lillian Roberts were the speakers, and the academy's superintendent read letters of praise from the Secretary of the Air Force and the Air Force Chief of Staff.[21]

Two years after Cochran's death, at the opening of the National Air and Space Museum's "Pioneers of Flight" exhibit, Claudia Oakes told *Washington Post* reporter Hank Burchard, "She had a personality like sandpaper. She had to be tough to fight her way out of really down-and-out poverty in the Florida panhandle into the sophisticated and expensive world of aviation. Jackie had to be hard." Burchard wrote, "Earhart, having disappeared in the Pacific on an attempted round-the-world flight, was canonized. Cochran was patronized."[22] Burchard should have added that, as a pilot, she was not patronized by the museum that included a display to match that given to Earhart, not by the Air Force Academy, and never by many of the men and women who flew with her.

30.1. Jackie's gravestone in the cemetery at Indio. There were thirteen—her lucky number—mourners in attendance at her funeral. (Courtesy Doris L. Rich.)

30.2. The U.S. Postal Service 50-cent stamp honoring Jackie.

On March 9, 1996, the U.S. Postal Service issued an international airmail stamp honoring Jacqueline Cochran. The dedication ceremony was held at the site of her former ranch in Indio. On the stamp was the title "Pioneer Pilot." The legend on a brass plate marking her grave read:

> Jacqueline Cochran 1906–1980—Colonel U.S. Air Force Reserve
> Leader Women's Air Force Service Pilots 1941–1944
> First Woman in the World to Fly Faster Than Sound.

Little Bessie Pittman would have been thrilled. Jacqueline Cochran might have been satisfied.

Abbreviations

AAFHS #55	"Women Pilots with the AAF: 1941–44." *Army Air Force Historical Studies #55*. USAF Historical Archives. Maxwell AFB, Alabama
CUOH	Columbia University Oral History Collection, Jacqueline Cochran
CVHS	Coachella Valley Historical Society. Papers of Jacqueline Cochran and Floyd Odlum
EL	Dwight D. Eisenhower Library, Abilene, Kansas. Cochran Papers
EL: AF	Air Force Series
EL: AFSS	Annual File Subseries
EL: Articles	Articles Series
EL: ATA	Air Transport Auxiliary Series
EL: ECS	Eisenhower Campaign Series
EL: GEF	General Election File
EL: GES	General Election Series
EL: GFS	General File Series
EL: PPFS	Primary Political File Series
EL: SANM	*Stars at Noon* Manuscript, including material for second autobiography
EL: Trips	Travel file of Jacqueline Cochran
LBJL	Lyndon Baines Johnson Library, Austin, Texas
NASM/Cochran	National Air and Space Museum. Jacqueline Cochran File, unpublished manuscripts from Billie Ayers and Beth Dees
OH/DAF	Department of the Air Force. Interview with Jacqueline Cochran, Washington, D.C., February 25, 1970
OH/USAFA	U.S. Air Force Oral History Interview #44. Jacqueline Cochran. U.S. Air Force Academy, March 11–12, 1976

TWU	Texas Woman's University. Woman's Collection, Mss. 281
WASPH/FW	"History of the Women's Air Force Service Pilots Program and Activities of the AAF Training Command." 220.0721-1. Completed at Headquarters AAF Training Command, Fort Worth, Texas. Research Studies, Institute Archives Branch, Maxwell AFB, Alabama
Wickman OH	Dr. John E. Wickman Oral History. Jacqueline Cochran, March 28, 1968. Eisenhower Campaign Series, Box 1
WPP 6–1262	"Final Report on Women Pilots Program." AAF Report, June–December 1962. Air Force Historical Archives, Maxwell AFB, Alabama

Notes

Chapter 1. Sawdust Road

1. Quinten Waters interview with author at Robertsdale, Ala., Nov. 7, 1998.

2. U.S. Census 1910. State of Florida, County of Escambia, Township of Pine Barren.

3. Ibid.

4. Ibid.

5. Ibid.; *St. Regis News*. Southern Edition. Vol. 2, no. 10. December 1971: St. Regis Lumber Company.

6. Jacqueline Cochran, *The Stars at Noon*. Boston: Little, Brown, 1954, p. 6. (Hereafter: SAN.)

7. Billie B. Ayers, Pensacola, Fla., interview with author, Nov. 9, 1998. (Hereafter: Ayers interview.) Ayers was the daughter of Jackie's older brother Joseph.

8. Dwight D. Eisenhower Library, Abilene, Kansas. Cochran Papers: The Stars at Noon Manuscript, Box 1. (Hereafter: EL: SANM.)

9. Jacqueline Cochran, "I Reached the Stars the Hard Way." *Life*, Aug. 16, 1954, p. 107.

10. *New York Times*, May 12, 1940, Sect. 2, p. 5; ibid., July 13, 1941; numerous others.

11. Ayers interview.

12. Ibid.

13. Jean Waters, Robertsdale, Ala., letter to author, April 14, 2000.

14. SAN, p. 15.

15. SAN, p. 10.

16. *St. Regis News*, December 1971.

17. Jacqueline Cochran and Maryanne Bucknum Brinley, *Jackie Cochran: The Autobiography of the Greatest Woman Pilot in Aviation History*. New York, Bantam, 1987, p. 22. (Hereafter: Brinley.)

18. SAN, p. 11.

19. Ibid.

20. Ibid., p. 19.

21. Ibid., p. 12.

22. Ibid., p. 17.

23. Virginia (Mrs. Fred) Waring telephone interview with author, July 2, 1998.

24. EL: SANM, Box 1.

25. Ibid.

26. Ibid., Box 6.

27. EL: Cochran Annual File Subseries, Box 197. Cochran to Brigadier General Slade Nash letter, Dec. 16, 1969. (Hereafter: EL: AFSS.)

28. SAN, pp. 20–21.

29. Ibid.

30. EL: SANM, Box 6.

31. Ibid.

32. Ayers interview with author, Nov. 9, 1998.

33. EL: SANM, Box 6.

34. Mayo Clinic report, Aug. 20, 1975.

35. SAN, p. 260.

36. Pike's Directory for Columbus, Georgia, 1914–16.

37. EL: SANM, Box 6.

38. Ibid.

39. Ibid.

40. Ibid.

41. Ibid., Box 1. Memorandum to Dudley Cloud, editor, Atlantic Monthly Press, Feb. 20, 1954.

42. Ibid., Box 11.

Chapter 2. Becoming Jackie

1. U.S. Census 1920. Florida Bureau of Archives and Records Management. Vol. 3, E.D. 148, Sheetline 75.

2. National Air and Space Museum, Washington, D.C. Cochran file, including correspondence from Billie Ayers and Beth Dees. (Hereafter: NASM/Cochran file. Ayers/Dees.)

3. Interrogatory submitted to Circuit Court of Montgomery County, Ala. (in Equity). January Term, 1926, in case of R. H. Cochran vs. Bessie Cochran.

4. NASM/Cochran file. Ayers/Dees.

5. SAN, pp. 29–30; Ann Lewis letter to author, July 28, 1998.

6. Ibid., pp. 30–31.

7. Ibid.

8. Ibid.; Ann Lewis letter to author, June 24, 1998.

9. EL: SANM, Box 7.

10. Ibid.

11. EL: AFSS, Box 17. Eli Futch to Cochran letter, May 10, 1949.

12. NASM/Cochran file. Ayers/Dees; Death Records, State of Florida. Robert Cochran Jr. in Walton County. Male, white, 1925. Vol. 267, no. 13758.

13. SAN, p. 32.

14. EL: Articles Series, Box 4. E. A. Smith, Route 2, Bayshore Road, Fort Myers, Florida, letter to *Life*, Oct. 12, 1954.

15. SAN, p. 32.

16. Ibid.

17. Ibid., pp. 32–33.

18. Mobile City Directory, 1927.

19. Interrogatory submitted to Circuit Court of Montgomery County, Ala. (in Equity). January Term, 1926, in case of R. H. Cochran vs. Bessie Cochran.

20. Ibid.

21. Divorce Decree, State of Alabama, Montgomery County. Department of Archives and History ADAH Divorce Index A–R.

22. Brinley, p. 21: Major General Fred Ascani.

23. Mobile City Directory, 1927.

24. Ibid.

25. SAN, p. 6.

26. Pensacola City Directory, 1928.

27. SAN, p. 35.

28. EL: SANM, Box 1.

29. Ibid., Box 7.

30. Ibid., Box 1, p. 37.

31. SAN, p. 35.

32. EL: SANM, Box 1. Cochran memo to Cloud concerning unpublished revised autobiography.

33. Ibid.

34. Ibid., Box 7.

35. SAN, p. 37.

36. Ibid.

37. *Life*, Aug. 16, 1954, p. 107; SAN, p. 46.

38. Brinley, p. 49.

39. Ibid.

40. EL: SANM, Box 1.

41. Ibid.; SAN, p. 37.

42. Ibid.

43. Ibid.

44. Waring telephone interview, July 2, 1998.

45. Brinley, p. 59.

46. Ibid., pp. 59–60.

Chapter 3. Floyd

1. EL: SANM, Box 1.

2. Ibid.

3. Ibid.

4. Brinley, p. 57.

5. SAN, p. 40.

6. *Time*, Aug. 19, 1935.

7. Ibid.

8. Ibid.

9. Coachella Valley Historical Society. Letter from University of Colorado Law School, Sept. 12, 1914. (Hereafter: CVHS.)

10. *Dun's Review*, May 1975, p. 14.

11. *Newsweek*, April 15, 1957.

12. Ibid.
13. *New York Times*, June 18, 1976.
14. *Dun's Review*, May 1975, p. 14.
15. *Newsweek*, May 5, 1934.
16. Ibid.
17. *Time*, Aug. 19, 1935.
18. Forrest Davis. "The Tinker of Wall Street," *Saturday Evening Post*, July 10, 1937.
19. NASM/Cochran file. Otherwise unidentified newspaper clipping bylined Adela Rogers St. John, Oct. 2, 1938.
20. Brinley, p. 68.
21. Hortense Odlum, *A Woman's Place: The Autobiography of Hortense Odlum*. New York: Arno Press, 1980. Reprint of edition published by Scribner, New York, 1939.
22. Ibid.
23. *New York Times*, Jan. 18, 1932.
24. EL: SANM, Box 7.

Chapter 4. Airborne

1. SAN, pp. 41–42; EL: General File Series, Box 260, Log Books. (Hereafter: EL: GFS); Columbia University Oral History Collection. Jacqueline Cochran, p. 4. (Hereafter: CUOH.)
2. CVHS: Floyd Odlum, "The Aviation Sequence."
3. *New York Times*, Aug. 2, 1932.
4. EL: GFS, Box 260.
5. Ibid.
6. CVHS: Floyd Odlum, "The Aviation Sequence."
7. *U.S. Air Services*, January 1938, p. 25.
8. Brinley, p. 59.
9. EL: GFS, Box 260.
10. *New York Times*, Aug. 14, 1932.
11. SAN, p. 43.
12. Ibid.
13. Ibid., pp. 43–44.
14. *New York Times*, Aug. 14, 1932.
15. Ibid., Aug. 26, 1932.
16. SAN, pp. 44–45.
17. EL: SANM, Box 9.
18. Ibid.
19. SAN, p. 45; EL: SANM, Box 1.
20. Brinley, p. 84.
21. EL: SANM, Box 1.
22. EL: Articles Series, Box 2. Jacqueline Cochran: "Flights and Fancies" manuscript. (Hereafter: EL: Articles.)
23. Ibid.
24. EL: SANM, Box 13.
25. Richard Sanders Allen, *The Northrop Story, 1929–1939*. Atglen, Pa.: Schiffer Publishing, 1995, p. 39. (Hereafter: R. S. Allen.)
26. *U.S. Air Services*, January 1938.
27. Donald C. Ferguson, letter to author Jan. 4, 1999.
28. SAN, p. 46.
29. EL: SANM, Box 1. Frank E. Wigelius, Captain USN (Ret.), letter to Cochran, October 1954.
30. EL: SANM, Box 7.
31. *U.S. Air Services*, January 1938.
32. SAN, p. 48.
33. Ibid.

Chapter 5. Transport Pilot

1. EL: SANM, Box 1; SAN, p. 48.
2. Brinley, p. 31.
3. Ibid.
4. Ayers interview.
5. Texas Woman's University, Woman's Collection, Mss. 281. (Hereafter: TWU.)
6. *Honolulu Advertiser*, Aug. 10, 1939.
7. Judith Odlum, Irvine, Calif., interview with author, Oct. 18, 2000. (Hereafter: J. Odlum interview.)
8. EL: SANM, Box 1.
9. NASM/Cochran file. Ayers/Dees.
10. EL: GFS, Box 260. Log Books.
11. EL: AFSS, Box 1. Mrs. Rex Terry to Cochran letter, March 23, 1955.
12. Ibid. Cochran to Terry letter, March 31, 1955.
13. NASM/Cochran file. Ayers/Dees.

14. Ibid.
15. EL: GFS, Box 260.
16. SAN, p. 49.
17. SAN, pp. 49–50.
18. *U.S. Air Services*, January 1938, p. 28.
19. EL: Articles, Box 2. "Flights and Fancies."
20. *New York American*, Dec. 9, 1933.
21. SAN, p. 50.
22. EL: SANM, Box 7.
23. SAN, p. 56.
24. J. Odlum interview, Oct. 18, 2000.
25. EL: AFSS, Box 199. Cochran to Howard Stern letter, Feb. 17, 1974.
26. SAN, p. 56.
27. EL: GFS, Box 260.

Chapter 6. Three-Time Loser

1. Brinley, p. 100.
2. EL: AFSS, Box 2. Floyd Odlum to Major General B. D. Foulois, Chief of the Army Air Corps, Washington, D.C., letter, May 1, 1934.
3. EL: AFSS, Box 1. Odlum to Granville, Miller, and DeLackner letter, May 15, 1934.
4. R. S. Allen, p. 39.
5. R. S. Allen to author, letter, July 26, 2000.
6. *New York Times*, May 31, 1934.
7. *Aero Digest*, June 1934.
8. R. S. Allen, p. 40.
9. F. M. S. Miller. "From England to Australia." *Western Flying*, November 1934.
10. Ibid.
11. EL: AFSS, Box 2. Unsigned summary of personnel, Aug. 18, 1934.
12. Miller. *Western Flying*, November 1934.
13. *New York American*, Aug. 29, 1934.
14. R. S. Allen, p. 41.
15. Ibid.
16. EL: AFSS, Box 3. Willebrandt to Cochran letter, Oct. 6, 1934; Richard S. Allen letter to author, July 26, 2000.
17. Brinley, pp. 104–6.
18. Ibid.
19. Brinley, p. 110.
20. EL: AFSS, Box 3. Willebrandt to Cochran letter, Oct. 6, 1934.
21. Ibid.
22. Ibid.
23. CUOH, p. 8.
24. SAN, p. 53; CUOH, p. 8.
25. EL: AFSS, Box 3. Associated Press dispatch from Mildenhall, England, Oct. 17, 1934.
26. *New York World-Telegram*, Oct. 18, 1934.
27. EL: AFSS, Box 3. Cochran press release, undated.
28. Brinley, pp. 110–12.
29. SAN, p. 54.
30. EL: AFSS, Box 2. Universal press release, Oct. 22, 1934.
31. Ibid.
32. Ibid.
33. SAN, p. 54.
34. Ibid.
35. EL: AFSS, Box 2. Cochran to U.S. Customs Department letter, Feb. 27, 1935.
36. EL: AFSS, Box 6. Cochran description of Gee Bee, May 24, 1939.
37. Ibid.
38. EL: GFS, Box 195. Cochran letter, undated.
39. EL: Articles, Box 8. Odlum to Jack S. Harris letter, Sept. 4, 1962.
40. SAN, p. 55; EL: SANM, Box 1.
41. EL: AFSS, Box 1. Cochran to Willebrandt, Dec. 18, 1934.
42. EL: AFSS, Box 1. Granville to Cochran letter, Dec. 31, 1934.

Chapter 7. In a Holding Pattern

1. SAN, p. 257.
2. Ibid.

3. EL: AFSS, Box 5. Ninety-Nines Newsletter, May 15, 1942.
4. Ibid. Cochran to Rivoli letter, Aug. 16, 1954.
5. Brinley, p. 119.
6. EL: AFSS, Box 5. Undated notes.
7. *Indio Daily News* (Calif.), Sept. 28, 1972.
8. EL: Eisenhower Campaign Series, Box 2. Cochran to Mamie Eisenhower letter, July 24, 1952. (Hereafter: EL: ECS.)
9. SAN, pp. 47–48.
10. *Indio Daily News* (Calif.), Sept. 28, 1972.
11. NASM/Cochran file. Ayers/Dees.
12. Ibid.
13. EL: SANM, Box 7.
14. Beverly Sfingi, La Quinta, Calif., interview with author Oct. 27, 2000.
15. Brinley, pp. 88–89.
16. Ibid.
17. EL: AFSS, Box 2. Smith to Cochran letter, March 16, 1935.
18. Gamma G2 records sent to author by Richard S. Allen, July 26, 2000.
19. Earhart Collection, NASM Library. Doris L. Rich, *Amelia Earhart, A Biography*. Washington, D.C.: Smithsonian Press, 1989, p. 181. (Hereafter: Rich.)
20. Ibid.
21. SAN, p. 62.
22. CUOH, p. 20.
23. Ibid.
24. Don Dwiggins, interview with Paul Mantz, May 13, 1964.
25. Richard S. Allen to author letter, July 26, 2000; *New York Times*, Aug. 31, 1935.
26. SAN, p. 63.
27. CUOH, p. 18.
28. EL: Articles, Box 5. Undated clipping from *Parade*; SAN, pp. 63–64.
29. CUOH, p. 19.
30. Ibid., pp. 19–20.

Chapter 8. Pygmalion and Galatea—with Wings

1. *New York Times*, Oct. 8, 1935.
2. Virginia (Mrs. Fred) Waring telephone interview with author, July 2, 1998.
3. *New York Times*, Jan. 13, 1970.
4. SAN, p. 7.
5. Chuck Yeager and Leo Janos, *Yeager: An Autobiography*. New York: Bantam Books, 1980, p. 214. (Hereafter: Yeager.)
6. J. Odlum interview, Oct. 18, 2000.
7. Wood-Kelly interview with author. Manchester-by-the-Sea, Mass., Aug. 10, 1998.
8. Yeager, p. 216.
9. Ibid., pp. 220–21.
10. Brinley, p. 126.
11. Clerk of Superior Court, Mohave County, Ariz., Certified Abstract of Marriage, Sept. 1, 2000.
12. Bill and Violet Kersteiner interview with author, Oct. 24, 2000.
13. *Time*, Aug. 19, 1935.
14. J. Odlum interview, Oct. 18, 2000.
15. U.S. Air Force Oral History Interview #44. Jacqueline Cochran, March 11–12, 1976, p. 131. (Hereafter: OH/USAFA.)
16. CVHS: Floyd Odlum, "Aviation Sequence," p. 3; Wood-Kelly interview.
17. Brinley, p. 69.
18. Arnold Steele interview with author, May 18, 2002.
19. *National Aeronautics*, February 1938.
20. Brinley, p. 152.
21. *Indianapolis Star*, July 4, 1936.
22. *New York Times*, July 13, 1941.
23. SAN, p. 74.
24. *Los Angeles Times*, May 5, 1976.
25. *Indianapolis Star*, July 11, 1936.
26. EL: SANM, Box 7.
27. *New York Herald-Tribune*, Sept. 2, 1936.
28. Ibid., Sept. 5, 1936.

Chapter 9. Jackie and Amelia

1. CUOH, p. 25.
2. EL: SANM, Box 11.
3. Rich, p. 229.
4. Ibid., p. 160.
5. EL: GFS, Box 233. Cochran and Odlum Oral History: Stern, Feb. 17, 1974.
6. Rich, p. 228.
7. EL: Articles, Box 1.
8. Ibid.
9. Ibid.
10. SAN, p. 86.
11. Ibid., pp. 88–89.
12. *New York Daily News*, Feb. 16, 1937.
13. SAN, p. 89.
14. Ibid.
15. EL: Articles, Box 1. "The Amelia I Knew."
16. NASM/Cochran file. Ayers/Dees.
17. EL: GFS, Box 233.
18. Ibid.
19. Ibid.
20. Rich, pp. 237–38.
21. Ibid., p. 249.
22. Ibid., p. 234.
23. Ibid., p. 241.
24. CUOH, p. 33.
25. *New York Times*, March 21, 1937.
26. CUOH, Ben Howard. Vol. 2, pp. 64–67.
27. Rich, p. 238.
28. EL: GFS, Box 233. Cochran and Odlum Oral History: Stern, Feb. 17, 1974.
29. SAN, p. 91.
30. Claudia Oakes interview with Cochran, May 20, 1979.

Chapter 10. Up, Up, and Away!

1. SAN, p. 75; *Indianapolis Star*, July 14, 1936.
2. EL: AFSS, Box 3. Olive Beech to Cochran letter, June 10, 1937.
3. SAN, pp. 245–46.
4. EL: AFSS, Box 3. Hawks to Odlum letter, July 7, 1937.
5. Ibid.
6. *Los Angeles Times*, July 29, 1937.
7. *National Aeronautics*, 1937.
8. Ibid.
9. EL: GFS, Box 195; Box 6; CUOH, p. 13.
10. CUOH, p. 14.
11. *New York Times*, Sept. 4, 1937; *U.S. Air Services*, January 1938.
12. Ibid.
13. CUOH, p. 14.
14. Ibid.
15. EL: SANM, Box 7.
16. CUOH, p. 15.
17. Ibid.
18. CVHS: Undated paper by Floyd B. Odlum, p. 4.
19. CUOH, p. 15.
20. Ibid.
21. Ibid.
22. *New York Times*, September 1, 1937.
23. EL: SANM, Box 9.
24. CUOH, p. 16.
25. *New York Times*, September 26, 1937.
26. Ibid.
27. *Detroit News*, September 21, 1937.
28. CUOH, p. 14.
29. EL: AFSS, Box 5. Mantz to Cochran letter, November 18, 1937.
30. Ibid.
31. Ibid.
32. *New York Herald-Tribune*, November 22, 1937.
33. EL: SANM, Boxes 7 and 9.
34. Ibid., Box 7.
35. *New York Times*, December 4, 1937.
36. Ibid.
37. EL: SANM, Box 9.
38. Ibid.
39. CVHS: Undated paper by Floyd Odlum.

40. EL: AFSS, Box 4. Cochran to F. William Zelcer letter, November 2, 1937.

41. Ibid., Box 3. Cochran to Dick Blythe letter, December 29, 1937.

42. *National Aeronautics*, December 1937.

43. Ibid.

44. *U.S. Air Services*, January 1938.

Chapter 11. First Lady of the Air Lanes

1. EL: AFSS, Box 4. Cochran to Winthrop Rockefeller letter, April 6, 1938.

2. Ibid., Box 5. M. Howard to Cochran letter, undated.

3. Ibid. M. Howard to Cochran letter, Jan. 24, 1938.

4. *New York Times*, Feb. 18, 1938.

5. Ibid.

6. Ibid., Feb. 20, 1938.

7. Ibid.

8. EL: AFSS, Box 5. Nichols to Howard telegram, Feb. 21, 1938.

9. EL: AFSS, Box 5. Agreement between Cochran and Seversky, March 12, 1938.

10. Ibid.

11. Ibid.

12. Ibid. Cochran to M. Howard letter, March 13, 1936.

13. *U.S. Air Services*, May 1938.

14. Rich, p. 259.

15. EL: AFSS, Box 5. Cochran to Mantz letter, April 11, 1938.

16. Ibid.

17. Ibid. Odlum to MacFadden letter, July 25, 1938.

18. Ibid. Radio script, April 12, 1938.

19. Ibid.

20. SAN, p. 15.

21. EL: SANM, Box 1.

22. EL: AFSS, Box 4. Cochran to Tex Rankin letter, May 24, 1938.

23. Bird, Nancy. *My God! It's a Woman: The Autobiography of Nancy Bird*. Sydney: Angus & Robertson, imprint of HarperCollins, 1990, p. 39. (Hereafter: Bird.)

24. EL: AFSS, Box 5.

25. Ibid. Nicholson to Olive Beech letter, June 22, 1938.

26. EL: SANM, Box 6.

27. Ibid.

28. Ibid.

29. *Western Flying*, September 1938.

30. EL: AFSS, Box 4. Cochran to Constant letter, Aug. 16, 1938.

31. Ibid., Box 5. M. Howard to Cochran letter, undated.

32. Ibid. Cochran to M. Howard letter, Aug. 22, 1938.

33. Brinley, pp. 158–59.

34. Ibid.

35. EL: AFSS, Box 4. Lovelace to Frye letter, Aug. 23, 1938.

36. Ibid. Cochran to Danton Floyd letter, Aug. 16, 1938.

37. Ibid., Box 5. Odlum to Cochran telegram, Aug. 29, 1938.

38. Ibid.

39. Ibid. Aug. 31, 1938.

40. *U.S. Air Services*, October 1938.

41. Ibid.

42. EL: SANM, Box 9.

43. Brinley, pp. 163–64; EL: Articles, Box 2. "Medical Aspects of Women as Pilots."

44. SAN, pp. 65–66; *Western Flying*, May 1939.

45. *Newsweek*, Sept. 12, 1938.

46. *Popular Aviation*, December 1938.

47. *Newsweek*, Sept. 12, 1938.

48. EL: AFSS, Box 5. William Enyart, Secretary of the National Aeronautics Association, to Cochran letter, Oct. 19, 1938.

49. *Atlanta Constitution*, Sept. 5, 1938.

50. EL: AFSS, Box 4. Cochran to Rankin letter, Aug. 23, 1938.

51. *New York Times*, Sept. 23, 1938.
52. *Popular Aviation*, December 1938.
53. EL: AFSS, Box 6. Cochran to H. S. Hoover letter, Sept. 9, 1938.
54. Ibid.
55. EL: AFSS, Box 4. Cochran to M. Howard letter, Sept. 17, 1938.
56. *New York Daily News*, Oct. 5, 1938.
57. Robert Gilliland telephone interview with author, June 11 and June 18, 1998.
58. EL: AFSS, Box 4. Kirkpatrick to Cochran letter, Sept. 23, 1938.
59. Ibid., Box 5. Beech to Cochran letter, Nov. 1, 1938.
60. Ibid. Cochran to M. Howard letter, Nov. 30, 1938.
61. *Detroit News*, Dec. 16, 1938.
62. *Business Week*, Dec. 17, 1938.

Chapter 12. Keeping the Crown

1. *New York Times*, March 25, 1939.
2. EL: AFSS, Box 5. Enyart to Cochran letter, Oct. 19, 1938.
3. Ibid., Box 6. Enyart to Cochran telegram, March 20, 1939.
4. SAN, pp. 60–62; *Western Flying*, May 1939; CUOH, p. 12.
5. Ibid.
6. *U.S. Air Services*, October 1927; EL: AFSS, Box 6. H. A. Bruno & Associates press release, March 24, 1939.
7. OH/USAFA, p. 15.
8. CUOH, p. 12.
9. EL: SANM, Box 9; CUOH, p. 12.
10. EL: AFSS, Box 6. Enyart to Cochran letter, March 26, 1939.
11. Ibid. Cochran to Enyart letter, April 13, 1939.
12. Ibid. Cochran to Harwood letter, April 4, 1939.
13. Ibid., Box 7. N.A.A. to Cochran telegram, April 11, 1939.
14. Ibid., Box 6. Cochran to Father Flaherty, a Roman Catholic priest, letter, April 7, 1939.
15. Ibid. B. Kerwood to Cochran letter, May 5, 1939.
16. Ibid. Odlum to Cochran telegram, May 16, 1939.
17. Ibid. E. Roosevelt to Cochran letter, May 7, 1939.
18. Ibid. White House to Cochran letter, May 13, 1939.
19. Ibid. Odlum to Cochran telegram, May 16, 1939.
20. Ibid. Cochran speech, undated.
21. Ibid. Cochran to E. Roosevelt letter, May 26, 1939.
22. Ibid. Cochran to Frye letter, May 26, 1939.
23. *Western Flying*, July 1939.
24. CVHS: Odlum, undated paper.
25. Ibid.; Warren M. Bodie, *Republic's P-47 Thunderbolt; From Seversky to Victory*. Hiawassee, Ga.: Widening Publications, 1994.
26. Ibid.
27. CVHS: Odlum, undated paper.
28. EL: AFSS, Box 7. W. Wallace Kellett to Cochran letter, July 18, 1939; *Newsday* (Garden City, N.Y.), July 21, 1944.
29. *Pittsburgh Press*, Aug. 9, 1939.
30. EL: SANM, Box 9.
31. *U.S. Air Services*, October 1939.
32. *Los Angeles Times*, Sept. 16, 1939.
33. Ibid.
34. *New York Times*, Sept. 29, 1939.
35. Ibid.
36. *New Republic*, April 1939.

Chapter 13. Women and War

1. Department of the Air Force, Washington, D.C. Interview with Jacqueline Cochran, Feb. 25, 1970, pp. 52–53. (Hereafter: OH/DAF.)
2. Ibid.

3. Ibid.
4. Ruth Ann Pfeiffer interview, June 12, 2001; Bird, p. 132.
5. OH/DAF, pp. 51–52.
6. Ibid.
7. EL: AFSS, Box 6. Cochran to E. Roosevelt letter, Sept. 28, 1939.
8. Ibid.
9. Ibid.
10. *Los Angeles Times*, May 11, 1936.
11. EL: AFSS, Box 7. Undated speech.
12. *New York Times*, May 12, 1940.
13. *National Aeronautics*, September 1939.
14. EL: AFSS, Box 6. Gardner Kidd to Cochran letter, Sept. 6, 1939.
15. Ibid., undated.
16. Ibid. Cochran to Gardner Kidd draft of letter, undated.
17. *New York Times*, Sept. 12, 1940.
18. OH/DAF, pp. 44–47.
19. EL: AFSS, Box 6. Odlum to W. W. Kellett letter, Oct. 24, 1939.
20. Ibid., Box 8. Odlum to Cochran telegram, March 12, 1940.
21. CVHS: Cochran Logbook and Instructions, undated; Department of Interior to Cochran letters, March 18 and April 17, 1940.
22. EL: Air Force Series, Box 7. (Hereafter: EL: AF.)
23. *Western Flying*, June 1940; EL: AFSS, Box 8. NAA to Cochran letter, June 6, 1940; Richard S. Allen to author letter, June 26, 2000.
24. CUOH, p. 41.
25. Ibid.
26. EL: AFSS, Box 9. Radio script, June 17, 1940.
27. Ibid., Box 18. Hoenes to Cochran letter, Jan. 2, 1949.
28. Ibid., Box 8. Cochran to Willebrandt letter, Aug. 16, 1940.
29. Ibid. Constant to Cochran letters, Nov. 9 and 21, 1940.
30. Ibid. Constant to Cochran letter, Aug. 24, 1940.
31. OH/DAF, pp. 45–46.
32. Brinley, p. 130.
33. OH/DAF, pp. 46–47.
34. Ibid.; EL: AFSS, Box 8. Arnold to Cochran letter, Sept. 24, 1940.
35. National Aeronautic Association Web site: USAF Almanac, Robert J. Collier Trophy.
36. OH/DAF, p. 47.
37. SAN, p. 98.
38. Jean Howard Phelan interview with author, April 8, 1998. (Hereafter: Phelan interview.)
39. EL: AFSS, Box 8. Cochran to Ninety-Nines letter, May 31, 1940.
40. SAN, pp. 99–100.
41. *Washington Times-Herald*, June 17, 1941.

Chapter 14. Testing the Waters

1. OH/USAFA, p. 9.
2. Ibid., p. 10.
3. Ibid., pp. 10–11.
4. Ibid., p. 11.
5. SAN, pp. 98–100.
6. Ibid., pp. 100–101.
7. *Washington Times-Herald*, June 17, 1941.
8. SAN, pp. 101–2.
9. *Washington Post*, June 21, 1941.
10. Ibid.
11. *Mobile Register*, June 21, 1941.
12. Ibid.
13. Ibid.
14. SAN, p. 105.
15. *New York Times*, July 21, 1941.
16. SAN, p. 106.
17. Sally Van Wagenen Keil, *Those Wonderful Women in Their Flying Machines*. New York: Rawson, Wade, 1979, p. 64. (Hereafter: Keil.)
18. "Women Pilots with the Army

Air Force: 1941–1944." Army Air Force Historical Studies #55. U.S. Air Force Historical Archives, Maxwell Air Force Base, Alabama, p. 5. (Hereafter: AAFHS #55.)

19. Ibid.

20. Ibid., pp. 5–6.

21. Ibid., p. 7.

22. Ibid., pp. 7–9.

23. SAN, p. 3. Sir Arthur Harris in foreword, British edition.

24. EL: SANM, Box 3; AAFHS #55, p. 9.

25. *Business Week*, Sept. 13, 1941.

26. *Newsweek*, Oct. 27, 1941.

27. EL: AFSS, Box 10. Odlum to Cochran telegram, Jan. 9, 1942.

28. Ibid.

29. AAFHS #55, pp. 10–11.

30. Ibid.

31. *New York Times*, Jan. 24, 1942.

32. SANM, Box 4; SAN, p. 109.

33. SAN, pp. 109–10.

34. Wood-Kelly interview with author. Manchester-by-the-Sea, Mass., Aug. 10, 1998.

35. Ibid.

36. Ibid.

37. Ibid.

38. SAN, p. 34.

39. Wood-Kelly interview.

40. OH/USAFA, p. 14.

41. EL: Air Transport Auxiliary Series, Box 4. (Hereafter: EL: ATA.)

42. Byrd Howell Granger, *On Final Approach*. Scottsdale, Ariz.: Falconer, 1991, p. 19. (Hereafter: Granger.)

43. SAN, pp. 112–13.

44. Granger, p. 19.

45. Ibid., p. 20.

Chapter 15. Taking Over

1. *New York Times*, Sept. 11, 1942.

2. Granger, p. 22.

3. Ibid., pp. 22, 26.

4. Ibid., p. 21.

5. AAFHS #55, p. 11.

6. Ibid., p. 13.

7. Ibid., p. 73.

8. Granger, pp. 19–26.

9. Ibid., pp. 29–30.

10. SAN, p. 118.

11. AAFHS #55, p. 17.

12. *New York Times*, Sept. 15, 1942.

13. Granger, p. 31.

14. OH/USAFA, p. 46.

15. Granger, pp. 314, 320, 410–11.

16. Brinley, pp. 202–3.

17. SAN, p. 120.

18. Phelan interview, April 8, 1998.

19. Jane Straughn interview with author, June 30, 1998.

20. Phelan interview, April 8, 1998.

21. SAN, p. 120; "History of the Women's Air Force Service Pilots Program and Activities of the AAF Training Command," 220.0721-1. Completed at Headquarters AAF Training Command, Fort Worth, Texas. Research Studies, Institute Archives Branch, Maxwell AFB, Ala. (Hereafter: WASPH/FW.)

22. Granger, p. 37.

23. Texas Woman's University Collections. Leoti Deaton Oral History by Ziggy Hunter. Edited by Dawn Letson. March 18, 1975, p. 62. (Hereafter: TWU: Deaton OH.)

24. Ibid.

25. WASPH/FW, p. 26.

26. TWU: Deaton OH, p. 26.

27. Ibid., p. 64.

28. Granger, p. 71.

29. EL: AFSS, Box 10. Schedule, Nov. 18–22, 1942.

30. TWU: Deaton OH, pp. 44–45.

31. Granger, p. 79.

32. WASPH/FW, pp. 39–40.

33. OH/DAF, pp. 18–19.

34. Ibid.

35. OH/USAFA, p. 31.
36. Granger, pp. 86–87.
37. Ibid., pp. 39–40.
38. CUOH, p. 14.
39. TWU: Deaton OH, p. 43.
40. Ibid., pp. 43, 46–47.
41. AAFHS #55, p. 83.
42. OH/USAFA, p. 39.
43. Ibid.
44. Ibid., p. 40.
45. Ibid., p. 41.
46. Ibid.
47. OH/DAF, p. 23.
48. Ibid., p. 24.

Chapter 16. Cochran's Convent

1. WASPH/FW, p. 20.
2. Ibid., p. 27.
3. Ibid., p. 21.
4. TWU: Deaton OH, p. 10.
5. Ibid., p. 38.
6. Margaret Kerr Boylan telephone interview with author, May 29, 2000; Brinley, p. 201.
7. Ibid.
8. Phelan interview, June 19, 1999.
9. OH/USAFA, p. 31.
10. SAN, p. 122.
11. OH/USAFA, p. 75.
12. TWU: Deaton OH, p. 2.
13. OH/DAF, p. 27.
14. Ibid., pp. 16–17.
15. EL: GFS, Box 261. Cochran log, Feb. 4, 1943.
16. EL: AFSS, Box 8. Max Constant to Talbert Abrams letter, Nov. 11, 1940; ibid., Box 10. War Department Army Air Forces Purchase Order, March 18, 1943.
17. OH/USAFA, p. 46.
18. Granger, pp. 111–14.
19. Ibid.
20. Ibid., pp. 318–19.
21. Iris Cummings Critchell. Telephone interview with author, June 29, 1998; Granger, p. 21.
22. Keil, pp. 139–40.
23. Ibid., p. 157.
24. Jasper L. Moore letter to author, Oct. 25, 1999.
25. Granger, pp. 119–120.
26. AAFHS #55, p. 44–45.
27. Ibid., pp. 85–86.
28. *Newsweek*, July 19, 1943.
29. AAFHS #55, pp. 44–45.

Chapter 17. The Rise and Fall of Jackie's Empire

1. AAFHS #55, p. 48.
2. Granger, p. 150.
3. Ibid., pp. 151–52.
4. Ibid., pp. 168–71.
5. Ibid., p. 171.
6. CUOH, pp. 31–32.
7. Ibid., p. 33.
8. SAN, p. 127.
9. Ibid.
10. http://www.af.mil/50th/library/wasp.html.
11. OH/DAF, p. 32.
12. Granger, p. 450.
13. Cochran: Final Report on Women Pilots Program, Army Air Force Report 6–1262, p. 28. Army Air Force Historical Archives, Maxwell Air Force Base, Ala. (Hereafter: WPP 6–1262.)
14. SAN, pp. 123–24.
15. EL: AFSS, Box 251. Agnes Morley Cleaveland to Cochran letter, Jan. 7, 1956.
16. AAFHS #55, p. 45.
17. Ibid., p. 48.
18. Granger, p. 144.
19. AAFHS #55, pp. 52–53.
20. Ibid., p. 53.
21. Granger, pp. 359–60.
22. Barbara Erickson, London, interview with author, Oct. 19,2000.
23. TWU: Deaton OH, p. 34.
24. WPP 6–1262, p. 17.
25. AAFHS #55, p. 99.

26. Ibid., p. 88.
27. Ibid., p. 92.
28. *New York Times*, March 23, 1944.
29. AAFHS #55, p. 97.
30. *New York Times*, June 20, 1944.
31. AAFHS #55, p. 97.
32. *New York Times*, June 22, 1944.
33. AAFHS #55, p. 98.
34. Ibid., pp. 93–94; *New York Times*, Aug. 5, 1944.
35. *Dallas Morning News*, Aug. 6, 1944.
36. *New York Times*, Aug. 8, 1944.
37. *Washington Post*, Aug. 8, 1944.
38. AAFHS #55, p. 100.
39. WASPH/FW, p. 1151.
40. Keil, p. 243; *Newsday* (Garden City, N.Y.), Sept. 21, 1944.
41. Sarah Rickman interview with James for the *International Women's Air and Space Museum Quarterly*, undated clipping.
42. WASPH/FW, pp. 59–60.
43. TWU: Deaton OH, pp. 33–34.
44. Brinley, p. 211.
45. EL: AFSS, Box 10. Odlum to Cochran letter, Oct. 16, 1944.
46. *New York Times*, Nov. 1, 1944.
47. Granger, p. 435.
48. Ibid., pp. 465–66.
49. WPP 6–1262, p. 1.
50. Ibid.
51. EL: GFS, Box 186. Cochran to Arnold letter, Nov. 4, 1944.

Chapter 18. War Correspondent

1. Granger, p. 469.
2. Federal Bureau of Investigation. Cochran file sent to Sherman Adams, assistant to the president, April 23, 1957.
3. OH/USAFA, p. 125.
4. Ibid.
5. *New York Times*, March 1, 1945.
6. OH/USAFA, p. 122.
7. Ibid., pp. 122–23.
8. *New York Times*, March 1, 1945.
9. EL: Trips, Box 1. Application for Foreign Flight. Department of Commerce, undated.
10. Ibid. War Department Bureau of Public Relations, Aug. 6, 1945; *Time*, Aug. 13, 1945.
11. OH/DAF, p. 40.
12. Ibid.
13. EL: Trips, Box 2. Odlum to Cochran letter, Aug. 13, 1945.
14. Jan Larson (Jan Wendell Conner). Interview with author. Aug. 14, 1998. New Canaan, Conn.
15. EL: Trips, Box 6. Notes, Aug. 11, 1945.
16. Ibid., Box 1. Cochran to Odlum letter, Aug. 19–26, 1945; SAN, pp. 138–39.
17. EL: GFS, Box 261. Logs, Aug. 21, 1945.
18. *Liberty*, Oct. 27, 1945; EL: Trips, Box 2. Cochran to Odlum letter, Aug. 31, 1945.
19. EL: Trips, Box 2. Cochran to Odlum letter, Aug. 26–30, 1945.
20. Ibid.
21. Ibid. Odlum to Cochran letter, Aug. 20, 1945.
22. Ibid. Cochran to Odlum letter, Aug. 26–30, 1945.
23. Ibid. Odlum to Cochran letter, Sept. 22, 1945.
24. Ibid. Cochran to Odlum letter, Sept. 6, 1945.
25. Ibid.
26. Ibid.
27. Ibid.
28. Ibid.
29. Ibid., Box 1. Affidavit, Sept. 11, 1945.
30. Ibid. Edward Maher to Odlum letter, Oct. 10, 1945.
31. SAN, p. 142.
32. EL: Trips, Box 2. Cochran to Odlum letters, Sept. 13, 1945, and Sept. 16, 1945.

33. Ibid., Sept. 16, 1945.
34. Ibid. Odlum to Cochran cable, Sept. 17, 1945.
35. Ibid. Cochran to Odlum note, Sept. 18, 1945.
36. Ibid.
37. Ibid. Odlum to Cochran letter, Oct. 3, 1945.
38. Ibid., Box 1. McCabe to Cochran letter, Sept. 24, 1945.
39. SAN, p. 151.
40. Ibid., pp. 152–53.
41. Ibid., pp. 161–62.
42. Ibid., p. 157.
43. Ibid., pp. 158–59.
44. Ibid., pp. 157–58.
45. EL: Trips, Box 2. Cochran to Odlum letter, Oct. 3, 1945.
46. SAN, p. 163.
47. EL: SANM, Box 6.
48. Ibid.
49. EL: Trips, Box 1. Headquarters, United States Forces, China Theater Memorandum, Oct. 20, 1945.
50. EL: SANM, Box 9.
51. Ibid.
52. SAN, pp. 170–71.
53. Ibid., p. 174.
54. EL: Trips, Box 2. Hammond to Odlum letter, Sept. 17, 1945.
55. Ibid. Dan Silberberg to Odlum letter, Sept. 24, 1945.
56. Ibid. Nurse Sherman to Cochran letter, Oct. 2, 1945.
57. Ibid. Odlum to Cochran cable, Oct. 14, 1945.
58. Ibid. Cochran to Odlum cable, Oct. 14, 1945.
59. Ibid., Box 1. Undated article.
60. SAN, p. 181.
61. EL: GFS, Box 189. Cochran to Rosemary Brogan letter, Oct. 9, 1972.
62. SAN, pp. 188–89.
63. EL: Trips, Box 2. Cochran to Odlum letter, Nov. 22, 1945.
64. Ibid. Cochran to Odlum cables, Nov. 29, Dec. 1, and Dec. 6, 1945.
65. EL: SANM, Box 6.

Chapter 19. The Colonel and the Air Force

1. OH/USAFA, pp. 40–41.
2. Ibid.
3. EL: AF, Box 11. *Time Radio Hour* script, April 17, 1946.
4. Ibid.
5. EL: AFSS, Box 10. Cochran to Tom Doland letter, June 15, 1946.
6. Ibid. Guest list, June 19, 1946.
7. OH/DAF, p. 43.
8. EL: SANM, Box 7.
9. Ibid.
10. CUOH, pp. 35–38; EL: SANM, Box 7.
11. EL: SANM, Box 7; *Newsweek*, Sept. 9, 1946.
12. *American*, April 1947.
13. EL: GFS, Box 185. Harry A. Bruno & Associates news release, Dec. 17, 1947.
14. EL: AFSS, Box 11. Held to Cochran letter, March 19, 1948.
15. EL: GFS, Box 11. Cochran to Held letter, March 26, 1948.
16. *Aviation Week*, May 31, 1948.
17. EL: Articles, Box 2. "Medical Aspects of Women as Pilots."
18. EL: AFSS, Box 11. Harry A. Bruno & Associates. News release, May 24, 1948.
19. *Dallas Morning News*, May 16, 1948.
20. EL: GFS, Box 196. Floyd Odlum to Dr. Donald H. Henzel letter, Oct. 15, 1970.
21. Lyndon Baines Johnson Library, Austin, Texas, File 81–17. Stuart Symington interview by J. B. Frantz, Oct. 6, 1976. (Hereafter: LBJL.)
22. Ibid., File AC 69–82. Warren Woodward interview by David C. McComb, May 26, 1969.
23. Ibid.

24. *Los Angeles Times*, May 5, 1974.
25. LBJL, File AC 81–17. Symington, Oct. 6, 1976.
26. Beverly Hanson Sfingi to author correspondence, Dec. 6, 2002; confirmed by telephone, Jan. 7, 2003.
27. EL: AFSS, Box 11. *U.S. Air Services*, October 1948.
28. Ibid. Unidentified news clip, Sept. 8, 1948.
29. SAN, p. 96.
30. EL: AFSS, Box 18. M. Howard to Cochran letter, Sept. 14, 1949.
31. SAN, p. 83.
32. EL: AF, Box 2. FBI report to Sherman Adams, Aug. 23, 1957.
33. EL: AFSS, Box 19. LBJ to Cochran letter, Dec. 31, 1948.
34. Ibid., Feb. 5, 1949.
35. *Life*, June 6, 1949.
36. *Washington Times-Herald*, June 14, 1949.
37. EL: AFSS, Box 19. Cochran to Helen and Otto Oberlander letter, Jan. 25, 1949.

Chapter 20. The Purposeful Traveler

1. EL: GFS, Box 261. Cochran to Vandenberg letter, April 22, 1949.
2. EL: AFSS, Box 16. Cochran to Georges de Sonchen letter, April 11, 1949.
3. Ibid.
4. Beverly Hanson Sfingi interview with author, Oct. 27, 2000. Indio, Calif.
5. Ibid.
6. EL: AFSS, Box 18. Cochran to Holmes letter, April 21, 1949.
7. Ibid., Box 16. Cochran to Carolyn and Radu Irimescu letter, July 5, 1949.
8. EL: SANM, Box 6.
9. Ibid.; EL: AFSS, Box 16. Cochran to Hughes letter, July 9, 1949.
10. EL: AFSS, Box 21. Cochran to Freda Marshall letter, July 9, 1949.
11. Ibid., Box 23. Walsh to Roseborough letter, May 20, 1949.
12. Ibid., Box 16. Cochran to Edwards letter, July 1, 1949.
13. Ibid. Cochran to White House Secretary Hasset letter, July 25, 1949.
14. Ibid. Odlum to Durning letter, July 13, 1949.
15. Ibid. Cochran to de Sonchen letter, Sept. 30, 1949.
16. Ibid. Walsh to Durning letter, Nov. 29, 1949.
17. EL: SANM, Box 6.
18. Ibid.
19. EL: Articles, Box 1. C. P. Cabell to Cochran letter, Oct. 3, 1950.
20. CVHS: Floyd Odlum, "Aviation Sequence," pp. 16–17; EL: SANM, Box 7.
21. EL: SANM, Box 6.
22. OH/USAFA, p. 129.
23. Ibid.
24. Ibid.
25. Kristin Norstad Jaffe telephone interview with author, May 31, 1998.
26. Isabelle Norstad telephone interview with author, June 3, 1998.
27. EL: AF, Box 3. Vandenberg to Cochran letter, Oct. 25, 1950.
28. EL: SANM, Box 6.
29. OH/USAFA, pp. 128–29.
30. EL: AF, Box 5. Cochran to Vandenberg memo, Dec. 6, 1950.
31. Ibid.
32. Major General Holm USAF (Ret.), *Women in the Military; An Unfinished Record*. Novato, Calif.: Presidio Press, 1982. Revised ed. 1992, pp. 141–42.
33. EL: AFSS, Box 18. Cochran to Hamilton letter, Sept. 7, 1949.
34. EL: AF, Box 5. Minutes of meeting, Jan. 24, 1951.
35. Ibid., Box 4. *Worcester Gazette* (Mass.), Feb. 6, 1952.
36. EL: AF, Box 4. Harvey, June 10, 1951.
37. Ibid. Cochran to Chief of Staff, Air Force, letter, Dec. 22, 1950.

38. *Washington News*, June 11, 1951.
39. Ibid.
40. EL: Trips, Box 3. Odlum to Cochran cable, June 13, 1951; *Newsday* (Garden City, N.Y.), June 19, 1951.
41. *Elmira Star Gazette* (N.Y.), June 19, 1951.
42. OH/DAF, p. 43.
43. EL: AF, Box 3. Cochran to Maj. Gen. E. S. Wetzel letter, Nov. 6, 1951.

Chapter 21. Ike

1. SAN, p. 213.
2. Doris Kearns Goodwin, *The Fitzgeralds and the Kennedys; An American Saga*. New York: St. Martin's, 1987, p. 875.
3. Eisenhower Campaign Series, Box 1. Statement by Floyd B. Odlum, April 19, 1954. (Hereafter: EL: ECS.)
4. EL: Trips, Box 2. Cochran to McCabe letter, Oct. 21, 1945.
5. EL: ECS, Box 1. John Wickman oral history, March 28, 1968, pp. 14–16. (Hereafter: Wickman OH.)
6. Waring interview, July 2, 1998.
7. Wickman OH, p. 17.
8. *St. Louis Post-Dispatch*, Feb. 9, 1952.
9. Wickman OH, pp. 18–20.
10. *St. Louis Post-Dispatch*, Feb. 9, 1952.
11. *Variety*, Feb. 27, 1952.
12. *New York Post*, Feb. 11, 1952.
13. SAN, pp. 216–17.
14. *Kiplinger Letter*, Feb. 16, 1952.
15. EL: Trips, Box 3. Cochran to Colonel Pierre Gallois letter, April 5, 1952.
16. Ibid. Cochran to Bacon letter, April 11, 1952.
17. Ibid. List prepared by Walsh, April 28, 1952.
18. Ibid. Lodestar log, April 25–June 27, 1952.
19. EL: ECS, Box 3. Cochran to Hoffman letter, June 15, 1952.
20. Ibid. Weintraub to Hertz letter with note from Hertz, June 12, 1952.
21. SAN, pp. 212–13.
22. EL: ECS, Box 2. Eisenhower to Cochran and Odlum letter, July 18, 1952.
23. Ibid., Box 1. Odlum to Clay letter, Sept. 15, 1952.
24. Ibid., Box 3. Minutes of the meeting, Sept. 25, 1952.
25. Ibid. F. Daniel Frost III to Cochran letter, Oct. 11, 1952.
26. *Los Angeles Times*, Oct. 11, 1952.
27. EL: ECS, Box 3. Cochran to Silberberg letter, Oct. 14, 1952.
28. Ibid., Box 2. Cochran to Disney letters, Sept. 30 and Oct. 10, 1952.
29. EL: AFSS, Box 266. William Anderson to Cochran letter, undated.
30. EL: ECS, Box 2. Cochran to Sidney Weinberg letter, Dec. 4, 1952.
31. SAN, pp. 168–69.
32. Ibid., p. 219.
33. *U.S. Air Services*, December 1952.
34. EL: ECS, Box 2. Cochran to M. Eisenhower letter, July 4, 1952.
35. Ibid. Cochran to M. Eisenhower letter, July 24, 1952.

Chapter 22. The Fastest Woman in the World

1. *Washington Star*, May 15, 1951; *American Aviation Daily*, May 19, 1953; NASM/Cochran file.
2. Marie-Josephe de Beauregarde. Letter to International Women's Air and Space Museum, February 2000.
3. EL: Trips, Box 3. Odlum to Cochran letter, May 20, 1951.
4. *Aviation Week*, April 6, 1953; *Aeroplane*, May 22, 1953.
5. SAN, p. 224.
6. Yeager, p. 211.
7. Ibid., p. 216.
8. Wil Hanson. "The Cochran-Odlum

Ranch," unpublished manuscript, p. 1, Nov. 1, 2000.

9. Yeager, p. 214.

10. Ibid., pp. 223–24.

11. EL: GFS, Box 261. Log, June 23, 1953.

12. Yeager, p. 220.

13. SAN, p. 238.

14. EL: Articles, Box 2. "Flights and Fancies."

15. Ibid., p. 225.

16. EL: SANM, Box 9.

17. EL: GFS, Box 261. Log, June 23, 1953; SAN, p. 237; CUOH, pp. 49–50.

18. EL: Articles, Box 2. "Flights and Fancies."

19. SAN, p. 237.

20. *American Aviation Daily*, May 19, 1953.

21. SAN, p. 240.

22. EL: GFS, Box 261. Log, May 12–June 3, 1953.

23. *Aviation Week*, June 22, 1953.

24. SAN, p. 231.

25. CUOH, p. 3.

26. Ibid.; EL: SANM, Box 9.

27. Yeager, p. 218.

28. *Aviation Week*, June 22, 1953.

29. TWU: Cochran file. Charles McAdams taped interview, Oct. 2, 2000.

30. Ibid.

31. *American Weekly*, July 19, 1953.

32. EL: Articles, Box 2. Cochran to Bruno letter, July 13, 1953.

33. *Aviation Week*, July 13, 1953.

34. *Newsweek*, Aug. 16, 1953.

Chapter 23. The Stars at Noon

1. EL: Articles, Box 2. Cochran to James H. Straubel, editor, *Air Force* letter, Aug. 26, 1953.

2. Ibid.

3. Ibid. Cochran to Reid letter, Sept. 3, 1953.

4. Ibid. Bruno to Durling letter, Sept. 15, 1953.

5. Ibid. Bruno to Durling letter, Sept. 15, 1953.

6. *New York Times*, Aug. 30, 1953.

7. EL: Articles, Box 2. Odlum to Bruno letter, Sept. 21, 1953.

8. *New York Times*, Sept. 24, 1953.

9. Ibid.

10. EL: Trips, Box 4. Odlum to Cochran letter, Sept. 26, 1953.

11. Ibid., Oct. 12, 1953.

12. Ibid., Oct. 16, 1953.

13. Ibid. Pan American itinerary, Oct. 31, 1953.

14. Bird, pp. 147–48.

15. SAN, pp. 219–20; EL: GFS, Box 9. Cochran to Eisenhower letter, Feb. 23, 1954.

16. Dr. Earl A. Thompson interview with author, Oct. 24, 2000.

17. EL: SANM, Box 1. Cloud to Cochran note, undated.

18. EL: Trips, Box 6. Itinerary, Feb. 26–March 26, 1954.

19. CBS-TV. "Person to Person" with Edward R. Murrow, May 21, 1954.

20. *New York Times*, July 5, 1954.

21. *Life*, Aug. 16, 1954.

22. EL: Articles, Box 3. Walsh to Carolyn Fraser, *Life* magazine letter, July 20, 1954.

23. EL: Trips, Box 5. Itinerary, Sept. 24–Oct. 7, 1954.

24. SAN, pp. 252–54.

25. Ibid., p. 55.

26. *Kirkus Reviews*, July 15, 1954.

27. *Saturday Review of Literature*, Oct. 6, 1954.

28. EL: Trips, Box 6. Itineraries, Oct. 6–31, 1954, and Nov. 11, 1954.

29. EL: SANM, Box 1. Odlum to Vaughn, Leguay and Cochran interoffice communication, Aug. 9, 1954.

Chapter 24. Life According to Jackie

1. EL: GFS, Box 200. Cochran to Evonne M. Weinberg letter, Dec. 10, 1969.
2. Wil Hanson manuscript to author, Nov. 1, 2000.
3. Hanson interview with author, Oct. 31, 2001.
4. Hanson manuscript to author, Oct. 10, 2000.
5. Frances Pearson interview with author, Oct. 24, 2001.
6. Dr. Earl Thompson and Frances Pearson interviews with author, Oct. 24, 2000.
7. Hanson interview with author, Nov. 1, 2000.
8. Hanson manuscript to author, Nov. 1, 2000.
9. Dr. Earl Thompson interview with author, Oct. 24, 2000.
10. Hanson interview with author, Oct. 31, 2001.
11. Beverly Sfingi interview with author, Oct. 27, 2000.
12. Hanson interview with author, Oct. 31, 2001.
13. Hanson manuscript to author, Nov. 1, 2000.
14. Ibid.
15. EL: Trips, Box 6. Cochran to Clinton Henry Green letter, June 13, 1955.
16. *New York Herald-Tribune*, July 19, 1955.
17. EL: Trips, Box 7. Cochran to Ker and Downey cable, July 25, 1955.
18. EL: SANM, Box 9.
19. *Business Week*, May 28, 1955.
20. Ibid.; Arnold Steele interviews with author, Sept. 18 and Oct. 21, 2002.
21. EL: GFS, Box 251. Cochran to Alford letter, Oct. 22, 1955.
22. Ibid., Box 260. Cochran to Hydle letter, Oct. 14, 1955.
23. EL: SANM, Box 1. Howard Mathison to Cochran letter, undated.
24. EL: GFS, Box 260. Cochran to Mathison letter, March 22, 1955.
25. Ibid. Cochran to Lovelace letter, Dec. 8, 1955.
26. *Time*, Nov. 7, 1955.

Chapter 25. The Candidate

1. EL: Articles, Box 2. "Involvement in California Politics and the 1952 Campaign."
2. EL: Trips, Box 2. Cochran to Odlum letter, Aug. 26–30, 1945.
3. Ibid.
4. EL: Primary Political File Series, Box 15. Cochran to Bennett letter, July 26, 1955. (Hereafter: EL: PPFS.)
5. Ibid. Bennett to Cochran letter, Aug. 6, 1955.
6. Ibid., Box 9. Odlum to Cochran memo, Nov. 9, 1955.
7. *San Francisco Chronicle*, Nov. 27, 1955.
8. EL: PPFS, Box 9. Cochran to Symington letter, Jan. 25, 1956.
9. *Tulsa Daily World*, Jan. 13, 1956.
10. EL: PPFS, Box 5. Undated paper, pp. 12–15.
11. Ibid., Box 17. Proffitt to Odlum report, Feb. 8, 1956.
12. Ibid., Box 4. List, March 5, 1956.
13. Ibid., Box 16. Eldridge to Harper letter, Feb. 7, 1956.
14. Ibid., Box 15. Undated memo.
15. Ibid. Memo, March 26, 1956.
16. Ibid., Box 17. Behrens to Cochran letter, March 17, 1956.
17. Ibid. John Hunter to Cochran report, undated.
18. Ibid., Box 7. *Calexico Chronicle*, April 12, 1956.
19. Ibid., Box 15. Cochran to Behrens letter, April 7, 1956.

20. Ibid. Bennett to Cochran memo, undated.
21. Ibid. Walsh to Cochran memo, April 5, 1956.
22. Ibid., Box 17. Odlum to Allen letter, May 4, 1956.
23. *New York Herald-Tribune*, 5/11/56.
24. *Indio News* (Calif.), May 29, 1956.
25. EL: PPFS, Box 9. "Outlook for the Election Campaign," undated.
26. Ibid., Box 8. Memo, June 8, 1956.
27. EL: Trips, Box 1. Security data, July–August 1956.
28. EL: GFS, Box 260. Flier, Aug. 13, 1956.
29. EL: General Election Files, Box 1. Habein to Cochran letter, Sept. 25, 1956. (Hereafter: EL: GEF.)
30. *Calexico Chronicle*, Sept. 27, 1956.
31. *Time*, Oct. 8, 1956.
32. Ibid.
33. EL: PPFS, Box 6. Bennett to Cochran letter, undated.
34. *New York Daily News*, Oct. 20, 1956.
35. EL: PPFS, Box 17. Cochran to Saund telegram, undated.
36. EL: GEF, Box 9. Cochran to Eldridge letter, Oct. 27, 1956.
37. Ibid. Eldridge to Cochran letter, Nov. 5, 1956.
38. Ibid. Cochran to Eldridge letter, Nov. 10, 1956.
39. EL: ECS, Box 1. Wickman OH, pp. 80–82; Dr. John E. Wickman interview with author, Sept. 28, 1999.
40. Ibid.

Chapter 26. Speed and Space

1. EL: GES, Box 2. Walsh to Currlin letter and list, April 2, 1958.
2. Ibid. Cochran to Hoover letter, May 1, 1958.
3. EL: Trips, Box 8. Marsh and McLennan Insurance letter, May 15, 1959.
4. Yeager, p. 256.
5. SAN, pp. 67–69.
6. CUOH, pp. 68–71.
7. Yeager, pp. 259–60.
8. EL: AFSS, Box 3. Cochran to Gladys Baker letter, Dec. 4, 1959.
9. EL: AF, Box 2. Script, Aug. 12, 1958.
10. EL: Trips, Box 7. List of addresses for correspondence, June 1958.
11. EL: AFSS, Box 2. Lieutenant Colonel V. J. Adduci recommendation letters, Dec. 1, 1957–Nov. 30, 1958.
12. *Columbus Dispatch*, June 7, 1960.
13. Henry D. Steele interview with author, June 11, 1998.
14. National Aeronautic Association news releases, Aug. 25, 1961, and Oct. 13, 1961.
15. *Parade*, April 30, 1961.
16. Ibid.
17. Deborah C. Douglas, *United States Women in Aviation. 1940–1985*. Washington, D.C.: Smithsonian Institution Press, 1991, p. 85.
18. *Washington Post*, July 13, 1998.
19. Ibid.
20. EL: Articles, Box 7. Statement of Jacqueline Cochran before the subcommittee of the House Committee on Science and Astronautics, July 12, 1962.
21. Leslie Haynesworth and David Toomey, *Amelia Earhart's Daughters: The Wild and Glorious Story of American Women from World War II to the Dawn of the Space Age*. New York: William Morrow, 1998, pp. 236–37 and 261–71.
22. Ibid.
23. Ibid.
24. *Washington Post*, July 13, 1998.
25. EL: GFS, Box 227. Cochran to Dr. T. O. Paine letter, Aug. 8, 1969.
26. *Life*, 6/28/63.
27. EL: Articles, Box 8. "Space for Women in Space," unpublished article by Cochran, undated.

Chapter 27. Mach 2

1. EL: Trips, Box 9. Strauss Diary, Aug. 10–Oct. 13, 1962.
2. Ibid.
3. Ibid. Undated telegram.
4. EL: SANM, Box 1; EL: GFS, Box 260. Eisenhower to Cochran letter, undated.
5. CVHS: Cochran papers. March calendar.
6. EL: Trips, Box 10. Andrew A. Lynn to Robert Ricci letter, March 22, 1963.
7. Ibid. Cochran to Adams letter, March 27, 1963.
8. *Flying*, September 1977. Cochran with Gordon Baxter interview.
9. EL: GFS, Box 225. Undated draft letter to a Mr. Ingalls.
10. Robert Gilliland telephone interview with author, June 11, 1998.
11. EL: SANM, Box 9.
12. EL: GFS, Box 225. List of records.
13. Ibid. Hopkins to Cochran letter, April 1, 1963.
14. *Washington Post*, June 4, 1964.
15. *Sports Illustrated*, July 9, 1963.
16. EL: GFS, Box 225. Odlum to Cochran letter, June 14, 1963.
17. Ibid. Odlum to Whitener letter, Oct. 4, 1963.
18. EL: SANM, Box 9.
19. CVHS: Cochran calendar, 1963.
20. *Whitehorse Star*, Aug. 12, 1963.
21. EL: SANM, Box 9.
22. TWU: Cochran File. Lockheed-California Company Newsbureau press release, June 4, 1964.

Chapter 28. Jackie's Circus

1. EL: GFS, Box 259. All correspondence concerning Myrtle Alford.
2. Ibid., Box 260. All correspondence concerning Mamie Hydle.
3. EL: Trips, Box 2. Cochran to Odlum letter, Aug. 11, 1966.
4. EL: AFSS, Box 224. Memo, Jan. 27, 1968.
5. Ibid. Cochran to M. Abbas letter, Nov. 22, 1968.
6. EL: Trips, Box 4. Odlum to Cochran letter, Nov. 13, 1953.
7. *Time*, March 25, 1957.
8. Waring interview, July 2, 1998.
9. J. Odlum interview, Oct. 18, 2000.
10. Ibid.
11. Waring interview, July 2, 1998.
12. Arnold Steele interview with author, May 18, 2002.
13. EL: Trips, Box 11. Itinerary, Sept. 11–18, 1964, and Dec. 6–9, 1964.
14. Ibid., Box 12. Cochran to Odlum letter, Aug. 11, 1966.
15. CVHS: Eisenhower to Odlum letter, Nov. 20, 1962.
16. LBJL WH Central File. Name File 289. Johnson to Cochran letter, Dec. 12, 1963.
17. Ibid. Ctn. 22. Telegram, July 23, 1964.
18. Ibid. Valenti to Cochran letter, Dec. 14, 1964.
19. Ibid. WH Office Files of John W. Macy, Jr., Ctn. 107. Cochran to Weisel letter, March 13, 1965.
20. Ibid. Weisel to Valenti letter, April 8, 1965.
21. Ibid. Macy to Valenti memo, April 20, 1965.
22. Ibid. Macy memo, Jan. 31, 1967.
23. Ibid. WH Central File. Name File 289. Cochran to Johnson letter, Aug. 27, 1965.
24. Ibid. Sept. 6, 1966, and March 30, 1967.
25. Ibid. Feb. 6, 1968.
26. Ibid. WH Appointment File. Drawer 61.
27. EL: SANM, Box 9.
28. EL: GFS, Box 192. Cochran to Patricia Hitt letter, Nov. 19, 1968.

Chapter 29. Grounded

1. EL: GFS, Box 224. Cochran to H. M. Hutches letter, April 25, 1969.

2. Ibid. Hutches to Cochran letter, undated.

3. Newcomer telephone interview with author, Oct. 1, 2003.

4. Ibid., Box 201. Odlum to Yeager letter, Sept. 6, 1969.

5. EL: Trips, Box 13. Cochran to Aldine Tarter letter, Sept. 18, 1969.

6. EL: GFS, Box 197. Odlum to Cochran letter, Dec. 23, 1969.

7. Ibid., Box 196. Odlum to Henzel letter, Oct. 15, 1970.

8. OH/DAF, p. 1.

9. EL: AF, Box 3. Cochran to Reed letter, June 8, 1970.

10. EL: GFS, Box 225. Mayo Clinic report, Aug. 20, 1970.

11. EL: Trips, Box 14. Log, July 24, 1970.

12. EL: GFS, Box 205. Cochran to Dr. Murray Green letter, Jan. 6, 1971.

13. Ibid., Box 230. Jewelry list, May 21, 1971.

14. FAA files, May 28, 1998.

15. EL: Trips, Box 14. Cochran to Indio staff memo, July 11, 1971.

16. *Congressional Record* E10159. Extension of Remarks, Sept. 28, 1971.

17. EL: GFS, Box 235. Odlum to Cochran telegram, Dec. 16, 1971.

18. EL: AF, Box 195. Cochran to Marston letter, Nov. 10, 1972.

Chapter 30. The Last Years

1. EL: AF, Box 187. Odlum to Brig. Gen. Murray A. Bywater (Ret.) letter, Nov. 9, 1972.

2. EL: GFS, Box 186. Cochran to Arnold letter, Jan. 2, 1973.

3. Ibid., Box 200. Cochran to Una Stannart letter, March 26, 1973.

4. Ibid., April 6, 1973.

5. Ibid., Box 191. Cochran to Harris letter, June 12, 1974.

6. Ibid.

7. Ibid., Box 190. Cochran to C. B. Albert Gee letter, Jan. 31, 1973.

8. EL: AFSS, Box 187. Cochran to Mrs. E. Grafton Carlisle letter, Jan. 6, 1971.

9. Ibid., Box 201. Cochran to Yeager letter, April 11, 1968.

10. Ibid., Box 200. Symington to Cochran letter, July 8, 1974.

11. Yeager, p. 413.

12. Brinley, p. 346.

13. Thompson interview, Oct. 24, 2000.

14. Phelan interview, April 8, 1998.

15. Claudia Oakes interview with author, April 2, 1998.

16. Claudia Oakes interview of Cochran, May 20, 1979.

17. NASM/Cochran file. Ayers/Dees.

18. Thompson interview, Oct. 24, 2000.

19. Brinley, p. 347.

20. Wood-Kelly interview, Aug. 10, 1998.

21. *Colorado Springs Gazette-Telegraph*, Nov. 7, 1980.

22. *Washington Post*, Feb. 12, 1982.

Bibliography

Allen, Richard Sanders. *The Northrop Story, 1929–1939*. Atglen, Pa.: Schiffer Publishing, 1995.

Ambrose, Stephen E. *Eisenhower. Vol. 2. The President*. New York: Simon and Schuster, 1984.

Arnold, H. H. *Global Mission*. New York: Harper and Brothers, 1949.

Barton, Charles. "Jackie and the Bendix." *Air Classics*, May 1985.

Baxter, Gordon. "Cochran." *Flying*, September 1977, p. 178.

de Beauregard, Marie Josephe. *Femmes de l'Air: Chronique d'une Conquête*. Paris: Editions France-Empire, 1993.

Bird, Nancy. *My God It's a Woman*. Sydney: Angus and Robertson (HarperCollins), 1990.

Birdwell, Russell. *Women in Battle Dress*. New York: Fine Editions Press, 1942.

Bodie, Warren M. *Republic's P-47 Thunderbolt: From Seversky to Victory*. Hiawassee, Ga.: Widening Publications, 1994.

Bowers, Peter M. "Streamlining." *Wings Magazine*, October 1991.

Brinley, Maryann Bucknum, and Jacqueline Cochran. *Jackie Cochran: An Autobiography of the Greatest Woman Pilot in Aviation History*. New York: Bantam, 1987.

Carl, Ann B. *A Wasp among Eaglets: A Woman Military Test Pilot in World War II*. Washington, D.C.: Smithsonian Institution Press, 1999.

Cobb, Jerrie, with Jan Rieker. *Woman into Space: The Jerrie Cobb Story*. Englewood Cliffs, N.J.: Prentice-Hall, 1963.

Cochran, Jacqueline. *The Stars at Noon*. Boston: Little, Brown, 1954.

———. "I Reached the Stars the Hard Way: A Great Flier Poignantly Recalls Her First Bleak Earthbound Years." *Life*, August 16, 1954.

Daso, Maj. Dik, USAF. *Architects of American Air Supremacy: General Hap Arnold and Dr. Theodore von Karman*. Maxwell Air Force Base, Ala.: Air University Press, 1997.

Davis, Forrest. "The Tinker of Wall Street." *The Saturday Evening Post*, July 10, 1937, p 13.

Douglas, Deborah G. *United States Women in Aviation, 1940–1985*. Washington, D.C.: Smithsonian Institution Press, 1991.

Dwiggins, Don. *Hollywood Pilot: The Biography of Paul Mantz*. Garden City, N.J.: Doubleday, 1967.

Earhart, Amelia. *The Fun of It*. New York: Harcourt Brace, 1932.

General Dynamics Corporation. *Dynamic America: A History of General Dynamics Corporation and Its Predecessor Companies*. Edited by John Niven, Erik Nitsche, Courtlandt Canby, and Vernon Welsh. New York: P. M. Publishers, 1935–42.

Glines, Carroll V. *Roscoe Turner: Aviation's Master Showman*. Washington, D.C.: Smithsonian Institution Press, 1995.

Goodwin, Doris Kearns. *The Fitzgeralds and the Kennedys: An American Saga*. New York: St. Martin's, 1987.

Granger, Byrd Howell. *On Final*

Approach: The Women Air Force Service Pilots of W.W. II. Scottsdale, Ariz.: Falconer, 1991.

Hanson, Wil. "The Cochran-Odlum Ranch." Unpublished manuscript.

Harting, Lt. Albert, USAF. "The Nation's First and Only Military School for Women." *U.S. Air Services,* July 1943, p. 30.

Hartmann, Susan M. *The Home Front and Beyond: American Women in the 1940s.* Boston: Twayne, 1982.

Haynesworth, Leslie, and David Toomey. *Amelia Earhart's Daughters: The Wild and Glorious Story of American Women Aviators from World War II to the Dawn of the Space Age.* New York: William Morrow, 1998.

Holm, Maj. Gen. Jeanne (USAF–Ret). *Women in the Military: An Unfinished Record.* Novato, Calif.: Presidio Press, 1982; rev. ed. 1992.

Keil, Sally Van Wagenen. *Those Wonderful Women in Their Flying Machines.* New York: Rawson, Wade, 1979.

Laflin, Patricia B. *Coachella Valley, California: A Pictorial History.* Virginia Beach, Va.: Donning, 1998.

May, Charles Paul. *Women in Aeronautics.* New York: Thomas Nelson, 1962.

Miller, F.M.S. "From England to Australia." *Western Flying,* November 1934.

Noggle, Ann. *For God, Country and the Thrill of It: Women Air Force Service Pilots in World War II.* College Station: Texas A&M University Press, 1990.

Odlum, Hortense. *A Woman's Place: The Autobiography of Hortense Odlum.* New York: Arno Press, 1980, reprint; Scribner, 1939.

Pourade, Richard P. *The Rising Tide.* Vol. 6 of *The History of San Diego.* San Diego: Union-Tribune Publishing, 1967.

Rich, Doris L. *Amelia Earhart: A Biography.* Washington, D.C.: Smithsonian Institution Press, 1989.

Yeager, Chuck, and Leo Janos. *Yeager: An Autobiography.* New York: Bantam, 1980.

Index

Journalist Doris L. Rich is the author of the widely praised *Amelia Earhart: A Biography* and *Queen Bess: Daredevil Aviator*.